ExamKrackers MCAT

INORGANIC CHEMISTRY

6TH EDITION

WITHDRAWN

OSOTE
PUBLISHING

Copyright ©2005 by ExamKrackers, Inc.,

All rights reserved under International and Pan-American Copyright Conventions.
Published in the United States of America by Osote Publishing, New Jersey.

ISBN 1-893858-40-5 (Volume 4)
ISBN 1-893858-42-1 (5 Volume Set)

6th Edition

To purchase additional copies of this book or the rest of the 5 volume set,
call 1-888-572-2536 or fax orders to 1-859-255-0066.

examkrackers.com

osote.com

audioosmosis.com

Inside layout design: Saucy Enterprizes (www.saucyenterprizes.com)

Cover design: Scott Wolfe, Visible Theory (626) 795-1885

Inside cover design consultant: Fenwick Design Inc. (212) 246-9722; (201) 944-4337

Illustrations by ExamKrackers staff.

Acknowledgements

Although I am the author, the hard work and expertise of many individuals contributed to this book. The idea of writing in two voices, a science voice and an MCAT voice, was the creative brainchild of my imaginative friend Jordan Zaretsky. I would like to thank Scott Calvin for lending his exceptional science talent and pedagogic skills to this project. I would like to thank Paul Foglino for his contribution to the lecture questions. I also must thank five years worth of ExamKrackers students for doggedly questioning every explanation, every sentence, every diagram, and every punctuation mark in the book, and for providing the creative inspiration that helped me find new ways to approach and teach inorganic chemistry. Finally, I wish to thank my wife, Silvia, for her support during the difficult times in the past and those that lie ahead.

READ THIS SECTION FIRST!

This manual contains all the inorganic chemistry tested on the MCAT and more. It contains more chemistry than is tested on the MCAT because a deeper understanding of basic scientific principles is often gained through more advanced study. In addition, the MCAT often presents passages with imposing topics that may intimidate the test-taker. Although the questions don't require knowledge of these topics, some familiarity will increase the confidence of the test-taker.

In order to answer questions quickly and efficiently, it is vital that the test-taker understand what is, and is not, tested directly by the MCAT. To assist the test-taker in gaining this knowledge, this manual will use the following conventions. Any term or concept which is tested directly by the MCAT will be written in **bold and underlined.** To ensure a perfect score on the MCAT, you should thoroughly understand all terms and concepts that are in bold and underlined in this manual. Sometimes it is not necessary to memorize the name of a concept, but it is necessary to understand the concept itself. These concepts will also be in bold and underlined. It is important to note that the converse of the above is not true: just because a topic is not in bold and underlined, does not mean that it is not important.

Any formula that must be memorized will be written in **large, red, bold type.**

If a topic is discussed purely as background knowledge, it will be written in *italics*. If a topic is written in italics, it is not required knowledge for the MCAT but may be discussed in an MCAT passage. Do not ignore items in italics, but recognize them as less important than other items. Answers to questions that directly test knowledge of italicized topics are likely to be found in an MCAT passage.

 Text written in this font is me, Salty the Kracker. I will remind you what is and is not an absolute must for MCAT. I will help you develop your MCAT intuition. In addition, I will offer mnemonics, simple methods of viewing a complex concept, and occasionally some comic relief. Don't ignore me, even if you think I am not funny, because my comedy is designed to help you understand and remember. If you think I am funny, tell the boss. I could use a raise.

Each chapter in this manual should be read three times: twice before the class lecture, and once immediately following the lecture. During the first reading, you should not write in the book. Instead, read purely for enjoyment. During the second reading, you should both highlight and take notes in the margins. The third reading should be slow and thorough.

The 24 questions in each lecture should be worked during the second reading before coming to class. The in-class exams in the back of the book are to be done in class after the lecture. Do not look at them before class.

Warning: Just attending the class will not raise your score. __You must do the work.__ Not attending class will obstruct dramatic score increases. If you have Audio Osmosis, then listen to the appropriate lecture before and after you read a lecture.

If you are studying independently, read the lecture twice before doing the in-class exam and then once after doing the in-class exam. If you have Audio Osmosis, listen to Audio Osmosis before taking the in-class exam and then as many times as necessary after taking the exam.

A scaled score conversion chart is provided on the answer page. This is not meant to be an accurate representation of your MCAT score. Do not become demoralized by a poor performance on these exams; they are not accurate reflections of your performance on the real MCAT. The thirty minute exams have been designed to educate. They are similar to an MCAT but with most of the easy questions removed. We believe that you can answer most of the easy questions without too much help from us, so the best way to raise your score is

Copyright © 2005 Examkrackers, Inc.

to focus on the more difficult questions. This method is one of the reasons for the rapid and celebrated success of the Examkrackers prep course and products.

If you find yourself struggling with the science or just needing more practice materials, use the Examkrackers 1001 Questions series. These books are designed specifically to teach the science. If you are already scoring 10s or better, these books are not for you.

You should take advantage of the bulletin board at www.examkrackers.com. The bulletin board allows you to discuss any question in the book with an MCAT expert at Examkrackers. All discussions are kept on file so you have a bank of discussions to which you can refer to any question in this book.

Although we are very careful to be accurate, errata is an occupational hazard of any science book, especially those that are updated regularly as is this one. We maintain that our books have fewer errata than any other prep book. Most of the time what students are certain are errata is the student's error and not an error in the book. So that you can be certain, any errata in this book will be listed as it is discovered at www.examkrackers.com on the bulletin board. Check this site initially and periodically. If you discover what you believe to be errata, please post it on this board and we will verify it promptly. We understand that this system calls attention to the very few errata that may be in our books, but we feel that this is the best system to ensure that you have accurate information for your exam. Again, we stress that we have fewer errata than any other prep book on the market. The difference is that we provide a public list of our errata for your benefit.

Study diligently; trust this book to guide you; and you will reach your MCAT goals.

Copyright © 2005 Examkrackers, Inc.

TABLE OF CONTENTS

Copyright © 2005 Examkrackers, Inc.

Copyright © 2005 Examkrackers, Inc.

Copyright © 2005 Examkrackers, Inc.

PHYSICAL SCIENCES

DIRECTIONS. Most questions in the Physical Sciences test are organized into groups, each preceded by a descriptive passage. After studying the passage, select the one best answer to each question in the group. Some questions are not based on a descriptive passage and are also independent of each other. You must also select the one best answer to these questions. If you are not certain of an answer, eliminate the alternatives that you know to be incorrect and then select an answer from the remaining alternatives. Indicate your selection by blackening the corresponding oval on your answer document. A periodic table is provided for your use. You may consult it whenever you wish.

PERIODIC TABLE OF THE ELEMENTS

1 H 1.0																		2 He 4.0
3 Li 6.9	4 Be 9.0											5 B 10.8	6 C 12.0	7 N 14.0	8 O 16.0	9 F 19.0	10 Ne 20.2
11 Na 23.0	12 Mg 24.3											13 Al 27.0	14 Si 28.1	15 P 31.0	16 S 32.1	17 Cl 35.5	18 Ar 39.9
19 K 39.1	20 Ca 40.1	21 Sc 45.0	22 Ti 47.9	23 V 50.9	24 Cr 52.0	25 Mn 54.9	26 Fe 55.8	27 Co 58.9	28 Ni 58.7	29 Cu 63.5	30 Zn 65.4	31 Ga 69.7	32 Ge 72.6	33 As 74.9	34 Se 79.0	35 Br 79.9	36 Kr 83.8
37 Rb 85.5	38 Sr 87.6	39 Y 88.9	40 Zr 91.2	41 Nb 92.9	42 Mo 95.9	43 Tc (98)	44 Ru 101.1	45 Rh 102.9	46 Pd 106.4	47 Ag 107.9	48 Cd 112.4	49 In 114.8	50 Sn 118.7	51 Sb 121.8	52 Te 127.6	53 I 126.9	54 Xe 131.3
55 Cs 132.9	56 Ba 137.3	57 La* 138.9	72 Hf 178.5	73 Ta 180.9	74 W 183.9	75 Re 186.2	76 Os 190.2	77 Ir 192.2	78 Pt 195.1	79 Au 197.0	80 Hg 200.6	81 Tl 204.4	82 Pb 207.2	83 Bi 209.0	84 Po (209)	85 At (210)	86 Rn (222)
87 Fr (223)	88 Ra 226.0	89 Ac† 227.0	104 Unq (261)	105 Unp (262)	106 Unh (263)	107 Uns (262)	108 Uno (265)	109 Une (267)									

	58 Ce 140.1	59 Pr 140.9	60 Nd 144.2	61 Pm (145)	62 Sm 150.4	63 Eu 152.0	64 Gd 157.3	65 Tb 158.9	66 Dy 162.5	67 Ho 164.9	68 Er 167.3	69 Tm 168.9	70 Yb 173.0	71 Lu 175.0
†	90 Th 232.0	91 Pa (231)	92 U 238.0	93 Np (237)	94 Pu (244)	95 Am (243)	96 Cm (247)	97 Bk (247)	98 Cf (251)	99 Es (252)	100 Fm (257)	101 Md (258)	102 No (259)	103 Lr (260)

Copyright © 2005 Examkrackers, Inc.

Lecture 1

Atoms, Molecules, and Quantum Mechanics

All mass consists of tiny particles called **atoms**. Each atom is composed of a **nucleus** surrounded by one or more electrons. The radius of a nucleus is on the order of 10^{-4} angstroms (Å). One angstrom is 10^{-10} m. The nucleus contains **protons** and **neutrons**, collectively called *nucleons*, held together by the *strong nuclear force*. (More precisely, the strong nuclear force holds together the three *quarks* that make up each nucleon, and it is the 'spill over' from the strong nuclear force that holds together the nucleons.) Protons and neutrons are approximately equal in size and mass. (Neutrons are very slightly heavier.) Protons have a positive charge and neutrons are electrically neutral.

1-1
Atoms

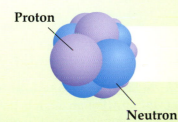

Proton

Neutron

Atomic radius
(reduced approximately 500 times
relative to the nucleons)

Electron
(magnified 1,000 times
relative to the nucleons)

Surrounding the nucleus at a distance of about 1 to 3 Å are **electrons**. The mass of one electron is over 1800 times smaller than the mass of a nucleon. Electrons and protons have opposite charges of equal magnitude. Although for convenience we often think of the charge on an electron as 1− and the charge on a proton as 1+, we should remember that this charge is in electron units 'e' called the *electronic charge*. A charge of 1 e is equal to 1.6×10^{-19} coulombs. An atom itself is electrically neutral; it contains the same number of protons as electrons.

Particle	Charge	Mass (amu)
Proton	Positive (1+)	1.0073
Neutron	Neutral	1.0087
Electron	Negative (1−)	5.5×10^{-4}

Of course, you want to know the charges on the particles, but don't memorize the masses in the table shown. Instead, recognize the disparity in size between electrons and nucleons. Also, notice that protons and neutrons have nearly the same mass, about one amu.

Since the nucleons are so small compared to the size of the atom, the atom itself is composed mostly of **empty space**. If an atom were the size of a modern football stadium, it would have a nucleus the size of a marble.

1-2
Elements

Any single atom must be one of just over 100 **elements**. Elements are the building blocks of all compounds and cannot be decomposed into simpler substances by chemical means. Any element can be displayed as follows:

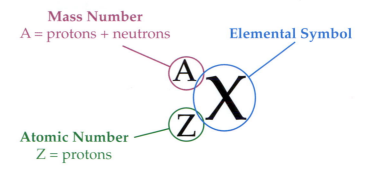

where **A** is the **mass number** or number of protons plus neutrons, and **Z** is the **atomic number** or number of protons. The atomic number is the identity number of any element. If we know the atomic number, then we know the element. This is not true of the mass number or the number of electrons. Any element may have any number of neutrons or electrons, but only one number of protons.

*Notice that 'A' stands for mass number and **NOT** atomic number.*

Two or more atoms of the same element that contain different numbers of neutrons are said to be **isotopes**. An atom of a specific isotope is called a *nuclide*. Isotopes have similar chemical properties. Hydrogen has three important isotopes: ^1H (*protium*), ^2H (*deuterium*), and ^3H (*tritium*). 99.98% of naturally occurring hydrogen is protium. Examples of three isotopes for carbon are:

The number of protons identifies which element. For a given element, the number of neutrons identifies which isotope.

$$^{12}C, \ ^{13}C, \text{ and } ^{14}C.$$

Each of carbon's isotopes contains 6 protons. 6 protons define carbon. ^{12}C (carbon-12) contains 6 neutrons, ^{13}C (carbon-13) contains 7 neutrons, and ^{14}C (carbon-14) contains 8 neutrons.

Think of an amu as approximately the mass of one proton or one neutron.

Biochemists call an amu a dalton.

Although the mass number is a good approximation of the mass of an atom, it is not exact. The **atomic weight** or **molar mass (*MM* or *M*)** of an atom is given in **atomic mass units** (abbreviated **amu** or with the less commonly used SI abbreviation **u**). The atomic weight of an element is actually a mass (or in some books a ratio) and not a weight. An amu is defined by carbon-12. By definition, one atom of ^{12}C has an atomic weight of 12 amu. All other atomic weights are measured against this standard. Since carbon naturally occurs as a mixture of its isotopes, the atomic weight of carbon is listed as the weighted average of its isotopes or 12.011 amu. (This is very close to 12 amu because almost 99% of carbon occurs in nature as ^{12}C.)

^{12}C also defines a **mole**. A mole (or **Avogadro's number, 6.022×10^{23}**) is the number of carbon atoms in 12 grams of ^{12}C. Keeping in mind the relationship between an amu and grams can be useful:

$$6.022 \times 10^{23} \text{ amu} = 1 \text{ gram}$$

We can read atomic weights from the periodic table as either amu or g/mol.

If you can't find moles from molecular or atomic weight, then you better get crackin'. This is basic stuff, but you need to have it down cold!

If we are given the amount of an element or compound in grams, we can divide by the atomic or molecular weight to find the number of moles in that sample.

$$\text{moles} = \frac{\text{grams}}{\text{atomic or molecular weight}}$$

Copyright © 2005 Examkrackers, Inc.

The periodic table lists the elements from left to right in the order of their atomic numbers. Each horizontal row is called a **period**. The vertical columns are called **groups or families**. There are at least two methods used to number the groups. The newer method is to number them 1 through 18 from left to right. An older method, which is still used, is to separate the groups into sections A and B. These sections are then numbered with Roman numerals as shown below.

The periodic table below divides the elements into three sections: 1) nonmetals on the right (dark orange); 2) metals on the left (light orange); and 3) metalloids along the yellow-shaded diagonal separating the metals from the nonmetals.

Metals are large atoms that tend to lose electrons to form positive ions or form positive oxidation states. To emphasize their loose hold on their electrons and the fluid-like nature of their valence electrons, metals are often described as atoms in a sea of electrons. The easy movement of electrons within metals gives them their metallic character. Metallic character includes ductility (easily stretched), malleability (easily hammered into thin strips), thermal and electrical conductivity, and a characteristic luster. Metal atoms easily slide past each other allowing metals to be hammered into thin sheets or drawn into wires. Electrons move easily from one metal atom to the next transferring energy or charge in the form of heat or electricity. All metals but mercury exist as solids at room temperature. Metals typically form ionic oxides such as BaO. (BeO is one exception that is not ionic.)

Nonmetals have diverse appearances and chemical behaviors. Generally speaking, nonmetals have lower melting points than metals. They form negative ions. Molecular substances are typically made from only nonmetals. Nonmetals form covalent oxides such as SiO_2 or CO_2.

1-3
The Periodic Table

Know the characteristics of metals: lustrous, ductile, malleable, thermally and electrically conductive.

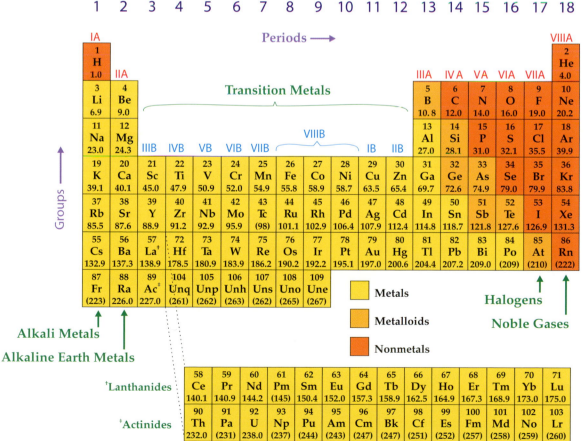

You need to know the names of the following groups: alkali metals, alkaline earth metals, halogens, and noble gases.

Copyright © 2005 Examkrackers, Inc.

<u>Metalloids</u> have some characteristics that resemble metals and some that resemble nonmetals.

You should also recognize the names of the following four groups: alkali metals; alkaline earth metals; halogens; and noble (or rare) gases. The section A groups are known as the *representative* or *main-group elements* and the section B groups are called the <u>transition metals</u>.

Elements in the same family on the periodic table tend to have similar chemical properties. For example, they tend to make the same number of bonds, and exist as similarly charged ions.

1-4
Characteristics Within Groups

Elements in the same family have similar chemical properties. Hydrogen is an exception to the rule.

You can remember that alkali metals are Group 1 and alkaline earth metals are Group 2 because alkali comes before alkaline in alphabetical order.

This is a lot of detail! Knowing some of details of the characteristics of each group on the periodic table as explained here will be helpful, but not required by the MCAT. Don't be too concerned with all this detail.

Hydrogen is unique and its chemical and physical characteristics do not conform well to any family. It is a nonmetal. Under most conditions, it is a colorless, odorless, diatomic gas.

As pure substances, Group 1A or alkali metals are soft metallic solids with low densities and low melting points. They easily form 1+ cations. They are highly reactive, reacting with most nonmetals to form ionic compounds. Alkali metals react with hydrogen to form hydrides such as NaH. Alkali metals react exothermically with water to produce the metal hydroxide and hydrogen gas. In nature, alkali metals exist only in compounds.

Group 2A or alkaline earth metals are harder, more dense, and melt at higher temperatures than alkali metals. They form 2+ cations. They are less reactive than alkali metals. Heavier alkaline earth metals are more reactive than lighter alkaline earth metals.

All the 4A elements can form four covalent bonds with nonmetals. All but carbon can form two additional bonds with Lewis bases. Of the 4A elements, only carbon forms *strong* pi bonds to make strong double and even triple bonds.

Group 5A elements can form 3 covalent bonds. In addition, all 5A elements except nitrogen can form five covalent bonds by using their *d* orbitals. These elements can further bond with a Lewis base to form a sixth covalent bond. Nitrogen forms strong pi bonds to make double and triple bonds. Phosphorous can form only weak pi bonds to make double bonds. The other 5A elements cannot make pi bonds. Nitrogen can also form four covalent bonds by donating its lone pair of electrons to form a bond.

Group 6A elements are called the *chalcogens*. Oxygen and sulfur are the important chalcogens for the MCAT. Oxygen is the second most electronegative element. Oxygen is divalent and can form strong pi bonds to make double bonds. In nature, oxygen exists as O_2 (*dioxygen*) and O_3 (ozone). Oxygen typically reacts with metals to form metal oxides. Alkali metals form peroxides (Na_2O_2) and *super oxides* (KO_2) with oxygen. The most common form of pure sulfur is the yellow solid S_8. Metal sulfides, such as Na_2S, are the most common form of sulfur found in nature. Sulfur can form two, three, four, or even six bonds. It has the ability to pi bond making strong double bonds.

The radioactively stable Group 7A elements (called halogens) are fluorine, chlorine, bromine, and iodine. Halogens are highly reactive. Fluorine and chlorine are diatomic gases at room temperature; bromine, a diatomic liquid; iodine, a diatomic solid. Halogens like to gain electrons. However, halogens other than fluorine can

Copyright © 2005 Examkrackers, Inc.

take on oxidation states as high as +7 when bonding to highly electronegative atoms like oxygen. When in compounds, fluorine always has an oxidation state of –1. This means that fluorine makes only one bond, while the other halogens can make more than one bond. Hydrogen combines with all the halogens to form gaseous hydrogen halides. The hydrogen halides are soluble in water forming the hydrohalic acids. Halogens react with metals to form ionic halides.

Noble gases are nonreactive. They are sometimes called the **inert gases**. Only the noble gas elements are normally found in nature as isolated atoms. They are all gases at room temperature.

The elements that tend to exist as diatomic molecules are hydrogen, oxygen, nitrogen, and the halogens. Typically, when these elements are discussed, it is assumed that they are in their diatomic form unless otherwise stated. In other words, the statement "Nitrogen is nonreactive." refers to N_2 and not N.

Notice that the size of an atom has a significant effect on its chemistry. If we examine the smallest element in a Group, we can sometimes see deviations in its behavior due to its size. Small atoms have less room to stabilize charge by spreading it out. This makes them bond more strongly to water resulting in greater heats of hydration. Because beryllium in its ionic form is not large enough to stabilize its charge, it forms a covalent oxide, whereas other alkaline earth metals make ionic oxides. This means that BeO is amphoteric whereas other alkaline earth metal oxides are basic. Small atoms don't have *d* orbitals available to them for bond formation. Atoms without *d* orbitals cannot form more than four bonds. Oxygen typically forms two bonds, while the larger sulfur can form up to six. On the other hand, the *p* orbitals on atoms that are too big don't overlap significantly, so large atoms can't easily form pi bonds. The second period elements carbon, nitrogen, and oxygen are small enough to form strong pi bonds while their larger third row family members form only weak pi bonds, if they form pi bonds at all.

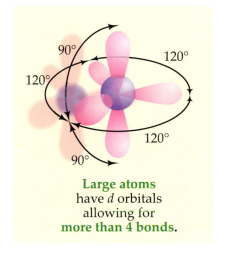

Large atoms have *d* orbitals allowing for more than 4 bonds.

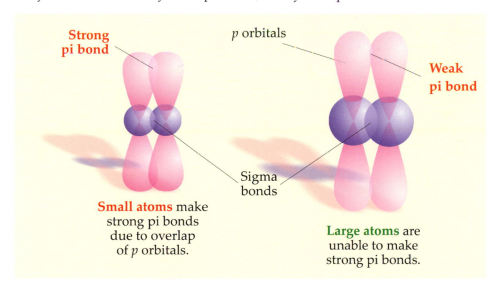

Strong pi bond

p orbitals

Weak pi bond

Sigma bonds

Small atoms make strong pi bonds due to overlap of *p* orbitals.

Large atoms are unable to make strong pi bonds.

Copyright © 2005 Examkrackers, Inc.

1-5

Ions

When an element has more or fewer electrons than protons, it becomes an ion. Positive ions are called cations; negative ions, anions. The representative elements make ions by forming the closest noble gas electron configuration. (Electron configurations are discussed later in this Lecture.) Metals form cations; nonmetals form anions. When the transition metals form ions, they lose electrons from their *s* subshell first and then from their *d* subshell. (Subshells will be discussed later in this lecture.) Below are some common ions formed by metals.

Easy here! You don't have to memorize the charge on every cation made by transition metals. This is background knowledge. But, you should be able to predict the charge based upon two things:

1. Atoms lose electrons from the highest energy shell first. In transition metals, this means that electrons are lost from the s subshell first, and then from the d subshell.

2. Ions are looking for symmetry. Representative elements form noble gas electron configurations when they make ions. Transition metals try to 'even-out' their d orbitals, so each orbital has the same number of electrons.

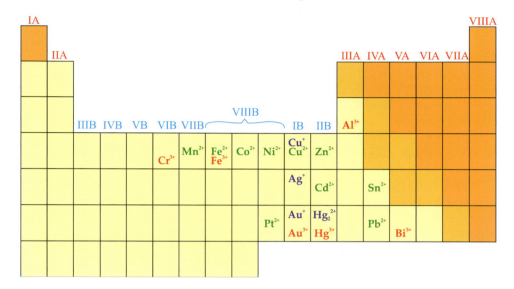

These are not all the possible ions; they are just some of the more common ions. Notice that Group 1B makes 1+ ions. There are six 3+ ions Cr^{3+}, Fe^{3+}, Au^{3+}, Al^{3+}, and Bi^{3+}. The rest are 2+ ions.

Cations are significantly smaller than their neutral atom counterparts. For instance, sodium's outermost electron is located by itself on an outer shell. When this outer electron is removed, the sodium cation is significantly smaller because the remaining electrons are located in inner shells. The reverse is true for anions. The additional electrons are added to an outer shell making the anion much larger than its neutral atom counter part. Isoelectronic ions (ions with the same number of electrons) tend to get smaller with increasing atomic number because more protons pull inward on the same number of electrons. The sizes of the oxygen, fluorine, sodium and magnesium ions reflect this trend.

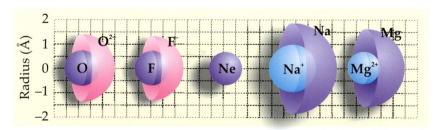

Ionic compounds are usually made from both metals and nonmetals.

Coulomb's law: $F = kq_1q_2/r^2$, describes the electrostatic forces holding an electron to its nucleus. The distance between the electron and the nucleus is r. For q_1 we might plug in the positive charge of the nucleus, Z, and for q_2, the charge on the given electron. This would work fine for hydrogen, where the lone electron *feels* 100% of the positive charge on the nucleus. However, in helium the first electron **shields** some of the nuclear charge from the second electron, so that the second electron doesn't

Copyright © 2005 Examkrackers, Inc.

feel the entire nuclear charge, Z. The amount of charge felt by the second electron is called the **effective nuclear charge** (Z_{eff}). You can see in the graph below that Z_{eff} for the outermost electron of helium is not 2, even though there are two protons in the helium nucleus. The Z_{eff} is the nuclear charge Z minus the average number of electrons between the nucleus and the electron in question. The Z_{eff}, and not Z, should be plugged in for q in Coulomb's law to find the force on the outermost electron. Note that the force is a function of both q (Z_{eff}) and r (the distance from the nucleus).

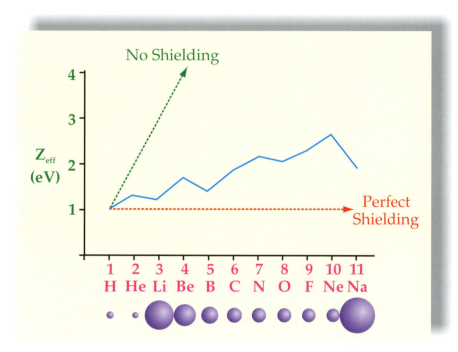

When considering the effect of Z_{eff}, consider the strength of Z_{eff} and the distance from the nucleus. The force pulling the electron inward goes up with Z_{eff} but goes down with distance according to Coulomb's law: *F = Kqq/r²*.

The graph above shows Z_{eff} values (given in electron volts) for the highest energy electron in each element through sodium. Notice the drop in Z_{eff} going from helium to lithium. This is because the last electron added to make lithium is added to an outer shell making the shielding effect strong. To form beryllium, an electron is added to the same shell and the shielding effect is not as great. To form boron, an electron is added to the $2p$ subshell, a higher energy subshell, and shielding is stronger again. (We'll discuss subshells later in this lecture.) Going from nitrogen to oxygen, the next electron must share an orbital with one of the three p orbitals resulting in some shielding and a reduction in Z_{eff}. Moving from neon to sodium, the next electron is added to an entirely new shell, the 3s subshell. This causes a strong reduction in Z_{eff}, but notice that the outermost electron in sodium still experiences a higher Z_{eff} than the outermost electron of the element immediately above it on the periodic table, lithium. For now, think of Z_{eff} as increasing going from left to right and from top to bottom on the periodic table.

With Z_{eff} in mind, we can make general predictions about the elements based upon their position in the periodic table. The totalities of these predictions are called the **periodic trends**. Since the effective nuclear charge increases when moving from left to right, each additional electron is pulled more strongly toward the nucleus. This results in a smaller **atomic radius**. Of course, with each added shell the atom grows larger. Thus, atomic radius also increases from the top of the periodic table to the bottom.

When an electron is more strongly attached to the nucleus, more energy is required to detach it. The energy necessary to detach an electron from a nucleus is called **ionization energy**. The energy necessary to detach an electron from a neutral atom is called the first ionization energy. (By definition, the atom being ionized is gaseous.) The energy for the removal of a second electron from the same atom is called the

Copyright © 2005 Examkrackers, Inc.

second ionization energy, and so on. The second ionization energy is always much greater than the first because when one electron is removed, the effective nuclear charge on the other electrons increases. Ionization energy generally increases along the periodic table from left to right and from bottom to top. This trend is explained by Z_{eff}. Z_{eff} increases when moving across a period to the right making it tougher to knock off an electron. Although Z_{eff} also increases when moving down the periodic table, the distance of the electron from the nucleus increases as well, thus decreasing the electric field at the point of the electron. The decreased electric field has less strength to hold the electron to the atom.

Electronegativity is the tendency of an atom to attract an electron in a bond that it shares with another atom. The most commonly used measurement of electronegativity is the *Pauling scale*, which ranges from a value of 0.79 for cesium to a value of 4.0 for fluorine. Electronegativity also tends to increase from left to right and bottom to top on the periodic table, and is related to Z_{eff} in a similar fashion to ionization energy. Electronegativity values are undefined for the noble gases.

Electron affinity is the willingness of an atom to accept an additional electron. More precisely, it is the energy released when an electron is added to a gaseous atom. Electron affinity tends to increase on the periodic table from left to right and from bottom to top, and is related to Z_{eff}. (**Warning:** Many books use the exothermic value for electron affinity, which is the negative of the energy released. We can state this as follows: Electron affinity is more exothermic to the right and up on the periodic table.) The noble gases do not follow this trend. Electron affinity values for the noble gases are endothermic.

The final important periodic trend, **metallic character,** tends to increase from right to left and top to bottom.

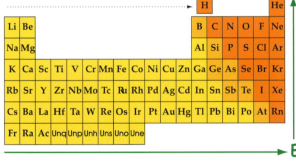

Energy of Ionization
Electron Affinity
Electronegativity

Atomic Radius
Metallic Character

An easy way to remember the 5 periodic trends is as follows: if it begins with an 'E', as shown here, then it increases going to the right and up; if it doesn't begin with an 'E', then it increases in the opposite direction. Be careful! This mnemonic requires that you think of 'ionization energy' as 'energy of ionization' so that it begins with an 'E'. Z_{eff} is not considered a periodic trend for this mnemonic. Keep in mind that the trends are just trends, and are violated frequently.

The noble gases do not follow the trends for electronegativity or for electron affinity.

Notice that I have moved hydrogen to a more appropriate position.

Copyright © 2005 Examkrackers, Inc.

1. Which of the following increases with increasing atomic number within a family on the periodic table?

    A. electronegativity
    B. electron affinity
    C. atomic radius
    D. ionization energy

2. Which of the following molecules has the greatest dipole moment?

    A. H_2
    B. O_2
    C. HF
    D. HBr

3. How many carbon atoms exist in 12 amu of ^{12}C?

    A. 1
    B. 12
    C. 6.02×10^{23}
    D. 7.22×10^{24}

4. Silicon has a silvery luster at room temperature. Silicon is brittle, and does not conduct heat or electricity well. Based on its position in the periodic table, silicon is most likely a:

    A. nonmetal
    B. metalloid
    C. metal
    D. chalcogen

5. Which of the following most likely represents the correct order of ion size from greatest to smallest?

    A. O^{2-}, F^-, Na^+, Mg^{2+}
    B. Mg^{2+}, Na^+, F^-, O^{2-}
    C. Na^+, Mg^{2+}, O^{2-}, F^-
    D. Mg^{2+}, Na^+, O^{2-}, F^-

6. A natural sample of carbon contains 99% of ^{12}C. How many moles of ^{12}C are likely to be found in a 48.5 gram sample of carbon obtained from nature?

    A. 1
    B. 4
    C. 12
    D. 49.5

7. In 1869 both Mendeleev and Meyer, working separately, published nearly identical classification schemes for the elements that were the forerunners of the modern periodic table. Although scientists of that time had no knowledge of atomic numbers, both schemes ordered the elements in nearly correct order from lowest to highest atomic number. Which of the following is the most likely explanation?

    A. Both scientists noticed similar patterns in chemical and physical behaviors among the elements.
    B. Atomic number generally increases with atomic weight and the scientist knew the atomic weights of the elements.
    C. The chemical identity was predictable from the number of valence electrons which was known at the time.
    D. Although the number of protons for each element was not known, the number of neutrons was.

8. Which of the following could be a stable molecular structure?

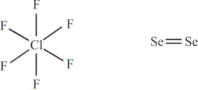

1-6
SI Units and Prefixes

By international agreement, SI units are used for scientific measurements. 'SI Units' stands for *Systeme International d'Unites*. SI units predominate on the MCAT.

There are seven base units in the SI system. The seven are listed in the table below:

Physical Quantity	Name of Unit	Abbreviation
Mass	Kilogram	kg
Length	Meter	m
Time	Second	s
Electric current	Ampere	A
Temperature	Kelvin	K
Luminous intensity	Candela	cd
Amount of substance	Mole	mol

Other SI units can be derived from these seven, such as a newton: $1 \text{ N} = 1 \text{ kg m s}^{-2}$. There are other units still commonly in use that you may also see on the MCAT, such as atm or torr for pressure. All such units will have an SI counterpart that you should know. We will point this out as we come across new units.

The SI system also employs standard prefixes for each unit. These prefixes are commonly seen on the MCAT. The table below lists these standard prefixes:

Prefix	Abbreviation	Meaning
Mega-	M	10^6
Kilo-	k	10^3
Deci-	d	10^{-1}
Centi-	c	10^{-2}
Milli-	m	10^{-3}
Micro-	μ	10^{-6}
Nano-	n	10^{-9}
Pico-	p	10^{-12}
Femto-	f	10^{-15}

PREPARE TO STOP

STOP! You were going to skip this page; weren't you? Memorize the SI units and the prefixes. They will help you in all the sciences.

1-7
Molecules

Atoms can be held together by **bonds**. In one type of bond, two electrons are shared by two nuclei. This is called a **covalent bond**. The negatively charged electrons are pulled toward both positively charged nuclei by electrostatic forces. This 'tug of war' between the nuclei for the electrons holds the atoms together. If the nuclei come too close to each other, the positively charged nuclei repel each other. These repulsive and attractive forces achieve a balance to create a bond. The diagram compares the internuclear distance between two hydrogen atoms to their electrostatic potential energy level as a system. The **bond length** is defined as the point where the energy level is the lowest. Two atoms will only form a bond if they can lower their overall energy level by doing so. Nature tends to seek the lowest energy state.

If we separate the atoms by an infinite distance, the forces between them, and thus the energy, go to zero. The energy necessary to achieve a complete separation is given by the vertical distance on the graph between the bond length and zero. This

Copyright © 2005 Examkrackers, Inc.

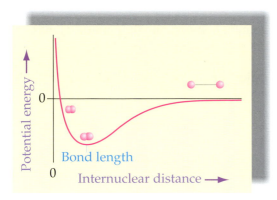

Bond length

Potential energy →

0

0

Internuclear distance →

is called **the bond dissociation energy or bond energy.** (Bond dissociation energy and bond energy are very closely related.)

A substance made from two or more elements in definite proportions is called a **compound**. In all pure compounds, the relative number of atoms of one element to another can be represented by a ratio of whole numbers. This ratio is called the **empirical formula**. In molecular compounds, groups of atoms form repeated, separate and distinct units called **molecules**. In molecular compounds, the exact number of elemental atoms in each molecule can be represented by a **molecular formula**. The empirical formula for glucose is CH_2O. The molecular formula is $C_6H_{12}O_6$.

From the empirical formula and the atomic weight of each atom, we can find the percent composition of a compound by mass. To do this, multiply an atom's atomic weight by the number of atoms it contributes to the empirical formula. Divide your result by the weight of all the atoms in the empirical formula. This gives you the mass fraction of the compound represented by the atom. Now multiply this fraction by 100, and you have the percent composition by mass.

To find the empirical formula from the percent mass composition, you assume that you have a 100 gram sample. Now the percent translates directly to grams. When you divide the grams by atomic weight, you get moles. Now divide by the greatest common factor. This is the number of atoms represented by each element in the empirical formula. In order to find the molecular formula, we would need more information.

Notice from the graph that energy is always required to break a bond. Conversely, no energy is ever released by breaking a bond. (Energy from ATP is released when the new bonds of ADP and iP are formed, and not when the ATP bonds are broken.)

The percent mass of carbon in glucose (empirical formula = CH_2O) is found as follows:

$$\frac{\text{molecular weight of carbon}}{\text{molecular weight of } CH_2O} = \frac{12}{30} = 0.4$$

$$0.4 \times 100 = 40$$

Glucose is 40% carbon by mass.

This stuff should be easy for you. You have to know it backwards and forwards. It will definitely be on the MCAT, and it should be a couple of fast and easy points. Practice this until you know it well.

If we are asked to find the empirical formula of a compound that is 6% hydrogen and 94% oxygen by mass, we do the following:

From a 100 gram sample:

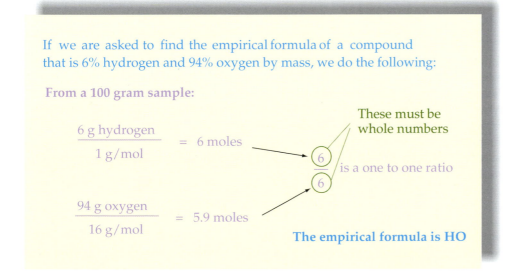

$$\frac{6 \text{ g hydrogen}}{1 \text{ g/mol}} = 6 \text{ moles}$$

$$\frac{94 \text{ g oxygen}}{16 \text{ g/mol}} = 5.9 \text{ moles}$$

These must be whole numbers

6

6

is a one to one ratio

The empirical formula is HO

Copyright © 2005 Examkrackers, Inc.

1-8
Naming Inorganic Compounds

There is very little tested concerning the naming of inorganic compounds. However, it is a good idea to be able to identify compounds when they are referred to.

Ionic compounds are named after their cation and anion. If the cation is metal and capable of having different charges, for example, copper can take on a charge of 1+ or 2+, then its name is followed by a Roman numeral in parentheses, as in copper(I) ion or copper(II) ion. An older method for naming cations that can take on different charges is to add –ic to the ending of the cation with the greater positive charge and –ous to the cation with the smaller charge, as in cupric (Cu^{2+}) and cuprous (Cu^+) ions. If the cation is made from a nonmetal, the cation name ends in –ium, such as ammonium (NH_4^+).

This nomenclature stuff is boring. Just memorize this stuff once and for all and get it over with. Don't get too involved in the myriad little rules in nomenclature. Keep it simple because the MCAT sure will.

Monatomic anions and simple polyatomic anions are given the suffix –ide, such as hydride ion (H^-) or hydroxide ion (OH^-). Polyatomic anions with multiple oxygens end with the suffix –ite or –ate depending upon the relative number of oxygens. The more oxygenated species will use the –ate suffix, such as nitrite ion (NO_2^-) versus nitrate ion (NO_3^-). If there are more possibilities, the prefixes hypo- and per- are used to indicate fewest and most oxygens respectively, such as the hypochlorite (ClO^-), chlorite (ClO_2^-), chlorate (ClO_3^-), and perchlorate (ClO_4^-) ions. If an oxyanion has a hydrogen, the word hydrogen is added as in hydrogen carbonate ion (HCO_3^-). The old name would have been bicarbonate ion.

To name an ionic compound, just put the cation name in front of the anion name as in barium sulfate ($BaSO_4$) or sodium hydride (NaH).

Acids are named based on their anions. If the name of the anion ends in –ide, the acid name starts with hydro- and ends in –ic, as in hydrosulfuric acid (H_2S). If the acid is an oxyacid, the ending –ic is used for the species with more oxygens and –ous for the species with fewer oxygens, as in sulfuric acid (H_2SO_4) and sulfurous acid (H_2SO_3).

For **binary molecular compounds** (compounds with only two elements), the name begins with the name of the element that is farthest to the left and lowest in the periodic table. The name of the second element is given the suffix –ide and a Greek number prefix is used on the first element if necessary (e.g., dinitrogen tetroxide, N_2O_4).

1-9
Chemical Reactions and Equations

When a compound undergoes a reaction and maintains its molecular structure and thus its identity, the reaction is called a **physical reaction**. Melting, evaporation, dissolution, and rotation of polarized light are some examples of physical reactions. When a compound undergoes a reaction and changes its molecular structure to form a new compound, the reaction is called a **chemical reaction**. Combustion, metathesis, and redox are examples of chemical reactions. Chemical reactions can be represented by a chemical equation with the molecular formulae of the reactants on the left and the products on the right.

$$CH_4 + 2O_2 \rightarrow CO_2 + 2H_2O$$

An unbalanced equation is a wrong answer unless specifically asked for. By the way, know the difference between a physical and chemical reaction.

Notice that there is a conservation of atoms from the left to the right side of the equation. In other words, there is the same number of oxygen, hydrogen, and carbon atoms on the right as on the left. This means the equation is balanced. On the MCAT, if the answer is given in equation form, the correct answer will be a balanced equation unless specifically indicated to the contrary.

Copyright © 2005 Examkrackers, Inc.

In the previous equation, O_2 is preceded by a coefficient of two. A coefficient of one is assumed for all molecules not preceded by a coefficient. Methane, then, has a coefficient of one. These coefficients indicate the relative number of molecules. They represent the number of single molecules, moles of molecules, dozens of molecules or any other quantity. They do not represent the mass, the number of grams, or kilograms.

	CH_4	$+ \ 2O_2 \ \rightarrow$	CO_2	$+ \ 2H_2O$
Starting amount:	4	6	0	0
Amount used up:	3	6	0	0
Ending amount:	1	0	3	6

To say that a reaction **runs to completion** means that it moves to the right until the supply of at least one of the reactants is depleted. (Reactions often don't run to completion because they reach equilibrium first.) As indicated by the equation above, two moles of oxygen (O_2) are needed to burn one mole of methane (CH_4). If we were to react four moles of methane with six moles of oxygen, and the reaction ran to completion, we would be left with 1 mole of methane. This is because, from the two to one ratio in the equation, six moles of oxygen are only enough to burn three moles of methane. Since we would run out of oxygen first, oxygen is our **limiting reagent**. Notice that the limiting reagent is not necessarily the reactant of which there is the least; it is the reactant that would be completely used up if the reaction were to run to completion. Also from the balanced equation, the one to one ratio of methane to carbon dioxide and the two to one ratio of methane to water, tells us that burning three moles of methane produces three moles of carbon dioxide and six moles of water.

If you don't understand where the numbers came from in the table, take another look. You should understand this for the MCAT.

1-10
Chemical Yield

The amount of product produced when a reaction runs to completion is called the **theoretical yield**. The amount of actual product after a real experiment is the actual yield. As mentioned above, reactions often don't run to completion, and sometimes there are competing reactions that reduce the actual yield. Actual yield divided by the theoretical yield, times 100, gives the **percent yield**.

MCAT would probably give you the equation for the percent yield. Just understand the concept.

$$\frac{Actual\ yield}{Theoretical\ yeild} \times 100 = Percent\ yield$$

1-11
Fundamental Reaction Types

Reactions can be categorized into types. The following lists four reaction types using hypothetical elements or molecules A, B, C, and D.

Combination: $A + B \rightarrow C$

Decomposition: $C \rightarrow A + B$

Single Displacement: $A + BC \rightarrow B + AC$ (also called single replacement)

Double Displacement: $AB + CD \rightarrow AD + CB$ (also called double replacement or metathesis)

Some important reaction types not shown here are redox, combustion, Bronsted-Lowry acid-base, and Lewis acid-base. We will cover these types later in this book. Reaction types are not mutually exclusive, so one reaction can fall into more than one type.

Nothing to do here but memorize these reaction types in case MCAT asks one question requiring you to identify which type. It won't be worth more than one question on an MCAT.

Copyright © 2005 Examkrackers, Inc.

1-12
Reaction Symbols

The symbol 'Δ' usually means "change in" but 'Δ' above or below a reaction arrow indicates that heat is added. When a chemical is written above the reaction arrow, it is often a catalyst. Two arrows pointing in opposite directions (like this '$\rightleftharpoons$') indicate a reaction that can reach equilibrium. If one arrow is longer than the other, the equilibrium favors the side to which the long arrow points. A single arrow pointing in both directions (like this '$\leftrightarrow$') indicates resonance structures. Square brackets [ ] around an atom, molecule, or ion indicate concentration. The naught symbol '$^{\circ}$' indicates standard state conditions.

1-13
Bonding in Solids

Solids can be *crystalline or amorphous*. A crystal has a sharp melting point and a characteristic shape with a well ordered structure of repeating units which can be atoms, molecules or ions. A crystal is classified as *ionic, network covalent, metallic,* or *molecular* depending upon the nature of the chemical bonding and the intermolecular forces in the crystal. Ionic crystals consist of oppositely charged ions held together by electrostatic forces. Salts are ionic crystals. Metallic crystals are single metal atoms bonded together by delocalized electrons. These delocalized electrons allow metallic crystals to efficiently conduct heat and electricity. They also make metallic crystals malleable and ductile. Network covalent crystals consist of an infinite network of atoms held together by polar and nonpolar bonds. Diamond and crystal SiO_2 are common examples of network covalent crystals. It is not possible to identify individual molecules in ionic, metallic, and network covalent crystals. Molecular crystals are composed of individual molecules held together by intermolecular bonds. Ice is an example of a molecular crystal.

An amorphous solid has no characteristic shape and melts over a temperature range. Glass (SiO_2) is an amorphous solid usually with some impurities added to lower the melting point. Some substances are capable of forming both crystalline and amorphous solids.

Polymers are solids with repeated structural units. They can be crystalline or amorphous. Generally, rapid cooling of liquid polymers results in amorphous solids and slow cooling results in crystalline solids. There are many polymers found in living systems. Examples of biopolymers are DNA, glycogen, and protein.

The MCAT does not directly test your knowledge of the structure of solids beyond ionic and molecular solids; however, it is good to at least be aware that atoms can form substances in many ways. Molecular solids are actually less common than other types of solids. There has been an MCAT passage on this topic.

Copyright © 2005 Examkrackers, Inc.

Questions 9 through 16 are **NOT** based on a descriptive passage.

9. What is the empirical formula of a neutral compound containing 58.6% oxygen, 39% sulfur, 2.4% hydrogen by mass?

    A. HSO_3^-
    B. HSO_4^-
    C. H_2SO_3
    D. H_2SO_4

10. Silica is a network solid of silicon and oxygen atoms. The empirical formula for silica is SiO_2. In silica, to how many oxygen atoms is each silicon bonded?

    A. 1
    B. 2
    C. 3
    D. 4

11. What is the percent by mass of carbon in CO_2?

    A. 12%
    B. 27%
    C. 33%
    D. 44%

12. Sulfur dioxide oxidizes in the presence of O_2 gas as per the reaction:

    $$2SO_2(g) + O_2(g) \rightarrow 2SO_3(g)$$

    Approximately how many grams of sulfur trioxide are produced by the complete oxidation of 1 mole of sulfur dioxide?

    A. 1 g
    B. 2 g
    C. 80 g
    D. 160 g

13. When gaseous ammonia is passed over solid copper(II)oxide at high temperatures, nitrogen gas is formed.

    $$2NH_3(g) + 3CuO(s) \rightarrow N_2(g) + 3Cu(s) + 3H_2O(g)$$

    What is the limiting reagent when 34 grams of ammonia form 26 grams of nitrogen in a reaction that runs to completion?

    A. NH_3
    B. CuO
    C. N_2
    D. Cu

14. Name the following compound: $Cu(ClO_4)_2$.

    A. copper(I) chlorate
    B. copper(II) perchlorite
    C. copper(II) chlorate
    D. copper(II) perchlorate

15. Polyethylene is a flexible plastic with many industrial uses. The synthesis of polyethylene is a radical reaction that follows the equation:

    $$n CH_2{=}CH_2 \rightarrow (CH_2CH_2)_n$$

    Polyethylene is a(n):

    A. molecular solid.
    B. polymer.
    C. ionic solid.
    D. network solid.

16. What type of reaction is shown below?

    $$2Mg(s) + O_2 \rightarrow 2MgO(s)$$

    A. combination
    B. single replacement
    C. metathesis
    D. decomposition

Copyright © 2005 Examkrackers, Inc.

STOP.

1-14
Quantum Mechanics

The MCAT requires a small amount of knowledge concerning quantum mechanics. Everything that you'll need to know is in this Lecture. Quantum mechanics basically says that elementary particles can only gain or lose energy and certain other quantities in discrete units. This is analogous to walking up stairs as opposed to walking up a ramp. If each stairstep is one foot, you can only raise or lower yourself by increments of one foot on the stairs, while on the ramp you can move along the ramp until you are raised one half foot or any other fraction of a foot. The discrete units of energy are so small that the gain or loss of one unit is insignificant on a macroscopic scale. Thus quantum mechanic effects are generally only important when dealing with elementary particles.

1-15
Quantum Numbers

A set of four quantum numbers is the address or ID number for an electron in a given atom. No two electrons in the same atom can have the same four quantum numbers.

The first quantum number is the **principal quantum number, n**. The principal quantum number designates the **shell** level. The larger the principal quantum number, the greater the size and energy of the electron orbital. For the representative elements the principal quantum number for electrons in the outer most shell is given by the period in the periodic table. The principal quantum number for the transition metals lags one shell behind the period, and for the lanthanides and actinides lags two shells behind the period.

Valence electrons, the electrons which contribute most to an element's chemical properties, are located in the outermost shell of an atom. Typically, but not always, only electrons from the s and p subshells are considered valence electrons.

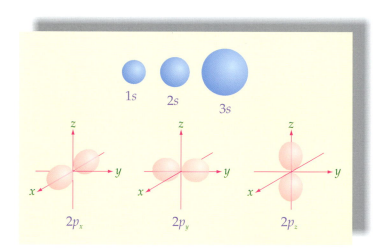

The second quantum number is the **azimuthal quantum number, ℓ**. The azimuthal quantum number designates the **subshell**. These are the orbital shapes with which we are familiar such as **s, p, d, and f**. If $\ell = 0$, we are in the s subshell; if $\ell = 1$, we are in the p subshell; and so on. For each new shell, there exists an additional subshell with the azimuthal quantum number **$\ell = n-1$**. Each subshell has a peculiar shape to its orbitals. The shapes are based on probability functions of the position of the electron. There is a 90% chance of finding the electron somewhere inside a given shape. You should recognize the shapes of the orbitals in the s and p subshells.

The third quantum number is the **magnetic quantum number, m_ℓ**. The magnetic quantum number designates the precise **orbital** of a given subshell. Each subshell will have orbitals with magnetic quantum numbers from **$-\ell$ to $+\ell$**. Thus for the first shell with $n = 1$, and $\ell = 0$, there is only one possible orbital, and its magnetic quantum number is 0. For the third shell with $n = 3$, and $\ell = 2$, there are 5 possible orbitals which have the magnetic quantum numbers of $-2, -1, 0, +1,$ and $+2$.

The fourth quantum number is the **electron spin quantum number, m_s**. The electron spin quantum number can have values of **$-\frac{1}{2}$ or $+\frac{1}{2}$**. Any orbital can hold up to two electrons and no more. If two electrons occupy the same orbital, they have the same first three quantum numbers. **The Pauli exclusion principle** says that no

Copyright © 2005 Examkrackers, Inc.

two electrons in the same atom can have the same four quantum numbers. Because two electrons in the same orbital have identical 1st, 2nd, and 3rd quantum numbers, they must have opposite electron spin quantum numbers.

The number of total orbitals within a shell is equal to n^2. Solving for the number of orbitals for each shell gives 1, 4, 9, 16… Since there are two electrons in each orbital, the number of elements in the periods of the periodic table is 2, 8, 18, and 32.

Number	Character	Symbol	Value
1st	Shell	n	n
2nd	subshell	ℓ	from zero to $n-1$
3rd	orbital	m_1	between ℓ and $-\ell$
4th	spin	m_s	$\frac{1}{2}$ or $-\frac{1}{2}$

Let's summarize: The first quantum number is the shell. It corresponds roughly to the energy level of the electrons within that shell. The second quantum number is the subshell. It gives the shape. You need to recognize the shape of *s* and *p* orbitals. The third quantum number is the specific orbital within a subshell. The fourth quantum number distinguishes between two electrons in the same orbital; one is a +1/2 and the other is a -1/2.

1-16 The Heisenberg Uncertainty Principle

The **Heisenberg Uncertainty Principle** arises from the dual nature (wave-particle) of matter. It states that there exists an inherent uncertainty in the product of the position of a particle and its momentum, and that this uncertainty is on the order of Planck's constant.

$$\Delta x \Delta p \approx h$$

Here's the story with the Heisenberg uncertainty principle: the more we know about the momentum of any particle, the less we can know about the position. The amount of uncertainty is very small; on the order of Planck's constant (6.63×10^{-34} J s). There are other quantities besides position and momentum to which the uncertainty principle applies, but position and momentum is the pair that you are likely to need to know for the MCAT.

1-17 Energy Level of Electrons

The **Aufbau principle** states that with each new proton added to create a new element, a new electron is added as well. Nature typically prefers a lower energy state. All other things being equal, the lower the energy level of a system, the more stable the system. Thus, electrons look for an available orbital with the lowest energy state whenever they add to an atom. The orbital with the lowest energy will be contained in the subshell with the lowest energy.

To see why the energy level rises as the electrons move further from the nucleus, we must consider the attractive force between the negatively charged electrons and the positively charged nucleus. Because the force is attractive, we must do work to separate them; we apply a force over a distance. Work is the transfer of energy into or out of a system. In this case, our system is the electron and the nucleus. We are

Copyright © 2005 Examkrackers, Inc.

doing work on the system, so we are transferring energy into the system. This energy shows up as increased electrostatic potential energy. Like the energy between bonding atoms, the energy between the electron and the nucleus increases from a negative to zero as the electron moves to an infinite distance away from the nucleus.

If, for a given atom, we list the shells and the subshells in order from lowest to highest energy level, and we add a superscript to show the number of electrons in each subshell, we have the **electron configuration** of that atom. (Electron configurations do not have to be from lowest to highest energy subshells, but they usually are.) Electron configurations for several atoms are given below:

$$Na => 1s^2\, 2s^2\, 2p^6\, 3s^1$$

$$Ar => 1s^2\, 2s^2\, 2p^6\, 3s^2\, 3p^6$$

$$Fe => 1s^2\, 2s^2\, 2p^6\, 3s^2\, 3p^6\, 4s^2\, 3d^6$$

$$Br => 1s^2\, 2s^2\, 2p^6\, 3s^2\, 3p^6\, 4s^2\, 3d^{10}\, 4p^5$$

An abbreviated electron configuration can be written by using the configuration of the next smallest noble gas as follows:

$$Na => [Ne]\, 3s^1$$

$$Ar => [Ar]$$

$$Fe => [Ar]\, 4s^2\, 3d^6 \text{ (sometimes written } [Ar]\, 3d^6\, 4s^2)$$

$$Br => [Ar]\, 4s^2\, 3d^{10}\, 4p^5$$

$$Cu => [Ar]\, 4s^1\, 3d^{10}$$

Above are the electron configurations for atoms whose electrons are all at their lowest energy levels. This is called the **ground state**. Electron configurations can also be given for ions and atoms with excited electrons:

$$Na^+ => 1s^2\, 2s^2\, 2p^6 \ \underline{or}\ [Ne]$$

$$Fe^{3+} => [Ar]\, 3d^5$$

$$Br^- => [Ar]\, 4s^2\, 3d^{10}\, 4p^6 \ \underline{or}\ [Kr]$$

$$Be_{\text{with an excited electron}} => 1s^2\, 2s^1\, 2p^1$$

A simple trick to find the relative energies of the subshells is to use this table. The chart grows like stair-steps. An arrow is drawn down each diagonal as shown. If we follow the arrows as they go down the steps, they show us the order of increasing energy for the subshells. Notice that the energy levels are not exactly in numerical order. For example, the 4s subshell is at a lower energy level than the 3d.

	s	p	d	f
1	1s			
2	2s	2p		
3	3s	3p	3d	
4	4s	4p	4d	4f
5	5s	5p	5d	5f

Be certain that the total number of electrons in your electron configuration equals the total number of electrons in the atom. Notice that for the ions of the representative elements, electron configuration resembles that of a noble gas. The electron configurations of the transition metal ions are not the same as the nearest noble gas. As noted before, for transition metals, ions are formed by losing electrons from the subshell with the highest principle quantum number first. Something else to know about transition metals is that their electron configurations aren't always that easy to predict. For instance, in the fourth period, the electron configurations of Cr and Cu have only one electron in the 4s orbital. This is because the 4s and 3d orbitals of these atoms are degenerate (at the same energy level). You don't have to memorize the electron configuration of each transition metal. Just be aware that they don't always follow the table given above, due to degenerate orbitals.

Also, notice that an electron can momentarily (for a matter of microseconds) absorb energy and jump to a higher energy level creating an atom in an excited state.

Copyright © 2005 Examkrackers, Inc.

Like charges repel each other. If we considered the energy of two particles with like charges, we would find that as the particles near each other, the mutual repulsion creates an increase in potential energy. This is the case when electrons approach each other. It explains why only two electrons can fit into one orbital. It also helps explain **Hund's rule**: electrons will not fill any orbital in the same subshell until all orbitals in that subshell contain at least one electron, and the unpaired electrons will have parallel spins. Hund's rule can be represented graphically as shown in the chart to the right. Electrons are represented by vertical arrows. Upward arrows represent electrons with positive spin, and downward arrows represent electrons with negative spin. When going from boron to carbon, the added electron has a choice of sharing the $2p_x$ orbital or taking the $2p_y$ orbital for itself. Hund's rule says that the electron prefers to have its own orbital when such an orbital is available at the same energy level.

Max Planck is considered the father of quantum mechanics. **Planck's quantum theory** demonstrates that electromagnetic energy is quantized (i.e. it comes only in discrete units related to the wave frequency). In other words, if we transfer energy from one point to another via an electromagnetic wave, and we wish to increase the amount of energy that we are transferring without changing the frequency, we can only change the energy in discrete increments given by:

$$\Delta E = hf$$

where h is Planck's constant (6.6×10^{-34} J s).

Einstein showed that if we considered light as a particle phenomenon with each particle as a photon, the energy of a single photon is given by the same equation: $E_{photon} = hf$. *Neils Bohr* applied the quantized energy theory to create an electron ladder model for hydrogen with each rung representing an allowed energy level for the electron. His model explained the line spectra for hydrogen but failed for atoms with more than one electron. *Louis de Broglie* then showed that electrons and other moving masses exhibit wave characteristics that follow the equation:

$$\lambda = \frac{h}{mv}$$

The energy levels of electrons are quantized as well. The possible energy levels of an electron can be represented as an energy ladder. Each energy level is analogous to a rung on a ladder or the spheres shown in the diagram on the next page. The electrons may occupy any rung, but do not occupy the space between rungs because this space represents forbidden energy levels.

When an electron falls from a higher energy rung to a lower energy rung, energy is released from the atom in the form of a photon. The photon must have a frequency which corresponds to the change in energy of the electron as per $\Delta E = hf$. Of course the reverse is also true. If a photon collides with an electron, it can only bump that electron to another energy level rung and not between energy level rungs. If the photon doesn't have enough energy to bump the electron to the next rung, the electron will not move from its present rung and the photon will be reflected away.

Copyright © 2005 Examkrackers, Inc.

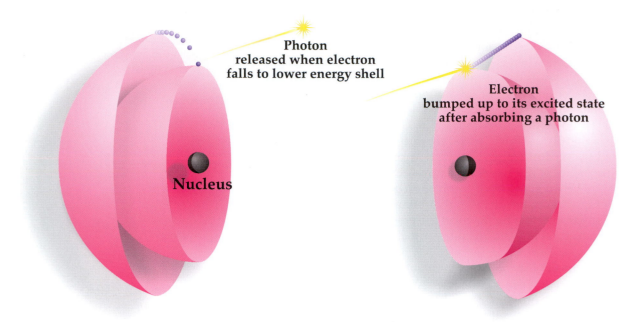

Photon released when electron falls to lower energy shell

Electron bumped up to its excited state after absorbing a photon

Nucleus

With the **photoelectric effect** Einstein demonstrated this one-to-one, photon to electron collision. He showed that the one-to-one collision proved that light was made up of particles. Einstein's reasoning went as follows: Light shining on a metal can cause the emission of electrons (sometimes called *photoelectrons* in the photoelectric effect). Since the energy of a wave is proportional to its intensity, we would expect that when the intensity of light shining on a metal is increased by increasing the number of photons, the kinetic energy of an emitted electron would increase accordingly. This is not the case. Instead, the kinetic energy of the electrons increases only when intensity is increased by increasing the frequency of each photon. If the frequency is low enough, no electrons at all will be emitted regardless of the number of photons. This demonstrates that the electrons must be ejected by one-to-one photon-electron collisions and not by the combined energies of two or more photons. It also shows that if a single photon does not have sufficient energy, no electron will be emitted. The minimum amount of energy required to eject an electron is called the *work function*, Φ, of the metal. The kinetic energy of the ejected electron is given by the energy of the photon minus the work function ($K.E. = hf - \Phi$).

Copyright © 2005 Examkrackers, Inc.

17. Which of the following species has an unpaired electron in its ground-state electronic configuration?

    A. Ne
    B. Ca^+
    C. Na^+
    D. O^{2-}

18. What is the electron configuration of chromium?

    A. $[Ar]\ 3d^6$
    B. $[Ar]\ 4s^1\ 3d^5$
    C. $[Ar]\ 4s^2\ 3d^3$
    D. $[Ar]\ 4s^2\ 4p^4$

19. If the position of an electron is known with 100% certainty, which of the following cannot be determined for the same electron?

    A. mass
    B. velocity
    C. charge
    D. spin quantum number

20. When an electron moves from a $2p$ to a $3s$ orbital, the atom containing that electron:

    A. becomes a new isotope.
    B. becomes a new element.
    C. absorbs energy.
    D. releases energy.

21. Compared to an electron with a principal quantum number of 1, an electron with a principal quantum number of 2 will have:

    A. a lower energy.
    B. a higher energy.
    C. a negative spin.
    D. a positive spin.

22. Which of the following best explains why sulfur can make more bonds than oxygen?

    A. Sulfur is more electronegative than oxygen.
    B. Oxygen is more electronegative than sulfur.
    C. Sulfur has $3d$ orbitals not available to oxygen.
    D. Sulfur has fewer valence electrons.

23. Hund's rule says that unpaired electrons in the same subshell:

    A. have opposite spins.
    B. have parallel spins.
    C. occupy the same orbital.
    D. cannot exist.

24. Aluminum has only one oxidation state, while chromium has several. Which of the following is the best explanation for this difference?

    A. Electrons in the d orbitals of Cr may or may not be used to form bonds.
    B. Electrons in the p orbitals of Cr may or may not be used to form bonds.
    C. Electrons in the d orbitals of Al may or may not be used to form bonds.
    D. Electrons in the p orbitals of Al may or may not be used to form bonds.

Gases, Kinetics, and Chemical Equilibrium

2-1
Gases

A typical real gas is a loose collection of weakly attracted atoms or molecules moving rapidly in random directions. In a gas, the volume of the molecules accounts for about 0.1 percent of the total volume occupied by the gas. By comparison, molecules in a liquid account for about 70 percent of the total volume occupied by the liquid. 0°C and 1 atm is called **standard temperature and pressure (STP)**. At STP, the average distance between gas molecules is about 35 Å. This is small on a macroscopic scale, but typically amounts to over a dozen molecular diameters on the microscopic scale. For instance, an oxygen molecule is about 2.5 Å from end to end. Gas molecules move at tremendous speeds. At STP, the average speed of oxygen molecules is about 1,078 mph (481 m/s). The **mean free path** is the distance traveled by a gas molecule between collisions. The mean free path of oxygen at STP is about 1600 Å, about 1 ten thousandth of a millimeter. Moving such small distances at such high speed results in one oxygen molecule making about 2,500,000,000 collisions with other molecules each second. This explains why some chemical reactions can appear to occur instantaneously.

If a gas is a mixture of compounds, then unlike liquids, the mixture will be homogeneous regardless of polarity differences. For instance, liquid gasoline and liquid water don't mix because gasoline is nonpolar while water is polar; however, water and gasoline vapors form a homogeneous mixture.

Although polarity differences do not cause gases to separate, when temperatures are low enough gravity causes denser gases to settle beneath less dense gases. Cold CO_2 gas from a fire extinguisher is heavier than air and smothers a fire by settling over the fire and displacing the air upward. Hot air rises because it is less dense than cold air.

Unlike liquids, all gases are miscible with each other; they mix regardless of polarity differences. However, given time and low temperatures, heavier gases tend to settle below lighter gases.

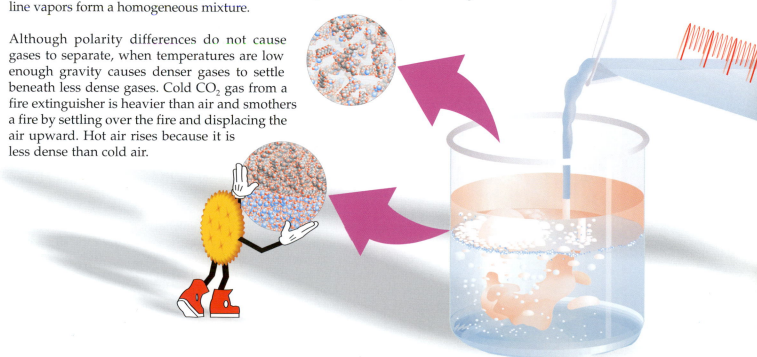

2-2
Kinetic Molecular Theory

Rather than memorizing Charles', Boyle's, and Avogadro's laws, you should have a good understanding of the ideal gas law. The equations associated with these laws have been left out purposely, so that you won't waste time memorizing them. The equations create confusion in the sense that they are true only within certain limitations. For instance, Charles' law requires constant pressure.

PV = nRT will solve any problem that the other three laws might solve. By the way, you won't need to memorize the name of each law either.

To better understand the complex behavior of gases, scientists have theorized a model of an **ideal gas**. This model is called the kinetic molecular theory. In the **kinetic molecular theory**, an ideal gas lacks certain real gas characteristics. Ideal gas has the following four characteristics not shared by a real gas:

1. Gas molecules have zero volume;

2. Gas molecules exert no forces other than repulsive forces due to collisions;

3. Gas molecules make completely elastic collisions;

4. The average kinetic energy of gas molecules is directly proportional to the temperature of the gas.

Ideal gas obeys the **ideal gas law**:

$$PV = nRT$$

where P is the pressure in atmospheres, V is the volume in liters, n is the number of moles of gas, T is the temperature in Kelvin, and R is the universal gas constant (0.08206 L atm K^{-1} mol^{-1} or 8.314 J K^{-1} mol^{-1}). Special cases of the ideal gas law include: *Charles' law*: The volume of a gas is proportional to temperature at constant pressure; *Boyle's law*: The volume of a gas is inversely proportional to pressure at constant temperature and; *Avogadro's law*: The volume of a gas is proportional to the number of moles at constant temperature and pressure.

Notice that there are four variables needed to define the state of a gas: P, V, n, and T. This can lead to confusion. For instance, it is possible to cool a gas by increasing the volume, even though the equation $PV = nRT$ indicates that temperature is directly proportional to volume. When a gas expands in a container, the gas does work on its surrounding by pushing outward on the walls of the container. The force on the walls times the distance that the walls expand is the work done by the gas. This work represents a transfer of energy from the gas to the surroundings. The energy comes from the kinetic energy of the gas molecules. Both the temperature and the pressure are related to the kinetic energy of the molecules. The pressure is related to the kinetic energy per volume, and the temperature is related to the average kinetic energy per mole. When the gas expands, the pressure decreases due to both the loss in kinetic energy and the increase in volume. The temperature decreases due to the loss in kinetic energy via work done. So, if the volume of a gas were doubled, and the kinetic energy remained the same, the pressure would be reduced by a factor of two. But if no heat were added, the kinetic energy would be reduced. If the kinetic energy were reduced as the volume doubles, the pressure would be reduced by more than a factor of two. Thus the temperature would also decrease to preserve the equality in $PV = nRT$.

Notice that the ideal gas law does not change for different gases behaving ideally. (Of course not, it's written for an ideal gas.) This means that all gases (behaving ideally) will have the same volume, if they have the same temperature, pressure, and number of molecules. At STP one mole of any gas (behaving ideally) will occupy the **standard molar volume of 22.4 liters**.

As well as pure gases, we can apply the kinetic molecular theory to mixtures of gases. In a mixture of gases, each gas contributes to the pressure in the same proportion as it contributes to the number of molecules of the gas. This makes sense, given the kinetic molecular theory, because molecules have no volume, no interactive forces other than collisions, and kinetic energy is conserved when they collide. Thus, each gas in a mixture essentially behaves as if it were in its container alone.

Copyright © 2005 Examkrackers, Inc.

You must recognize the standard molar volume and understand what it means. Learn to use this volume with the ideal gas law. For instance, 2 moles of gas at 0°C occupying 11.2 liters will have a pressure of 4 atm. To get this result, we start with the standard molar volume, 22.4 L, at STP. First, we double the number of moles, so, according to the ideal gas law, the pressure doubles. Second, we halve the volume, so pressure doubles again.

x2 x2

$PV = nRT$

x2

$PV = nRT$

÷2

1 atm	2 atm	4 atm
22.4 L	22.4 L	11.2 L
1 mole	2 moles	2 moles
0°C (273 K)	0°C	0°C

The amount of pressure contributed by any gas in a gaseous mixture is called the partial pressure of that gas. The **partial pressure** of a particular gas is the total pressure of the gaseous mixture times the mole fraction of the particular gas. The equation for the partial pressure is:

$$P_a = \chi_a P_{total}$$

where P_a is the partial pressure of gas 'a', and χ_a is the mole fraction of gas 'a'. (The mole fraction is the number of moles of gas 'a' divided by the total number of moles of gas in the sample.)

Dalton's law states that the total pressure exerted by a gaseous mixture is the sum of the partial pressures of each of its gases.

$$P_{total} = P_1 + P_2 + P_3 \ldots$$

From the ideal gas law, we can derive the following equation relating average translational kinetic energy and the temperature of a gas:

$$K.E._{avg} = \frac{3}{2}RT$$

Dalton's law is a good way to understand an ideal gas. Each gas behaves like it is in the container by itself so all the partial pressures added together equal the total pressure.

where the average translational kinetic energy is found from the root-mean-square (rms) velocity. (rms velocity is the square root of the average of the squares of the molecular velocities. rms velocity is slightly greater than the average speed.) $K.E. = 3/2\ RT$ is valid for any fluid system, including liquids. Notice that the kinetic energy derived from this equation is the average kinetic energy for a mole of gas molecules and not the energy of every, or maybe even any, of the molecules. A gas molecule chosen at random may have almost any kinetic energy associated with it.

Since the temperature dictates the average kinetic energy of the molecules in a gas, the gas molecules of each gas in any gaseous mixture must have the same average kinetic energy. For instance, the air we breathe is made up of approximately 21% O_2 and 79% N_2 by number. The molecules of O_2 and N_2 in a sample of air have the same

Copyright © 2005 Examkrackers, Inc.

In a sample of gas, the kinetic energy of the molecules will vary from molecule to molecule, but there will be an average kinetic energy of the molecules that is proportional to the temperature and independent of the type of gas.

average kinetic energy. However, since O_2 and N_2 have different masses, their molecules have different rms velocities. By setting their kinetic energies equal to each other, we can derive a relationship between their rms velocities. This relationship, which gives the ratio of the rms velocities of two gases in a homogeneous mixture, is called **Graham's law**:

$$\frac{v_1}{v_2} = \frac{\sqrt{m_2}}{\sqrt{m_1}}$$

Notice that the subscripts are reversed from one side of the equation to the other.

Graham's law also tells us that the average speed of the molecules of a pure gas is inversely proportional to the square root of the mass of the gas molecules.

Interestingly, Graham's law gives information about the rates of two types of gaseous spreading: effusion and diffusion. **Effusion** is the spreading of a gas from high pressure to very low pressure through a 'pinhole'. (A 'pinhole' is defined as an opening much smaller than the average distance between the gas molecules.) Because molecules of a gas with higher rms velocity will experience more collisions with the walls of a container, the rate at which molecules from such a gas find the pinhole and go through is likely to be greater. In fact, Graham's law predicts the comparative rates of effusion for two gases at the same temperature. The ratio of the rates of effusion of two gases is equal to the inverse of the ratio of the square roots of their molecular weights and equal to the ratio of their rms velocities.

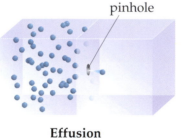

pinhole

Effusion

$$\frac{\text{effusion rate}_1}{\text{effusion rate}_2} = \frac{\sqrt{M_2}}{\sqrt{M_1}}$$

Diffusion is the spreading of one gas into another gas or into empty space. The ratio of the diffusion rates of two gases (acting ideally) is approximated by Graham's law. The diffusion rate is much slower than the rms velocity of the molecules because gas molecules collide with each other and with molecules of other gases as they diffuse. For example, if we wet two cotton balls, one with aqueous NH_3 and the other with aqueous HCl, and place them into opposite ends of a glass tube, gaseous NH_3 and HCl will diffuse toward each other through the air inside the tube. Where they meet, they will react to form NH_4Cl, which will precipitate as a white solid. Graham's law accurately predicts that NH_3 will travel 1.5 times further than HCl. However, any particular molecule is likely to follow a very crooked path similar to those shown in the diagram. Recall that the mean free path of a gas molecule is on the order of a few hundred nanometers.

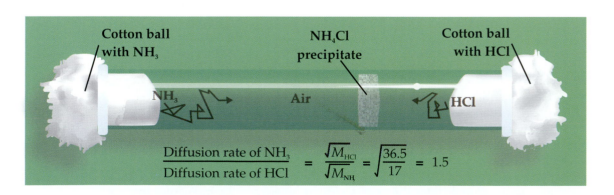

Cotton ball with NH_3 NH_4Cl precipitate   Cotton ball with HCl

NH_3 Air   HCl

$$\frac{\text{Diffusion rate of } NH_3}{\text{Diffusion rate of HCl}} = \frac{\sqrt{M_{HCl}}}{\sqrt{M_{NH_3}}} = \sqrt{\frac{36.5}{17}} = 1.5$$

Copyright © 2005 Examkrackers, Inc.

Real gases deviate from ideal behavior when their molecules are close together. When molecules are close together, the volume of the molecules become significant compared to the volume around the molecules. Also, as can be seen by Coulomb's law ($F = kqq/r^2$), when molecules are close together, the electrostatic forces increase and become significant. High pressure pushes gas molecules together causing deviations from ideal behavior. Low temperatures cause gas molecules to settle close together also resulting in deviations from ideal behavior. Gases generally deviate from ideal behavior at pressures above ten atmospheres and temperatures near their boiling points. Substances that we typically think of as gases closely approximate ideal behavior.

Once again, be careful about the confusion with PV = nRT. It seems like increasing pressure also increases temperature, so how can ideal behavior deviations occur with either an increase in pressure or a decrease in temperature? The answer is that to create deviations in ideal behavior, we just want to move the molecules closer together; in other words, decrease the volume. We can decrease the volume by squeezing the molecules together with high pressure, or by lowering the temperature and letting the molecules settle close together. From PV = nRT, we see that volume decreases with either increasing pressure or decreasing temperature.

2-3
Real Gases

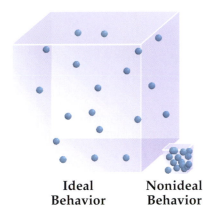

Ideal Behavior   **Nonideal Behavior**

You should be aware of how real gases deviate from ideal behavior. Van der Waals equation:

$$[P + a(n/V)^2](V - nb) = nRT]$$

approximates the real pressure and real volume of a gas, where a and b are constants for specific gases. The variable b is a measure of the actual volume occupied by a mole of gas. The variable a reflects the strength of intermolecular attractions. The values of a and b generally increase with the molecular mass and molecular complexity of a gas.

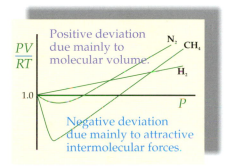

You do not need to know van der Waals equation for the MCAT. It is more important that you have a qualitative understanding of real gas deviations from ideal behavior. First, since molecules of a real gas do have volume, their volume must be added to the ideal volume. Thus:

$$V_{real} > V_{ideal}$$

where V_{ideal} is calculated from $PV = nRT$.

Second, molecules in a real gas do exhibit forces on each other, and those forces are attractive when the molecules are far apart. In a gas, repulsive forces are only significant during molecular collisions or near collisions. Since the predominant intermolecular forces in a gas are attractive, gas molecules are pulled inward toward the center of the gas, and slow before colliding with container walls. Having been slightly slowed, they strike the container wall with less force than predicted by the kinetic molecular theory. Thus a real gas exerts less pressure than predicted by the ideal gas law.

$$P_{real} < P_{ideal}$$

where P_{ideal} is calculated from $PV = nRT$.

From PV = nRT, we expect PV/RT to equal one for one mole of ideal gas at any temperature and pressure. Since volume deviates positively from ideal behavior and pressure deviates negatively, if PV/RT is greater than one for one mole of gas, then the deviation due to molecular volume must be greater than the deviation due to the intermolecular forces. If PV/RT is less than one for one mole of gas, then the deviation due to intermolecular forces must be greater than the deviation due to molecular volume.

Copyright © 2005 Examkrackers, Inc.

25. A 13 gram gaseous sample of an unknown hydrocarbon occupies a volume of 11.2 L at STP. What is the hydrocarbon?

    A. CH
    B. C_2H_4
    C. C_2H_2
    D. C_3H_3

26. If the density of a gas is given as ρ which of the following expressions represents the molecular weight of the gas?

    A. $P\rho/RT$
    B. $\rho RT/P$
    C. $nRT/P\rho$
    D. $P\rho/RT$

27. Ammonia burns in air to form nitrogen dioxide and water.

    $$4NH_3(g) + 7O_2(g) \rightarrow 4NO_2(g) + 6H_2O(l)$$

    If 8 moles of NH_3 are reacted with 14 moles of O_2 in a rigid container with an initial pressure of 11 atm, what is the partial pressure of NO_2 in the container when the reaction runs to completion? (Assume constant temperature.)

    A. 4 atm
    B. 6 atm
    C. 11 atm
    D. 12 atm

28. At moderately high pressures, the PV/RT ratio for one mole of methane gas is less than one. The most likely reason for this is:

    A. Methane gas behaves ideally at moderate pressures.
    B. The temperature must be very low.
    C. At such pressures, molecular volume causes a greater deviation to ideal behavior than intermolecular forces for methane.
    D. At such pressures, intermolecular forces cause a greater deviation to ideal behavior than molecular volume for methane.

29. A force is applied to a container of gas reducing its volume by half. The temperature of the gas:

    A. decreases.
    B. increases.
    C. remains constant.
    D. The temperature change depends upon the amount of force used.

30. Equal molar quantities of oxygen and hydrogen gas were placed in container *A* under high pressure. A small portion of the mixture was allowed to effuse for a very short time into the vacuum in container *B*. Which of the following is true concerning partial pressures of the gases at the end of the experiment?

    A. The partial pressure of hydrogen in container *A* is approximately four times as great as the partial pressure of oxygen in container *A*.
    B. The partial pressure of oxygen in container *A* is approximately four times as great as the partial pressure of hydrogen in container *A*.
    C. The partial pressure of hydrogen in container *B* is approximately four times as great as the partial pressure of oxygen in container *B*.
    D. The partial pressure of oxygen in container *B* is approximately four times as great as the partial pressure of hydrogen in container *B*.

31. HCl gas and NH_3 gas form NH_4Cl precipitate according to the following equation:

    $$HCl(g) + NH_3(g) \rightarrow NH_4Cl(s)$$

    When cotton balls are moistened with the aqueous solutions of the respective gases and inserted into either end of a glass tube, the gases diffuse toward the middle of the glass tube to form the precipitate. If a 10 cm glass tube is used, at what distance *x* will the precipitate form?

    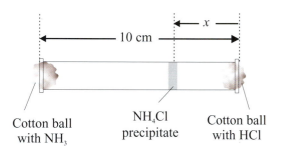

    Cotton ball with NH_3 NH_4Cl precipitate   Cotton ball with HCl

    A. 1.5 cm
    B. 2.5 cm
    C. 3.0 cm
    D. 4.0 cm

32. At STP, one liter of which of the following gases contains the most molecules?

    A. H_2
    B. He
    C. N_2
    D. Each gas contains the same number of molecules at STP.

Chemical kinetics is the study of reaction mechanisms and rates. As of yet, there are no unifying principles of kinetics, which means kinetics is a complicated field with many opposing theories as to how reactions proceed. Additionally, the mathematics of kinetics is complicated and well beyond the scope of MCAT. MCAT will address kinetics only in its simplest form. Keep in mind that kinetics deals with the rate of a reaction typically as it moves toward equilibrium, while thermodynamics deals with the balance of reactants and products after they have achieved equilibrium. Kinetics tells us how fast equilibrium is achieved, while thermodynamics tells us what equilibrium looks like. The two disciplines are intricately related, but they should not be confused.

2-4
Chemical Kinetics

The **collision model** of reactions provides an enlightening method for visualizing chemical reactions. In order for a chemical reaction to occur, the reacting molecules must collide. However, for most reactions, the rate of a given reaction is found to be much lower than the frequency of collisions. This indicates that most collisions do not result in a reaction.

2-5
The Collision Theory

There are two requirements for a given collision to create new molecules in a reaction. First, the relative kinetic energies of the colliding molecules must reach a threshold energy called the **activation energy.** The relative kinetic energy refers to the kinetic energy due to relative velocity only. In other words, velocity in a direction away from another molecule decreases the relative kinetic energy of a collision. Second, the colliding molecules must have the proper spatial orientation.

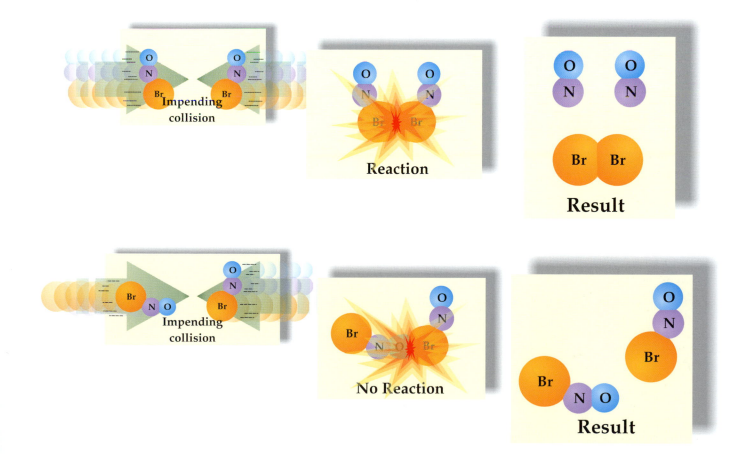

Copyright © 2005 Examkrackers, Inc.

The product of the collision frequency z, the fraction of collisions having the effective spatial orientations p (called the *steric factor*), and the fraction of collisions having sufficient relative energy $e^{-Ea/RT}$ (where E_a is the activation energy) gives the rate constant k of a reaction. This relationship is called the *Arrhenius equation*:

$$k = zpe^{-Ea/RT}$$

Does the rate of an exothermic reaction increase with temperature? You bet it does. Remember, do not confuse kinetics with thermodynamics. Increasing the rate is not necessarily a statement about the equilibrium. It simply means that equilibrium is achieved more quickly.

(often written as $k = Ae^{-Ea/RT}$). The value of the rate constant depends upon pressure, catalysts, and temperature. Pressure dependence is typically negligible. Catalysts will be discussed later in this Lecture. The temperature dependence is seen in the Arrhenius equation. The rate constant generally doubles to triples with each increase of 10°C. Since the effect of temperature on E_a is negligible for most reactions, the fraction of collisions that have at least the activation energy ($e^{-Ea/RT}$) increases with the temperature. This, in turn, indicates that the rate constant k increases with increasing temperature for nearly all reactions. As demonstrated by the rate law (discussed later in this lecture), the rate constant is directly proportional to the rate of a reaction. **The rate of a reaction increases with temperature** mainly because more collisions with sufficient relative kinetic energy occur each second.

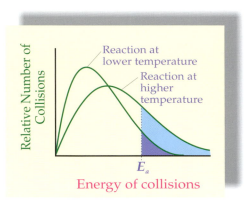

Energy of collisions

The temperature dependence of rate is demonstrated by the graph to the left, which compares two samples of identical gaseous mixtures reacting at different temperatures. The area under any section of the curve represents the relative number of collisions in that energy range. Notice the area to the right of the activation energy is greater at higher temperature. At higher temperature there are more collisions with enough energy to create a reaction. Notice that the energy of activation does not change with temperature. (Actually, E_a is temperature dependent, but for most reactions the dependence is extremely small, and, for the MCAT, E_a should be considered independent of temperature.)

2-6 Equations for Reaction Rates

For MCAT purposes we will consider only reactions occurring in gases and ideally dilute liquids at constant temperature. The rate of a reaction tells us how quickly the concentration of a reactant or product is changing. Rates are most often given in terms of molarity per second ($mol\ L^{-1}\ s^{-1}$). Factors affecting the rate of a reaction are temperature, pressure, and concentration of certain substances in the reacting system; however, pressure effects on reaction rates are usually small enough to be ignored.

The rate of a reaction can be viewed in terms of the change in concentration of any one of the reacting participants. Consider the following elementary reaction where the lower case letters are the stoichiometric coefficients of the balanced equation:

$$a\mathrm{A} + b\mathrm{B} \rightarrow c\mathrm{C} + d\mathrm{D}$$

In an elementary reaction, the coefficient tells you how many molecules participate in a reaction producing collision.

An *elementary reaction* is a reaction that occurs in a single step. The stoichiometric coefficients of an elementary equation give the *molecularity* of the reaction. The molecularity is the number of molecules colliding at one time to make a reaction. There are three possible molecularities: *unimolecular*, *bimolecular*, and *termolecular*. Since the reaction above is elementary, its molecularity is given by $a + b$. Chemical equations often represent multistep reactions called complex or composite reactions. There is no way to distinguish an elementary reaction from a complex reaction by inspection of the chemical equation. On the MCAT, the only way to know if a reaction is elementary is if you are told that it is.

The average reaction rate for any brief time interval t during the above reaction is:

$$rate = -\frac{1}{a}\frac{\Delta[A]}{t} = -\frac{1}{b}\frac{\Delta[B]}{t} = \frac{1}{c}\frac{\Delta[C]}{t} = \frac{1}{d}\frac{\Delta[D]}{t}$$

Don't confuse the rate constant with the rate of the reaction. They are proportional, but they are NOT identical.

'Δ' means "change in". The negative signs indicate that the reactant concentrations are decreasing as the reaction moves forward. Although the rate equation above is strictly correct only for an elementary reaction, it is a good approximation for a multistep reaction if the concentration of any intermediates is kept low. **Intermediates** are species that are products of one reaction and reactants of a later reaction in a reaction chain. The concentration of intermediates is often very low because they are often unstable and react as quickly as they are formed.

Chemical reactions are reversible; as the products are formed, products begin to react to form the reactants. This reverse reaction complicates the study of kinetics. For the time being, we will consider only the forward reactions. If we consider only the forward reaction, we can write a **rate law** for the reaction above as:

$$rate_{forward} = k_f[A]^{\alpha}[B]^{\beta}$$

The important thing to know here is the form of the rate law.

where k_f is the rate constant for the forward reaction. α and β are the **order of each respective reactant** and the sum $\alpha + \beta$ is the **overall order** of the reaction. If the reaction is elementary, $\alpha = a$ and $\beta = b$.

Both the order of the reactants and the value of the rate constant must be determined through experiment. Finding the rate law on the MCAT is a relatively simple matter. Consider the hypothetical reaction:

**2-7
Determining the Rate Law by Experiment**

$$2A + B + C \rightarrow 2D$$

In this case, we will assume that no reverse reaction occurs. We are given the following table with experimental data:

Trial	Initial Concentration of A (mol/L)	Initial Concentration of B (mol/L)	Initial Concentration of C (mol/L)	Measured Initial Rate (mol/L s)
1	0.1	0.1	0.1	8.0×10^{-4}
2	0.2	0.1	0.1	1.6×10^{-3}
3	0.2	0.2	0.1	6.4×10^{-3}
4	0.1	0.1	0.2	8.0×10^{-4}

We can find the order of each reactant by comparing the rates between two Trials in which only the concentration of one of the reactants is changed. For instance, comparing Trial 1 to Trial 2, the initial concentration of A is doubled and the concentrations of B and C remain the same. The reaction rate also doubles. Thus the rate of this reaction is directly proportional to the concentration of A. In the rate law, [A] receives an exponent of 1, and the reaction is considered first order with respect to reactant A. Comparing Trials 2 and 3 we find that when only the concentration of B is doubled, the reaction rate is quadrupled. This indicates that the rate is proportional to the square of the concentration of B. [B] receives a 2 for its exponent in the rate law and the reaction is second order with respect to B. Comparing Trials 1

For MCAT, you must be able to derive the rate law from a table of trials as done in this section. When given a rate law, you must be able to predict what changing the concentration of a reactant will do to the rate.

Copyright © 2005 Examkrackers, Inc.

The Rate Law **will** be determined by experiment!

and 4, the concentration of C is doubled, but there is no resulting change in the rate. The rate is independent of the concentration of C, so [C] receives an exponent of zero in the rate law. The reaction is zero order with respect to C. The complete rate law for our hypothetical reaction is:

$$rate_{forward} = k_f[A]^1[B]^2[C]^0$$

also written:

$$rate_{forward} = k_f[A][B]^2$$

By adding the exponents we find that the reaction overall is third order. Notice that the coefficients in the balanced chemical equation were not used to figure out the order.

Once we have derived the rate law from the experimental data, we can plug in the rate and concentrations from __any__ of the experiments into the rate law, and solve for the rate constant k.

Notice that the rate may be increased by increasing the concentration of the reactants. If we consider the collision model, this makes sense. The greater the concentration of a species, the more likely are collisions.

2-8 Recognizing Reaction Orders

The different orders of reactions have recognizably different characteristics. Keeping in mind that we are assuming that there is no reverse reaction taking place, we can compare graphs of the different orders of reaction for a single reactant. Plotting [A] with respect to time t for a zeroth order reaction results in a straight line with a slope $-k_f$.

In a first order reaction of the form:

$$A \rightarrow products \qquad rate = k_f[A]$$

where there is no reverse reaction, [A] decreases exponentially. A graph of a first order reaction comparing ln[A] with time t gives a straight line with a slope of $-k_f$. The same first order reaction has a constant half life that is independent of the concentration of A. The molecularity of a first order reaction implies that no collision takes place since there is only one molecule reacting. However, current theory requires a collision with any other molecule, boosting the reactant to a higher energy state resulting in a reaction. Although this is a two step process, it exhibits first order kinetics (except under low pressure). This is referred to as *pseudo-first order kinetics*.

For a graph of an irreversible second order reaction with a single reactant of the form:

$$2A \rightarrow products \qquad rate = k_f[A]^2$$

plotting 1/[A] gives a straight line with a slope of k_f. The half life of this type of second order reaction is dependent upon the concentration of A. It has the interesting characteristic that each consecutive half-life is twice as long as the last. For instance, the time required to reduce the concentration of A from 100% to 50% is half as long as the time required to reduce the concentration from 50% to 25%.

The second order reaction of the form:

$$A + B \rightarrow products \qquad rate = k_f[A][B]$$

Copyright © 2005 Examkrackers, Inc.

does not reveal the same graph, and does not have an easily predictable half life.

For a graph of an irreversible third order reaction with a single reactant of the form:

$$3A \rightarrow products \qquad rate = k_f[A]^3$$

plotting $1/2[A]^2$ gives a straight line with a slope of k_f.

To avoid the complications of reverse reactions, the technique of initial rates is often employed. In the initial moments of a reaction starting with all reactants and no products, the rate of the reverse reaction is zero. The rate law in section 2-7 was determined with initial rates.

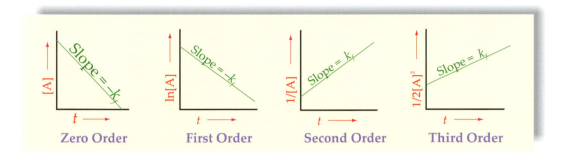

| Zero Order | First Order | Second Order | Third Order |

Any complex reaction can be separated into elementary steps. The rate of the slowest elementary step determines the rate of the overall reaction and is called the <u>rate determining step</u>. If the slow step is the first step, the rate law can be derived directly from this step and no other. If the slow step is other than the first step, the slow step is still the rate determining step, but steps prior to the slow step will contribute to the rate law. Steps after the slow step will make no contribution to the rate law.

2-9
Rates of Reversible Reactions

Consider the following reaction:

$$NO_2(g) + CO(g) \rightarrow NO(g) + CO_2(g)$$

This reaction has two elementary steps:

1. $NO_2(g) + NO_2(g) \rightarrow NO_3(g) + NO(g)$ *slow step*
2. $NO_3(g) + CO(g) \rightarrow NO_2(g) + CO_2(g)$ *fast step*

Notice that if we add these two equations together, we arrive at the original equation. Elementary steps must add to give the complex reaction. Since the first step is the slow step, the rate law for the overall reaction is given by this step and is:

$$rate = k_1[NO_2]^2$$

We know that the exponent for $[NO_2]$ is 2 because we derived the rate law from an elementary equation, and in the elementary equation two NO_2 molecules collide to create a reaction. Automatically using the coefficient of the balanced equation for the exponent in the rate law works only if the equation is elementary. Don't forget, the rate law above assumes negligible contribution from the reverse reaction, and it also assumes a sufficient concentration of CO for the fast step to occur.

When the first step of a reaction series is the fast step, things can be a little tricky. If the first reaction is the fast reaction, the rate of the overall reaction is still equal to

Remember that the slow step determines the rate.

Copyright © 2005 Examkrackers, Inc.

the rate of the slowest step. However, now one of the products of the fast step is a reactant in the slow step. Such a species is called an intermediate. The concentration of the intermediate is tricky to predict. An intermediate is usually not stable. If we assume that the fast reaction reaches equilibrium very quickly, the concentration of the intermediate remains at its equilibrium concentration. We can use the equilibrium concentration of the intermediate in predicting the slow step. For instance:

$$2NO(g) + Br_2(g) \rightarrow 2NOBr(g)$$

This reaction has two elementary steps:

1. $NO(g) + Br_2(g) \rightarrow NOBr_2(g)$ *fast step*

2. $NOBr_2(g) + NO(g) \rightarrow 2NOBr(g)$ *slow step*

The rate law for this reaction is:

$$rate = k_2[NOBr_2][NO]$$

Keep it simple:

When a fast step precedes the slow step, the slow step still determines the rate, but the concentration of one or more of the reactants in the slow step will be determined by the fast step. In such a case, assume that the fast step reaches and maintains equilibrium throughout the reaction, and use the equilibrium concentration of any intermediates.

However, the concentration of $NOBr_2$ depends upon the first step. If we assume that the first step reaches equilibrium very quickly, the concentration of $NOBr_2$ can be written in terms of the equilibrium constant K_c for step 1, $[NOBr_2] = K_c[NO][Br_2]$. Alternatively, since the first step is considered to be in equilibrium, we can set the forward reaction rate, $k_1[NO][Br_2]$, equal to the reverse rate, $k_{-1}[NOBr_2]$, and solve for $[NOBr_2]$. $[NOBr_2] = k_1/k_{-1}[NO][Br_2]$. The resulting rate law is:

$$rate = k_2 k_1/k_{-1}[NO]^2[Br_2]$$

This method is called the *equilibrium approximation*, which assumes that all steps prior to the rate limiting step are in equilibrium. The equilibrium approximation requires that the slow step be significantly slower than the fast steps. Since k_2k_1/k_{-1} is a constant, it is usually replaced by a single constant, $k_{observed}$.

If there is not a step that is significantly slower than the others, we can use the steady state approximation. In the *steady state approximation*, the concentration of the intermediate is considered to be small and hardly changing. This leads to the same result as the equilibrium approximation.

2-10
Catalysis

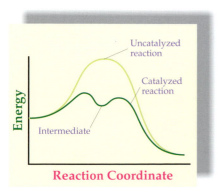

Reaction Coordinate

A catalyst creates a new reaction pathway which typically includes an intermediate.

A **catalyst** is a substance that increases the rate of a reaction without being consumed or permanently altered. Catalysts are capable of enhancing product selectivities and reducing energy consumption. A catalyst may lower the activation energy, E_a, or increase the steric factor (p from the Arrhenius equation). Most catalysts work by lowering the activation energy. The reaction rate depends exponentially on the activation energy. When the activation energy is lowered, more collisions have sufficient relative kinetic energy to create a reaction. This leads to more reactions and an increase in the overall reaction rate. This effect is shown in the energy vs. reaction coordinate diagram at the top of the next page.

A catalyst works by providing an alternative reaction mechanism that competes with the uncatalyzed mechanism. A catalyst cannot alter the equilibrium constant of a reaction, so it must increase the rate of both the forward and the reverse reaction. Although a catalyst cannot change the equilibrium constant, it can, in some cases, change the composition of the mixture at equilibrium; however, the effect is usually very small and should be ignored for the MCAT. For the MCAT, catalysts do not change the equilibrium composition.

Copyright © 2005 Examkrackers, Inc.

A catalyst can be either heterogeneous or homogeneous. A <u>**heterogeneous catalyst**</u> is in a different phase than the reactants and products. Heterogeneous catalysts are usually solids while the reactants and products are liquids or gases. A reactant may physically adsorb (via van der Waals forces) or, more often, chemically adsorb (usually via covalent bonds) to the surface of a solid catalyst. (Adsorption is the binding of molecules to a surface as opposed to absorption which refers to the uptake of molecules into an interior.) Molecules bind to a metal surface because, unlike metal atoms in the interior, metal atoms at the surface have unfulfilled valence requirements. The binding is almost always exothermic and the rate of catalysis depends upon the strength of the bond between the reactant and the catalyst. If bonds are too weak, not enough adsorption occurs; if bonds are too strong, too much energy is required to remove the reactant. Depending on the reaction, reactant molecules may bind to any of the atoms at the surface, or they may bind only to surface imperfections. Once adsorbed, molecules migrate from one adsorption site to the next. The more binding that occurs, the greater the reaction rate. Thus, reaction rates can be enhanced by increasing the surface area of a catalyst.

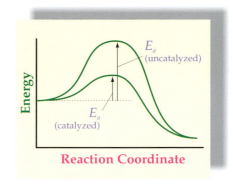

Reaction Coordinate

A <u>**homogeneous catalyst**</u> is in the same phase as the reactants and products, usually in the gas or liquid phase. Aqueous acid or base solutions often act as homogeneous catalysts. Some reactions exhibit autocatalysis by generating the catalyst as a product. The acid catalyzed hydrolysis of an ester is an example of autocatalysis, where the carboxylic acid product acts as a catalyst to the reaction.

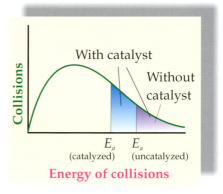

Energy of collisions

In the lab, concentrations of catalysts are usually small compared to the concentration of the reactants and products. In such cases, increasing the concentration of the catalyst increases the rate of the reaction. If the concentration of the catalyst is large compared to the reactants and products, the rate changes little or not at all with the catalyst concentration. Since catalysts alter reaction mechanisms, reactions with catalysts require separate rate constants. Remember, a catalyst doesn't prevent the original reaction from proceeding, so the total rate is given by the sum of the rates for both reactions. For instance, a first order uncatalyzed reaction may follow the rate law:

Remember that a catalyst increases the rate of a reaction by lowering the activation energy of that reaction. A catalyst doesn't change equilibrium and is not used up.

$$rate = k_0[\text{A}]$$

When the same reaction is catalyzed by acid, the new rate law would be:

$$rate = k_0[\text{A}] + k_{\text{H+}}[\text{H}^+][\text{A}]$$

Typically, the rate of the original reaction is negligible compared to the catalyzed rate.

Almost every chemical reaction in the human body is quickened by a protein catalyst called an enzyme. Enzymes are far more effective than inorganic catalysts. The number of reactions occurring at one active site on one enzyme is typically 1,000 per second and can be tens of thousands of times greater for the fastest enzymatic reactions. This number is called the *turnover number*.

Copyright © 2005 Examkrackers, Inc.

2-11
Effects of Solvent on Rate

Roughly speaking, liquid molecules make around 100 times more collisions per second than gas molecules because liquid molecules are much closer to each other. However, most of the collisions in a liquid are with the solvent resulting in no reaction.

The rate constant in a liquid is a function of the solvent as well as the temperature. The reactant in a liquid is solvated. These solvent-reactant bonds must be broken before a reaction can take place. In addition, the bonds may stabilize an intermediate. The degree of solvation affects k. Solvents can electrically insulate reactants reducing the electrostatic forces between them. The dielectric of the solvent affects k. Solvent viscosity can affect k as per the '*cage effect*' described below.

Reactants in a liquid can be trapped in a cage of solvent molecules. They rattle around in such a cage at tremendous rates making hundreds of collisions before squeezing between solvent molecules and into a new solvent cage. If they are trapped in the cage with another reactant, many of their collisions are with the other reactant and a reaction is likely to occur, but if there is not another reactant in the solvent cage, they cannot react until they escape the cage. The net result is that reactants in a liquid make an approximately equal number of collisions with other reactants as they would in a gas with equal concentrations; collisions in a liquid occur at about the same rate as in a gas.

Copyright © 2005 Examkrackers, Inc.

Questions 33 through 40 are **NOT** based on a descriptive passage.

33. Which of the following changes to a reaction will always increase the rate constant for that reaction?

    A. decreasing the temperature
    B. increasing the temperature
    C. increasing the concentration of the reactants
    D. increasing the concentration of the catalyst

34. All of the following may be true concerning catalysts and the reaction which they catalyze EXCEPT:

    A. Catalysts are not used up by the reaction.
    B. Catalysts lower the energy of activation.
    C. Catalysts increase the rate of the reverse reaction.
    D. Catalysts shift the reaction equilibrium to the right.

35. The table below shows 3 trials where the initial rate was measured for the reaction:

    $$2A + B \rightarrow C$$

    Which of the following expressions is the correct rate law for the reaction?

T	Molarity of A	Molarity of B	Initial Rate
1	0.05	0.05	5×10^{-3}
2	0.05	0.1	5×10^{-3}
3	0.1	0.05	1×10^{-2}

    A. rate = 0.1[A]
    B. rate = [A]
    C. rate = [A][B]
    D. rate = $[A]^2[B]$

36. The reaction below proceeds via the two step mechanism as shown.

    Overall Reaction: $2NO_2 + F_2 \rightarrow 2NO_2F$

    Step 1: $NO_2 + F_2 \rightarrow NO_2F + F$

    Step 2: $NO_2 + F \rightarrow NO_2F$

    X is the rate of step 1, and Y is the rate of step 2. If step 1 is much slower than step 2, then the rate of the overall reaction can be represented by:

    A. X
    B. Y
    C. $X + Y$
    D. $X - Y$

37. As temperature is increased in an exothermic gaseous reaction, all of the following increase EXCEPT:

    A. reaction rate.
    B. rate constant.
    C. activation energy.
    D. rms molecular velocity.

38. A container holds a pure sample of compound X shown at $t = 0$ min. Compound X undergoes a first order reaction to form compound Y. The same container is shown at $t = 15$ min. (Compound X is shown as white circles and compound Y is shown as black circles.)

    If the rate of the reverse reaction is negligible, which of the following might represent the container at $t = 30$ min?

    A.   C.

    B.   D.

39. The conversion of cis-2-butene to trans-2-butene takes place in a reaction that is first-order with respect to cis-2-butene. The conversion was observed in two separate trials under identical conditions except that in the second trial, the concentration of cis-2-butene was doubled. In the second trial:

    A. the reaction rate will be halved.
    B. the reaction rate will be doubled.
    C. the rate constant will be halved.
    D. the rate constant will be doubled.

40. When a radioactive isotope undergoes nuclear decay, the concentration of the isotope decreases exponentially with a constant half-life. It can be determined from this that radioactive decay is a:

    A. zeroth order reaction.
    B. first order reaction.
    C. second order reaction.
    D. third order reaction.

Copyright © 2005 Examkrackers, Inc.   **STOP.**

2-12
Equilibrium

Notice that by the rate definition:

$$rate = -\frac{1}{a}\frac{\Delta[A]}{t}$$

the rate at equilibrium is zero. Understand that zero is the net reaction rate, but there is a forward and a reverse reaction rate at equilibrium. Equilibrium is a dynamic process.

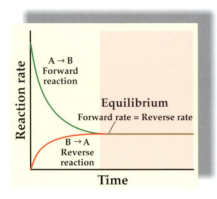

Chemical reactions are reversible. As reactants are converted to products, the concentration of the reactants decreases, and the concentration of the products increases. Since rates are related to concentrations, the rate of the forward reaction begins to slow, and the rate of the reverse reaction quickens as a reaction proceeds. Eventually, the two rates become equal. This condition, where the forward reaction rate equals the reverse reaction rate, is called **chemical equilibrium**. At chemical equilibrium, there is no change in the concentration of the products or reactants. Equilibrium will be reached from either direction, beginning with predominantly reactants or predominantly products. Equilibrium is the point of greatest entropy.

Consider the hypothetical first order elementary reaction:

$$A \rightarrow B$$

Notice from the diagram on the left that the forward rate changes faster than the reverse rate as the reaction proceeds. This indicates that the forward rate constant is greater than the reverse rate constant. The rate law for the forward and reverse reactions are rate = $k_f[A]$ and rate = $k_r[B]$ respectively. The rate of the forward reaction is directly proportional to [A]. From the diagram, the rate of the forward reaction is reduced by more than half, so [A] is also reduced by more than half. For every molecule of A lost, a molecule of B is created, so at equilibrium [B] must be greater than [A]. Setting the rates equal, $k_f[A] = k_r[B]$, we see that k_f must be greater than k_r if [B] is greater than [A] at equilibrium.

For a homogeneous reaction, where all species are in the same phase, there will always be some of each species present at equilibrium; however, in some cases, the rate constant for the forward reaction is so much greater than the rate constant for the reverse reaction that, for all practical purposes, the reaction runs to completion. Alternatively, if a product is continually removed as the reaction proceeds (perhaps in the form of a gas leaving an aqueous solution), the reaction can run to completion.

Consider the hypothetical elementary reaction: $aA + bB \rightarrow cC + dD$. Since the reaction is elementary, we can use the stoichiometric coefficients for the forward and reverse rate laws:

$$rate_{forward} = k_f[A]^a[B]^b$$

$$rate_{reverse} = k_r[C]^c[D]^d$$

(**WARNING:** For the MCAT, never use the coefficients as the exponents in the rate law. We do it here because we are told that the reaction is elementary.) Since equilibrium occurs when these two rates are equal, then, for equilibrium conditions only, we set them equal to each other as shown below:

$$k_f[A]^a[B]^b = k_r[C]^c[D]^d$$

With a little algebraic manipulation we have:

$$\frac{k_f}{k_r} = \frac{[C]^c[D]^d}{[A]^a[B]^b}$$

Since both k's are constants, we can replace them with a new constant called the **equilibrium constant K**. (**2nd WARNING:** This simple relationship between K equilibrium and k rate is only true for elementary equations.) The relationship between a chemical equation and the equilibrium constant is called **the law of mass action** and is written as follows:

$$K = \frac{[C]^c[D]^d}{[A]^a[B]^b} = \frac{\text{Products}^{coefficients}}{\text{Reactants}^{coefficients}}$$

Copyright © 2005 Examkrackers, Inc.

The value of K has no dimensions because the concentrations are actually approximations for a dimensionless quantity called an *activity*. The law of mass action is good for all chemical equations, including non-elementary equations. In other words, for equilibrium constants, use the chemical equation coefficients as the exponents of the concentrations regardless of molecularity. Notice that the equilibrium constant is a capital K and the rate constant is represented by lowercase k. Also notice that the equilibrium constant for the reverse reaction is the reciprocal of the equilibrium constant of the forward reaction. This is true regardless of whether or not the reaction is elementary. Following this same line of reasoning will demonstrate that the equilibrium constant for a series of reactions is equal to the product of the equilibrium constants for each of its elementary steps. Since the rate constant depends upon temperature, the equilibrium constant must also depend upon temperature.

> The equilibrium constant depends upon temprerature only. Don't confuse the equilibrium constant with equilibrium.

The concentration of a pure liquid or a pure solid is usually given a value of one for the equilibrium expression. Concentrations are only approximations for activities. Activities for pure solids and pure liquids are like 'effective' mole fractions. The mole fraction of a pure solid or liquid is one. Although solvents are not actually pure, they are usually considered ideally dilute on the MCAT, which means that their mole fraction is one. The activity then of a pure solid or liquid is approximately one. Be aware that pure solids or liquids can still participate in the equilibrium. When they do, they must be present in order for equilibrium to exist.

> Don't use solids or pure liquids such as water in the law of mass action.

2-13
The Partial Pressure Equilibrium Constant

For reactions with more than one pathway, and for reactions with more than one step, *the principle for detailed balance* states that, at equilibrium, the forward and reverse reaction rates for each step must be equal, and any two or more single reactions or series of reactions resulting in the same products from identical reactants must have the same equilibrium constant for a given temperature. The equilibrium constant does not depend upon whether or not other substances are present.

For reactions involving gases, the equilibrium constant can be written in terms of partial pressures. The concentration equilibrium constant and the partial pressure equilibrium constant do not have the same value, but they are related by the equation:

$$K_p = K_c(RT)^{\Delta n}$$

where K_p is the partial pressure equilibrium constant and n is the sum of the coefficients of the products minus the sum of the coefficients of the reactants. This equation is not required for the MCAT, but you must be able to work with partial pressure equilibrium constants.

2-14
The Reaction Quotient

The equilibrium constant describes only equilibrium conditions. For reactions not at equilibrium, a similar equation gives information about the reaction:

$$Q = \frac{\text{Products}^{\text{coefficients}}}{\text{Reactants}^{\text{coefficients}}}$$

where Q is called the **reaction quotient**. Of course, Q is not a constant; it can have any positive value.

> Use the reaction quotient Q to predict the direction in which a reaction will proceed.

Copyright © 2005 Examkrackers, Inc.

Since reactions always move toward equilibrium, Q will always change toward K. Thus we can compare Q and K for a reaction at any given moment, and learn in which direction the reaction will proceed.

- If Q is equal to K, then the reaction is at equilibrium.

- If Q is greater than K, then the ratio of the concentration of products to the concentration of reactants, as given by the reaction quotient equation above, is greater than when at equilibrium, and the reaction increases reactants and decreases products. In other words, the reverse reaction rate will be greater than the forward rate. This is sometimes called a leftward shift in the equilibrium. Of course, the equilibrium constant does not change during this type of equilibrium shift.

- If Q is less than K, then the ratio of the concentration of products to the concentration of reactants, as given by the reaction quotient equation above, is less than when at equilibrium, and the reaction increases products and decreases reactants. In other words, the forward reaction rate will be greater than the reverse rate. This is sometimes called a rightward shift.

2-15
Le Châtelier's Principle

There is a general rule called Le Châtelier's principle that can often be applied to systems at equilibrium. **Le Châtelier's principle** states that when a system at equilibrium is stressed, the system will shift in a direction that will reduce that stress.

There are three types of stress that usually obey Le Châtelier's principle: 1) addition or removal of a product or reactant; 2) changing the pressure of the system; 3) heating or cooling the system.

The Haber Process is an all gas reaction commonly used on the MCAT to test Le Châtelier's principle. The Haber Process is an exothermic reaction, so it creates heat. For Le Châtelier purposes, we can think of heat as a product in the Haber Process:

$$N_2(g) + 3H_2(g) \rightarrow 2NH_3(g) + \text{Heat}$$

Imagine a rigid container with N_2, H_2, and NH_3 gas at equilibrium. If we add N_2 gas to our system, the system attempts to compensate for the increased concentration of nitrogen by reducing the partial pressure of N_2 with the forward reaction. The forward reaction uses up H_2 as well, reducing its partial pressure. NH_3 and heat are created by the forward reaction.

If we raise the temperature by adding heat, the reaction is pushed to the left. The concentrations of N_2 and H_2 are increased, while the concentration of NH_3 is decreased.

If the size of the container is reduced at constant temperature, total pressure increases. Since there are four gas molecules on the left side of the reaction and only 2 on the right, the equilibrium shifts to the right producing heat and raising the NH_3 concentration. Interestingly, a similar effect is found when a solution is concentrated or diluted. If one side contains more moles than the other, the equilibrium shifts to the side with fewer moles when the solution is concentrated.

Warning: Le Châtelier's Principle does not always predict the correct shift. Notable exceptions are solvation reactions, and pressure increase due to the addition of a nonreactive gas. The solubility of salts generally increase with increasing temperature, even when the reaction is exothermic. This is largely due to the significant entropy increase that occurs with dissolution. The entropy factor becomes more

Copyright © 2005 Examkrackers, Inc.

important as the temperature increases. An example of a pressure increase where equilibrium is not affected is the addition of He to the Haber Process. If we add He gas to our container of N_2, H_2, and NH_3, the total pressure increases, but there is no shift in equilibrium. This can be seen by examining the partial pressure equilibrium constant. Adding He to a rigid container, does not change the partial pressures of the other gases, so the equilibrium does not shift

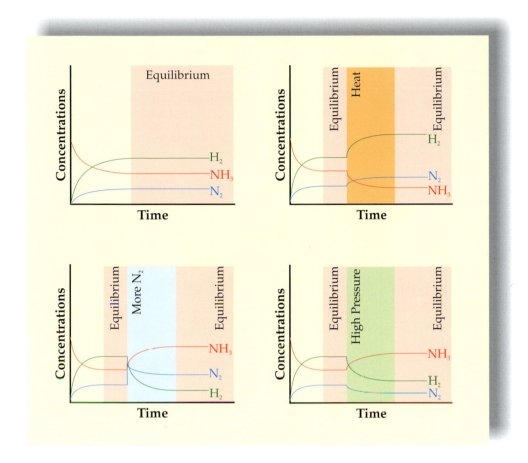

Copyright © 2005 Examkrackers, Inc.

Questions 41 through 48 are **NOT** based on a descriptive passage.

41. As temperature is increased, the equilibrium of a gaseous reaction will always:

A. shift to the right.
B. shift to the left.
C. remain constant.
D. The answer cannot be determined from the information given.

42. All of the following are true concerning a reaction at equilibrium EXCEPT:

A. The rate of the forward reaction equals the rate of the reverse reaction.
B. There is no change in the concentrations of both the products and the reactants.
C. The activation energy has reached zero.
D. The Gibbs free energy has reached a minimum.

43. Nitric acid is produced commercially by oxidation in the Oswald process. The first step of this process is shown below.

$$4NH_3(g) + 5O_2(g) \rightleftharpoons 4NO(g) + 6H_2O(g)$$

A container holds 4 moles of gaseous ammonia, 5 moles of gaseous oxygen, 4 moles of gaseous nitric oxide, and 6 moles of water vapor at equilibrium. Which of the following would be true if the container were allowed to expand at constant temperature?

A. Initially during the expansion the forward reaction rate would be greater than the reverse reaction rate.
B. The equilibrium would shift to the left.
C. The partial pressure of oxygen would increase.
D. The pressure inside the container would increase.

44. Nitrous oxide is prepared by the thermal decomposition of ammonium nitrate.

$$NH_4NO_3(s) \rightarrow N_2O(g) + 2H_2O(g)$$

The equilibrium constant for this reaction is:

A. $[NH_4NO_3]/[N_2O][H_2O]^2$
B. $[N_2O][H_2O]^2/[NH_4NO_3]$
C. $[N_2O][H_2O]^2$
D. $[N_2O][H_2O]$

45. Which of the following is true concerning a reaction that begins with only reactants and moves to equilibrium?

A. The rate of the forward and reverse reactions decreases until equilibrium is reached.
B. The rate of the forward and reverse reactions increases until equilibrium is reached.
C. The rate of the forward reaction decreases, and the rate of the reverse reaction increases until equilibrium is reached.
D. The rate of the forward reaction increases, and the rate of the reverse reaction decreases until equilibrium is reached.

Copyright © 2005 Examkrackers, Inc.

GO ON TO THE NEXT PAGE.

Questions 46 through 48 refer to the diagram below.

Calcium carbonate decomposes to calcium oxide and carbon dioxide gas via the following reversible reaction:

$$CaCO_3(s) \rightleftharpoons CaO(s) + CO_2(g)$$

Beaker I contains pure $CaCO_3$ and Beaker II contains pure CaO. The container is sealed.

46. Which of the following statements could be true about the system upon achieving equilibrium?

   A. Beaker I is empty.
   B. The number of calcium atoms in Beaker II has decreased.
   C. The number of calcium atoms in Beaker II has increased.
   D. Beaker II contains a mixture of $CaCO_3$ and CaO.

47. What is the equilibrium expression for the reaction?

   A. $K = [CO_2]$

   B. $K = [CaO][CO_2]$

   C. $K = \dfrac{[CaO][CO_2]}{[CaCO_3]}$

   D. $K = \dfrac{[CO_2]}{[CaCO_3]}$

48. The partial pressure equilibrium constant for the decomposition of $CaCO_3$ is K_p. If Beaker II is removed, under which of the following conditions would equilibrium NOT be achieved?

   A. K_p is less than the partial pressure of CO_2.
   B. K_p is greater than the partial pressure of CO_2.
   C. K_p is equal to the partial pressure of CO_2.
   D. Equilibrium could not be achieved under any conditions because solid CaO is required to achieve equilibrium.

Copyright © 2005 Examkrackers, Inc.

STOP.

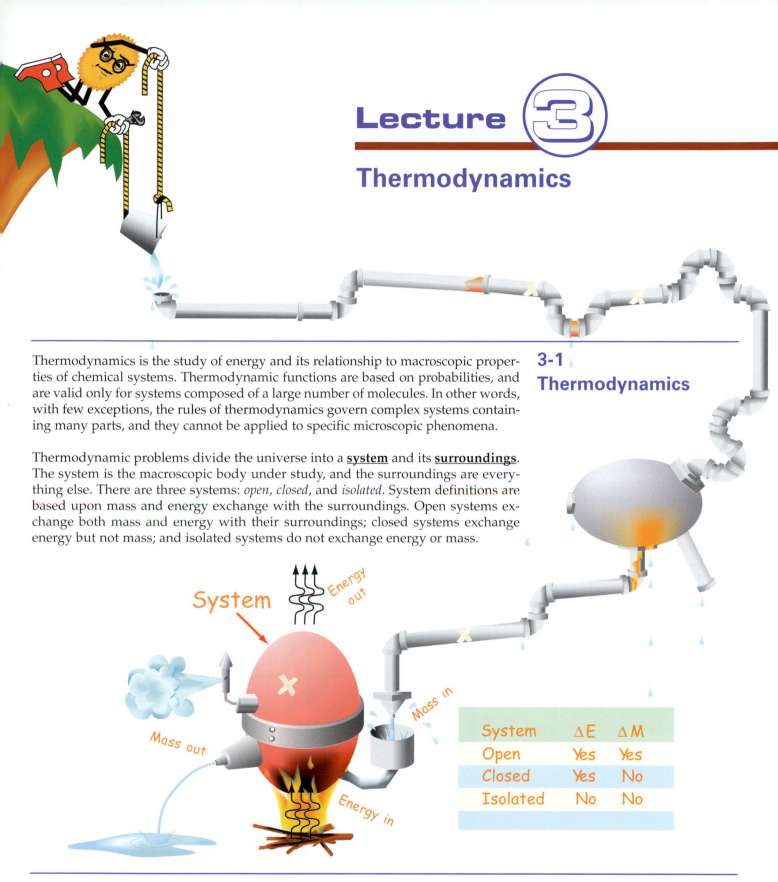

Lecture 3

Thermodynamics

Thermodynamics is the study of energy and its relationship to macroscopic properties of chemical systems. Thermodynamic functions are based on probabilities, and are valid only for systems composed of a large number of molecules. In other words, with few exceptions, the rules of thermodynamics govern complex systems containing many parts, and they cannot be applied to specific microscopic phenomena.

Thermodynamic problems divide the universe into a **system** and its **surroundings**. The system is the macroscopic body under study, and the surroundings are everything else. There are three systems: *open*, *closed*, and *isolated*. System definitions are based upon mass and energy exchange with the surroundings. Open systems exchange both mass and energy with their surroundings; closed systems exchange energy but not mass; and isolated systems do not exchange energy or mass.

System

Energy
out

Mass out

Mass in

Energy in

System	ΔE	ΔM
Open	Yes	Yes
Closed	Yes	No
Isolated	No	No

A state is the physical condition of a system described by a specific set of thermodynamic property values. There are two types of properties that describe the macroscopic state of a system: 1) *extensive* and; 2) *intensive*. Extensive properties are proportional to the size of the system; intensive properties are independent of the size of the system. If you combine two identical systems and a property is the same for both the single system and the combined system, that property is intensive. If a

Copyright © 2005 Examkrackers, Inc.

Extensive properties change with amount; intensive properties do not.

You need to know what a state function is. State functions are pathway independent. State properties describe the state of a system. In other words, the change in a state property going from one state to another is the same regardless of the process via which the system was changed.

Three state properties, one being extensive, describe the state of a system unambiguously.

property doubles when the systems are combined, the property is extensive. If you divide one extensive property by another, the result is an intensive property. Volume V and number of moles n are examples of extensive properties. Pressure P and temperature T are examples of intensive properties.

The macroscopic state of any one-component fluid system in equilibrium can be described by just three properties, of which at least one is extensive. All other properties of the state of the same system are necessarily specified by the chosen three properties. For instance, if for a single component gas in equilibrium, pressure, temperature, and volume are known, all other properties which describe the state of that gas (such as number of moles, internal energy, enthalpy, entropy, and Gibbs energy) must have a specific single value. Since the state of a system can be described exactly by specific properties, it is not necessary to know how the state was formed or what reaction pathway brought a state into being. Such properties that describe the state of a system are called **state functions**. Properties that do not describe the state of a system, but depend upon the pathway used to achieve any state, are called *path functions*. Work and heat are examples of path functions.

3-3
Heat

Heat is movement of energy via conduction, convection, or radiation always from hot to cold.

There are only two ways to transfer energy between systems: **heat** q and **work** w. Heat is the natural transfer of energy from a warmer body to a cooler body. Any energy transfer that is not heat is work.

Heat has three forms: conduction, convection, and radiation. **Conduction** is thermal energy transfer via molecular collisions. Conduction requires direct physical contact. In conduction, higher energy molecules of one system transfer some of their energy to the lower energy molecules of the other system via molecular collisions. Heat can also be conducted through a single object. An object's ability to conduct heat is called its thermal conductivity k. The thermal conductivity of an object depends upon its composition and, to a much lesser extent, its temperature. A slab of a given substance with face area A, length L, and thermal conductivity k will conduct heat Q from a hot body at temperature T_h to a cold body at temperature T_c in an amount of time t.

The temperature difference in thermal conductivity is like the pressure difference in fluids or the potential difference in electricity. The rate of heat flow is like volume flow rate or current. Notice the similarity in these equations for the conduction of heat, fluids, and electricity.

$$\Delta T = I\,R$$
$$\Delta P = Q\,R$$
$$V = i\,R$$

You can use this similarity to help you understand heat flow, fluid flow, and electron flow. For instance, in all cases, thicker conduits allow for greater flow, longer conduits impede flow, and flow rate depends upon the difference in a property of the reservoirs at either end of the conduit.

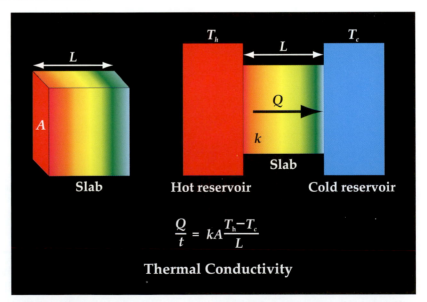

$$\frac{Q}{t} = kA\frac{T_h - T_c}{L}$$

Thermal Conductivity

Q/t is the rate of heat flow or *heat current I*. The resistance to heat flow R can be written as $L/(kA)$. A little algebra results in $\Delta T = IR$, an equation similar in form to Ohm's law in electricity. Similar to the rate of fluid flow in an ideal fluid (see Physics Lecture 6) or to the flow of electric current through resistors in series (see Physics

Lecture 7), in a steady state system the rate of heat flow is constant across any number of slabs between two heat reservoirs. In other words, if a series of slabs were lined up end to end between hot and cold reservoirs, the rate of heat flow, Q/t, would be the same in all slabs even if they each had different lengths, thicknesses, and different thermal conductivities. Conservation of energy explains why. If the rate of energy transfer were not steady across all slabs, the slab that conducted heat the fastest would become cold. A cold slab could not conduct heat to warmer slabs because heat moves from hot to cold. It also follows that since the rate of energy transfer is the same for each slab, the order in which we place the slabs does not affect the overall conductivity. Finally, since the rate of heat flow is the same through each slab, a higher conductivity results in a lower temperature difference across any slab of a given length.

Let's see how well you understand thermal conductivity. If I have a heavy blanket and a light blanket, which blanket should I place on top in order to stay warmer? The answer is: the order of the blankets will not make any difference since it will not change the rate of conduction.

Convection is thermal energy transfer via fluid movements. In convection, differences in pressure or density drive warm fluid in the direction of cooler fluid. For instance, on a warm sunny day at the beach the air above the land heats up faster than the air above the water. As the air above the land warms, it becomes less dense and rises carrying its thermal energy with it. Ocean and air currents are common examples of convection.

Convection

Radiation

Conduction
(hand warming
the glass)

3 types of Heat

Radiation is thermal energy transfer via electromagnetic waves. When metal is heated, it glows red, orange-yellow, white, and finally blue-white. The hot metal radiates visible electromagnetic waves. But even before the metal begins to glow, it radiates electromagnetic waves at a frequency too low to be visible to the human eye. In fact, all objects with a temperature above 0 K radiate heat. The rate at which an object radiates electromagnetic radiation (its power P) depends upon its temperature and surface area, and is given by the *Stefan-Boltzman law*:

$$P = \sigma\varepsilon AT^4$$

where A is the surface area of the object, T is the temperature of the object in kelvins, σ is the Stefan-Boltzman constant (5.67×10^{-8} W m^{-2} K^{-4}), and ε is the emissivity of the object's surface, which has a value between 0 and 1. If we substitute the temperature of the environment for the temperature of the object, we find the rate at which the object absorbs radiant heat from its environment. The net rate of heat transfer will always be from hot to cold, and is given by:

$$P = \sigma\varepsilon A(T_e^{\,4} - T_o^{\,4})$$

where the T_e is the temperature of the environment and T_o is the temperature of the object. *Newton's law of cooling* states that the rate of cooling of a body is approximately proportional to the temperature difference between the body and its environment.

When radiation strikes an opaque surface, only a fraction is absorbed. The remainder is reflected. The fraction absorbed is indicated by the emissivity ε of the surface. The emissivity depends upon surface composition. As stated above, the emissivity of any surface is between 0 and 1. An object with an emissivity of 1 is called a black-

Notice that an object that radiates heat faster also absorbs heat faster. This means that an object that is a more efficient radiator comes to equilibrium with its environment more quickly. With this in mind, is it better to paint your house black or white?

Copyright © 2005 Examkrackers, Inc.

Answer: White is better. In Summer, your house is cooler than the environment and white reflects away the heat. In Winter, your house is warmer than the environment and white radiates away less heat.

body radiator and is possible only in theory. All other objects reflect as well as absorb and radiate. Dark colors tend to radiate and absorb better than light colors, which tend to reflect.

Radiation is the only type of heat that transfers through a vacuum.

3-4
Work

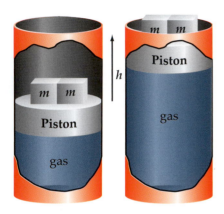

From our discussion of heat, we know that work is any energy transfer that is not heat. In Physics Lecture 3 we defined work as an energy transfer due to a force. In physics problems, work typically changes the motion or position of a body. However, now we want to look at work as it applies to a chemical system at rest. For our purposes, a system at rest may change its size or shape, but does not translate or change its position. A system at rest, with no gravitational potential energy and no kinetic energy, may still be able to do **PV work**. Imagine a cylinder full of gas compressed by a piston. If we place two blocks of mass m on the top of the piston and allow the gas pressure to lift the masses to a height h, the system has done work on the mass in the amount of the gravitational energy change $2mgh$. Thus negative work has been done on the system. This work is called PV work because, at constant pressure, it is equal to the product of the pressure and the change in the volume ($P\Delta V$).

From Newton's second law $F = ma$, we know that if the masses are lifted at constant velocity, the force on the masses is constant and equal to $2mg$. From the definition of pressure $P = F/A$, we know that if the force remained constant, the pressure also remained constant. Constant pressure conditions allow us to calculate the work done using:

$$w = P\Delta V_{\text{(constant pressure)}}$$

If pressure is not constant, then calculus is required to find the amount of PV work done. In such a case, the MCAT will not require you to calculate the work.

If the volume remains constant, no PV work is done at all.

The start point and end point of the expansion could also have been achieved by removing one mass, allowing the piston to rise, increasing the pressure to $2mg$ while holding the piston steady, and then replacing the second mass. This would have been a different pathway to achieve the same result. Since work is a path function, a different pathway results in a different amount of work; in this case the work would have been mgh.

Finally, the start and end point of the expansion could have been achieved by changing the pressure as the piston rose. In this case, PV work is done, but it does not equal $P\Delta V$. To calculate the work in this case, you would need to use calculus.

If we examine a pressure vs. volume graph for each case, the work done is given by the area under the curve. Notice that the area is different for each case.

An MCAT problem asking about PV work will likely specify constant pressure. However, you should understand these graphs and understand that PV work takes place when a gas expands against a force regardless of whether or not the pressure is constant.

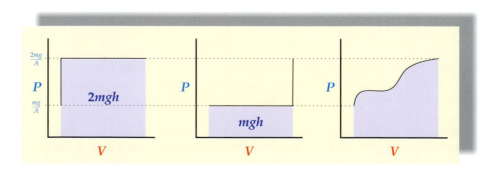

Copyright © 2005 Examkrackers, Inc.

The First Law of Thermodynamics states that energy of the system and surroundings is always conserved. Thus any energy change to a system must equal the heat flow into the system plus the work done on the system.

$$\Delta E = q + w$$

Warning: We have chosen the convention where work *on* the system is positive. It is possible that an MCAT passage could define work done *by* the system as positive, in which case the formula would be $\Delta E = q - w$.

3-5

The First Law of Thermodynamics

To simplify things by removing significant gravitational forces, let's turn our cylinder and piston on its side. The gas pushes against the piston which is now held by an outside force that we can control. By heating the gas, we can allow it to expand while maintaining a constant temperature. For a heat source, we can use a large hot body which we will call a *hot reservoir*. Since temperature is the kinetic energy per mole of gas molecules, and we are holding temperature constant, the total energy of the gas does not change as it expands. But the energy that we added as heat must be going somewhere. It is changed completely into *PV* work done by the force against the piston. (By the way, the force cannot be constant if the temperature is constant because at constant temperature, the pressure must go down as the gas expands [$PV = nRT$].)

This experiment seems to suggest that heat can be changed completely into work. But there is a problem. In the real world, we will run out of cylinder and we will have to push the piston back to its start point to begin again. When we do so, we must do work on the gas to compress it. In fact, compressing the gas as is will raise its temperature, requiring more work to compress it than was gained by expanding it. So we must cool the gas first. Heat flows from hot to cold, so we cannot cool the gas by allowing heat to flow to the hot reservoir. Instead, we must have a cold reservoir into which we dump the heat energy. Once the gas is sufficiently cooled, it can be compressed to its original state with less work than was gained. The expansion

3-6

Heat Engines

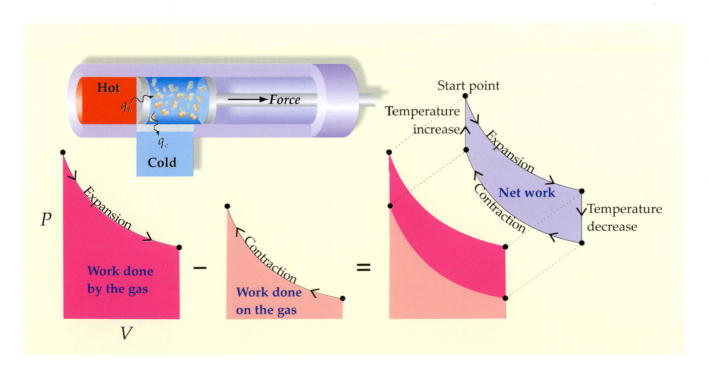

The heat engine stuff is given here in order to help you understand the relationship between heat and work. If it is on the MCAT, it will be explained in a passage. However, don't just ignore it. It is a possible passage topic and a good way to learn to understand heat and work. At the very least, know the second law of thermodynamics in terms of heat and work: Heat cannot be completely converted to worked in a cyclical process.

process can begin again and, as can be seen by the graph, we have turned some, but not all, of the heat into work. Our cylinder and piston is called a heat engine.

This is a demonstration of **the second law of thermodynamics** which says "Heat cannot be changed completely into work in a cyclical process."

A machine that converts heat to work is called a heat engine. A heat engine can be diagrammed as shown. Notice that, via conservation of energy, the heat entering the engine q_h must equal the net work done by the engine w plus the heat leaving the engine q_c. ($q_h = w + q_c$)

We can reverse a heat engine to create a refrigerator. If we change the directions of the arrows in the diagram, the inside of the refrigerator is represented by the cold reservoir. Notice that a refrigerator requires work, and that the heat that it generates is greater than the heat that it removes from the cold reservoir. The second law of thermodynamics requires this result.

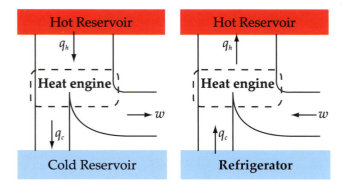

If we put a running refrigerator in a small closet, close the closet door and open the refrigerator door what will happen to the temperature of the closet?

Answer: The closet will warm up because q_h is greater than q_c.

The most effective cyclical conversion of heat into work is produced by the hypothetical Carnot engine and depends upon the temperature difference of the two reservoirs. The further apart the temperatures of the two reservoirs, the more effective the conversion. The fraction of heat that can be converted to work with a Carnot engine is called the efficiency e, and is given by:

$$e = 1 - \frac{T_C}{T_H}$$

where T_H and T_C are the temperatures of the hot and cold reservoirs respectively.

Copyright © 2005 Examkrackers, Inc.

Questions 49 through 56 are **NOT** based on a descriptive passage.

49. Which of the following is true concerning an air conditioner that sits inside a thermally sealed room and draws energy from an outside power source?

   A. It requires more energy to cool the room than if part of the air conditioner were outside the room.
   B. It will require more time to cool the room than if part of the air conditioner were outside the room.
   C. It will require less energy to cool the room than if part of the air conditioner were outside the room.
   D. It cannot cool the room on a permanent basis.

50. Three blocks made from the same insulating material are placed between hot and cold reservoirs as shown below.

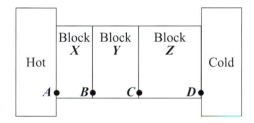

   Which of the following must be true?

   I. The temperature difference between points A and B is less than the temperature difference between points C and D.
   II. The rate of heat flow through Block X is greater than the rate of heat flowing through Block Z.
   III. Switching the positions of Block X and Block Z would decrease the rate of heat flow.

   A. I only
   B. III only
   C. I and III only
   D. I, II, and III

51. Immediately upon bringing a hot piece of metal into a room, the heat is felt from 5 meters away. The type of heat transfer is probably:

   A. convection
   B. transduction
   C. radiation
   D. conduction

52. A box sliding down an incline increases in temperature due to friction. The name for this type of heat is:

   A. convection
   B. conduction
   C. radiation
   D. The energy transfer here is due to work and not to heat.

53. Which of the following gas properties is needed to calculate the work done by an expanding gas?

   I. The initial and final pressures
   II. The initial and final volumes
   III. The path followed during the expansion.

   A. I only
   B. II only
   C. I and II only
   D. I, II, and III

54. The heating bill for a homeowner is directly proportional to the rate at which heat is conducted out of the house and into the surroundings. The average temperature inside and outside of a house is measured on different months and recorded in Table 1.

Month	Temperature outside (°C)	Temperature inside (°C)
Nov	8	22
Dec	5	25
Jan	3	20
Feb	13	26

For which month would the homeowner expect to have the largest heating bill?

   A. November
   B. December
   C. January
   D. February

55. A rigid container of constant volume is used to store compressed gas. When gas is pumped into the container, the pressure of the gas inside the container is increased and the temperature of the container also increases. Which statement is true of the work done on the container?

A. The work is equal to the increase in the pressure inside the container.

B. The work is equal to the increase in the temperature inside the container.

C. The work is equal to the sum of the pressure and temperature increases.

D. There is no work done on the container.

56. Under the best possible conditions, a steam engine will have an efficiency of slightly more than 20 percent. A normal steam engine has an efficiency of about 10 percent. This means that for a normal steam engine:

A. 10 percent of the input energy contributes to the work done by the engine.

B. 90 percent of the input energy contributes to the work done by the engine.

C. the internal temperature will increase by 10 percent during operation.

D. the internal temperature will increase by 90 percent during operation.

To understand thermodynamics, you must be familiar with seven state functions:

1. internal energy U
2. temperature T
3. pressure P
4. volume V
5. enthalpy H
6. entropy S
7. Gibbs energy G

3-7 Thermodynamic Functions

3-8 Internal Energy

Since thermodynamics is mainly concerned with chemical energy, most problems will not deal with macroscopic mechanical energies. Instead, problems will be concerned with internal energy. Internal energy is the collective energy of molecules measured on a microscopic scale. This energy includes vibrational energy, rotational energy, translational energy, electronic energy, intermolecular potential energy, and rest mass energy. Internal energy does not include mechanical energy. In other words, internal energy is all the possible forms of energy imaginable on a molecular scale. *Vibrational energy* is created by the atoms vibrating within a molecule. *Rotational energy* is molecular movement where the spatial orientation of the body changes, while the center of mass remains fixed and each point within a molecule remains fixed relative to all other points. *Translational energy* is the movement of the center of mass of a molecule. *Electronic energy* is the potential electrical energy created by the attractions between the electrons and their respective nuclei. The *intermolecular potential energy* is the energy created by the intermolecular forces between molecular dipoles. *Rest mass energy* is the energy predicted by Einstein's famous equation $E = mc^2$. The sum of these energies for a group of molecules is called the internal energy.

The MCAT doesn't generally ask about internal energy directly. The study of internal energy is beyond the MCAT. However, in order to understand and use conservation of energy you must consider internal energy.

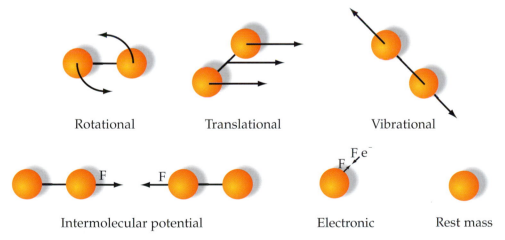

Rotational   Translational   Vibrational

Intermolecular potential   Electronic   Rest mass

Internal Energy Types

The MCAT may refer to internal energy as 'heat energy', 'thermal energy', or even 'heat'. Heat energy and thermal energy are really the vibrational, rotational, and translational parts of internal energy. They are called thermal energy because they affect temperature. Heat is a transfer of energy, and using it as another name for internal energy can create confusion. Unfortunately, this is a common mistake.

If we have a closed system at rest with no electric or magnetic fields, the only energy change will be in internal energy, and the first law of thermodynamics can be rewritten as: $\Delta U = q + w$. For a reaction within such a system involving no change in volume, there is no work of any kind and the change in internal energy is equal to the heat: $\Delta U = q$.

Copyright © 2005 Examkrackers, Inc.

Tidbits of info that may help your understanding but won't be tested by MCAT.

Internal energy is a state function. For an ideal gas, any state function can be expressed as a function of temperature and volume only. For an ideal gas, internal energy is independent of volume and is a function of temperature only.

3-9
Temperature

The zeroth law of thermodynamics just states that temperature exists. It's called the zeroth law because after the first, second, and third laws were already established it was realized that they depended upon a law that established the existence of temperature.

The *zeroth law of thermodynamics* states "Two systems in thermal equilibrium with a third system are in thermal equilibrium with each other." The zeroth law declares that two bodies in thermal equilibrium share a thermodynamic property, and that this thermodynamic property must be a state function. The thermodynamic property described by the zeroth law is **temperature**.

There are several methods used to define temperature. One definition is based upon the volume of an ideal gas. For an ideal gas the volume vs. temperature graph is exactly linear for any given pressure. Although all real gases become liquids at low temperatures, if we extrapolate back along the volume vs. temperature line, the lines for all pressures intersect at the same point on the temperature axis. We can define the temperature of this point as 0 K or –273°C. To establish the size of a unit of temperature, we can arbitrarily choose the freezing point and boiling point of water along the 1 atm line, and label those points 0°C and 100°C respectively.

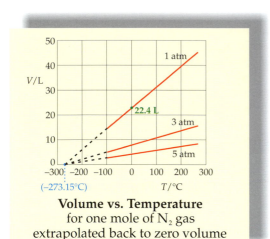

Volume vs. Temperature
for one mole of N_2 gas
extrapolated back to zero volume

This and other definitions of temperature do not give a satisfying intuitive notion for what temperature really is. For an intuitive feel of temperature, we need to examine the motion of the molecules. When we look at internal energy, we see that the translational, rotational, and vibrational energies describe the energies of molecular motion. The sum of these energies is called *thermal energy.* Any increase in thermal energy increases temperature.

Think of temperature as a measurement of how fast the molecules are moving or vibrating. When substances get hot, it is because their molecules move faster.

For a fluid, temperature is directly proportional to the translational kinetic energy of its molecules. Translational motion can be divided into three *degrees of freedom* or *modes*: 1) along the x axis; 2) along the y axis; and 3) along the z axis. The *equipartition theory* states that for a normal system each mode of motion will have the same average energy and that the energy will be equal to $\frac{1}{2}kT$, where T is the temperature, and k is the Boltzmann constant (1.38×10^{-23} J K^{-1}). The Boltzmann constant k is related to the ideal gas constant R by Avagadro's number N_A: $R = N_A k$. Since there are three modes of kinetic energy each averaging $\frac{1}{2}kT$ joules, the average kinetic energy of a single molecule in any fluid is given by:

$$K.E._{avg} = \frac{3}{2}kT$$

MCAT won't test the equipartition theory. Just know the formula:

$K.E. = \frac{3}{2}kT$

This is a variation of an equation from Lecture 2. The equipartition theorem is derived from classical physics and breaks down when quantum effects are significant. Quantum effects are greater for rotation than for translation, and greater still for vibration. The molecules of a solid do not translate or rotate; they vibrate. For solids at high temperatures where quantum effects are less important, temperature is proportional to the average kinetic energy of the vibration of molecules about their equilibrium position. For solids at low temperatures, there is deviation from this rule due to quantum effects.

The greater the random translational energy of gas molecules per mole , the greater the temperature. So ideally, temperature can be thought of as the thermal energy per molecule or mole of molecules. Recall that when we divide one extensive property by another, we get an intensive property. Energy and number of moles are extensive properties. This makes temperature an intensive property.

Copyright © 2005 Examkrackers, Inc.

The MCAT will use two measurement systems for temperature: degrees Celsius and Kelvin. Celsius is just the centigrade system with a new name. At 1 atm, water freezes at 0°C and boils at 100°C. The lowest possible temperature is called absolute zero, and is approximately –273°C. To find approximate Kelvin from degrees Celsius, simply add 273. An increase of 1°C is equivalent to an increase of 1 K.

Virtually all physcial properties change with temperature.

When in doubt, use kelvin. In chemistry, you are always safe using the Kelvin scale because the Kelvin scale is absolute.

Good to know for the MCAT!

3-10 Pressure

Loosely speaking, pressure of an ideal gas is the random translational kinetic energy per volume. Pressure is an intensive state function. Pressure and volume are discussed in depth in Chemistry Lecture 2 and Physics Lecture 5.

The greater the random translational kinetic energy of gas molecules per volume, the greater the pressure

---

3-11 Enthalpy

Two systems at rest may have the same amount of internal energy, and, if they are at different pressures, they have different capacities to perform PV work. (This is one demonstration of why "energy is the capacity to perform work" is a poor definition of energy. See Physics Lecture 3.) **Enthalpy** is a man-made property that accounts for this extra capacity to do PV work. Unlike functions such as pressure, volume, and temperature, enthalpy is not a measure of some intuitive property. Enthalpy is defined as an equation rather than as a description of a property. Enthalpy H is defined as:

$$H \equiv U + PV$$

From our inexact but intuitive concept of pressure as the random translational kinetic energy per unit volume, we see that enthalpy actually counts random translational kinetic energy twice! Although enthalpy is measured in units of energy (joules), enthalpy itself is not conserved like energy. Enthalpy of the universe does not remain constant.

Since U, P, and V are state functions, enthalpy is also a state function. Like internal energy, for an ideal gas enthalpy depends only on temperature. Enthalpy is an extensive property.

As with many state functions, we are interested in the *change* in enthalpy and not its absolute value. For the MCAT, we will be interested in the change in enthalpy under constant pressure conditions only:

$$\Delta H = \Delta U + P\Delta V \quad \text{(const. } P\text{)}$$

There are no absolute enthalpy values, so scientists have assigned enthalpy values to compounds based upon their standard state. **Standard state** should not be confused with STP. Standard state is a somewhat complicated concept that varies with phase and other factors and even has differnet values based upon which convention you choose to follow. As usual, we can simplify things greatly for the MCAT. Recall that a 'state' is described by a specific set of thermodynamic property values. For a pure solid or liquid, the standard state is the **reference form** of a substance at any chosen temperature T and a pressure of 1 bar (about 750 torr or exactly 10^5 pascals). The reference form is usually the form that is most stable at 1 bar and T. For a pure gas there is an additional requirement that the gas behave like an ideal gas. An element in its standard state at 25°C is arbitrarily assigned an enthalpy value of 0

Enthalpy cannot be intuited. Just memorize the equation.

Don't confuse standard state and STP.

An element in its standard state at 25°C is arbitrarily assigned an enthalpy value of 0 J/mol.

J/mol. From this value we can assign enthalpy values to compounds based upon the change in enthalpy when they are formed from raw elements in their standard states at 25°C. Such enthalpy values for compounds are called standard enthalpies of formation. The **standard enthalpy of formation** $\Delta H°_f$ is the change in enthalpy for a reaction that creates one mole of that compound from its raw elements in their standard state. The symbol '°' (called naught) indicates standard state conditions. Standard enthalpies of formation can be found by experiment, and are available in books. An example of the enthalpy of formation of water is:

$$H_2(g) + \tfrac{1}{2}O_2(g) \rightarrow H_2O(l) \quad \Delta H°_f = -285.8 \text{ kJ/mol}$$

For reactions involving no change in pressure, the change in enthalpy is equal to the heat:

$$\mathbf{\Delta H = q} \quad \text{(const. } P, \text{ closed system at rest, } PV \text{ work only)}$$

Basically, if gas is not part of the reaction, enthalpy change is equal to heat which, in the absence of work, is equal to a change in energy.

Many liquid and solid chemical reactions performed in the lab take place at constant pressure (1 atm) and nearly constant volume. For these reactions (any reactions involving only solids and liquids at moderate pressures) $\Delta U \approx \Delta H$.

Since, in many reactions in the lab, enthalpy approximates heat, the change in enthalpy from reactants to products is often referred to as the **heat of reaction**.

$$\Delta H°_{reaction} = \Delta H°_{f\ products} - \Delta H°_{f\ reactants}$$

Hess' law says that when you add reactions, you can add their enthalpies. Hess' law works because enthalpy is a state function.

Since enthalpy is a state function, the change in enthalpy when converting one group of compounds to another is not dependent upon what reaction or even series of reactions take place. The change in enthalpy depends only on the identities and thermodynamic states of the initial and final compounds. Thus, in any reaction, the steps taken to get from reactants to products do not affect the total change in enthalpy. **Hess' law** states "The sum of the enthalpy changes for each step is equal to the total enthalpy change regardless of the path chosen." For example:

$N_2 + O_2 \rightarrow 2NO$	$\Delta H = 180$ kJ	step 1
$2NO + O_2 \rightarrow 2NO_2$	$\Delta H = -112$ kJ	+ step 2
$N_2 + 2O_2 \rightarrow 2NO_2$	$\Delta H = 68$ kJ	= complete reaction

Exothermic reactions ($-\Delta H$) release heat making the reaction system hot; endothermic reactions ($+\Delta H$) absorb heat making the reaction system cold.

Hess's law also indicates that a forward reaction has exactly the opposite change in enthalpy as the reverse. If the enthalpy change is positive, the reaction is said to be **endothermic**; if it is negative, it is said to be **exothermic**. If we consider a reaction where the change in enthalpy is equal to the heat (a constant pressure reaction), then an exothermic reaction produces heat flow to the surroundings, while an endothermic reaction produces heat flow to the system.

We can see this graphically if we compare the progress of a reaction with the energy of the molecules. (Due to the close relationship between internal energy and enthalpy, the term energy is used loosely for these types of graphs. You may see the y axis labeled as enthalpy, Gibbs free energy, or simply energy.) You can see from the graph that if the reaction progress is reversed, the enthalpy change is exactly reversed. Notice that there is an initial increase in energy regardless of which direction the reaction moves. This increase in energy is called the **activation energy** (the same activation energy as in Chemistry Lecture 2). The peak of this

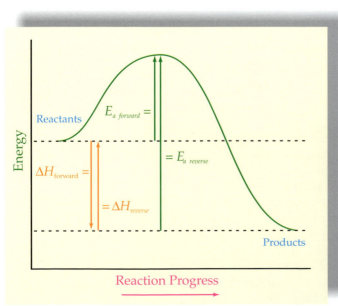

Copyright © 2005 Examkrackers, Inc.

energy hill represents the molecules in a **transition state** where the old bonds are breaking and new bonds are forming. The transition state occurs during the reaction collision. Do not confuse the transition state with **intermediates**, which are the products of the first step in a two step reaction. A two step reaction has two humps as shown on page 34. The intermediates exist in the trough between the two humps.

Notice, on an energy diagram, how a **catalyst** lowers the activation energy. The activation energy for both the forward and the reverse reactions is lowered. Although the relative amount by which the activation energies are lowered is different, if we used the Arrhenius equation (Chemistry Lecture 2) to find the new rate constants, we would find that the rate constants are raised by the same relative amounts; thus, equilibrium is unaffected by a catalyst. For the MCAT you must remember that a catalyst affects the rate and not the equilibrium. Notice that a catalyst does not affect the enthalpy change either.

Copyright © 2005 Examkrackers, Inc.

57. What is the enthalpy change in the following reaction?

Compound	ΔH_f°
$CH_4(g)$	−75 kJ/mol
$CO_2(g)$	−394 kJ/mol
$H_2O(l)$	−286 kJ/mol

$$CH_4(g) + 2O_2(g) \rightarrow CO_2(g) + 2H_2O(l)$$

A. −755 kJ
B. −891 kJ
C. −1041 kJ
D. 891 kJ

58. Which of the following properties of a gaseous system affect its enthalpy?

I. pressure
II. volume
III. internal energy

A. III only
B. I and II only
C. II and III only
D. I, II, and III

59. A catalyst will change all of the following EXCEPT:

A. enthalpy
B. activation energy
C. rate of the forward reaction
D. rate of the reverse reaction

60. In an exothermic reaction, which of the following will most likely increase the ratio of the forward rate to the reverse rate?

A. adding thermal energy to the system
B. removing thermal energy from the system
C. using a catalyst
D. lowering the activation energy

61. The heats of combustion for graphite and diamond are as follows:

$$C_{graphite}(s) + O_2(g) \rightarrow CO_2(g) \quad \Delta H = -394 \text{ kJ}$$

$$C_{diamond}(s) + O_2(g) \rightarrow CO_2(g) \quad \Delta H = -396 \text{ kJ}$$

Diamond spontaneously changes to graphite. What is the change in enthalpy accompanying the conversion of two moles of diamond to graphite?

A. −790 kJ
B. −4 kJ
C. 2 kJ
D. 4 kJ

62. The standard enthalpy of formation for liquid water is:

$$H_2(g) + \tfrac{1}{2}O_2(g) \rightarrow H_2O(l) \quad \Delta H^\circ_f = -285.8 \text{ kJ/mol}$$

Which of the following could be the standard enthalpy of formation for water vapor?

A. −480.7 kJ/mol
B. −285.8 kJ
C. −241.8 kJ/mol
D. +224.6 kJ/mol

63. For a particular reversible reaction, the forward process is exothermic and the reverse process is endothermic. Which of the following statements must be true about this reaction?

A. The forward reaction will be spontaneous under standard conditions.
B. The reverse reaction will be spontaneous under standard conditions.
C. The activation energy will be greater for the forward reaction than for the reverse reaction.
D. The activation energy will be greater for the reverse reaction than for the forward reaction.

64. Sulfur dioxide reacts with oxygen in a reversible reaction to form sulfur trioxide as shown.

$$2SO_2(g) + O_2(g) \rightleftharpoons 2SO_3(g) \quad \Delta H^\circ = -200 \text{ kJ}$$

If the temperature at which the reaction takes place is increased, which of the following will take place?

A. The rates of both the forward and reverse reactions will increase.
B. Only the rate of the forward reaction will increase.
C. Only the rate of the reverse reaction will increase.
D. The rates of neither the forward nor reverse reactions will increase.

Copyright © 2005 Examkrackers, Inc.

STOP.

If you have studied entropy before, you have probably heard the following example: "Over time, a clean room will tend to get dirty. This is entropy at work." Entropy is nature's tendency toward disorder. A better definition of entropy incorporates the concept of probability. **Entropy S** is nature's tendency to create the most probable situation that can occur within a system. For instance, imagine four identical jumping beans that bounce randomly back and forth between two containers. If we label each bean A, B, C, and D respectively, we will find that the most likely situation is to have two beans in each container. The least likely situation is to have all four beans in either of the containers. For example, if we choose the left container, there is only one way for all four beans to be in the left container, but there are 6 possible ways that two beans can be in each container. Two beans in each container is six times more likely than four beans in the left container. Since the two-bean container situation is more likely, it has greater entropy.

If we replace the four jumping beans with millions of molecules moving randomly back and forth between two glass spheres connected by a glass tube, you should be able to see how the odds against having all the molecules in one sphere become astronomical. The odds are so poor, in fact, that **the second law of thermodynamics** states that it will never happen without some outside intervention, namely work. The second law of thermodynamics states that the entropy of an isolated system will never decrease.

We can apply the second law of thermodynamics to any type of system, if we recall that the surroundings of any system include everything that is not in the system. Thus, the system and the surroundings together make up the entire universe. The universe itself is an isolated system. Therefore, the sum of the entropy changes of any system and its surroundings equals the entropy change of the universe, which must be equal to or greater than zero.

$$\Delta S_{system} + \Delta S_{surroundings} = \Delta S_{universe} \geq 0$$

So the entropy of a system can decrease, only if, at the same time, the entropy of the surroundings increases by a greater or equal magnitude.

Entropy is a state function. This means that the entropy change of a forward reaction is equal to the negative entropy change of a reverse reaction. This is true for the entropy change of the system, the surroundings, and the universe. Since the change in entropy of the universe must be positive or zero for all reactions, only a reaction with zero universal entropy change can be reversible. Only ideal reactions create zero change in the entropy of the universe, so only ideal reactions are **reversible** from a thermodynamic definition of reversibility. On a macroscopic scale, all real reactions are **irreversible**. Recall from the beginning of this lecture that we said that thermodynamics properties are valid only for macroscopic systems with many particles. On a microscopic scale, all real chemical reactions are reversible. The terms reversible and irreversible are most often used in a relative sense where their meaning is ambiguous and not as often used in the molecular or thermodynamic senses where there meanings are exact. In the relative sense, if the activation energy of a chemical reaction is sufficiently high for the reverse direction, the probability that it will occur may be sufficiently low for chemists to call the reaction irreversible. The MCAT is most likely to use the terms reversible and irreversible in their relative sense.

An intuitive way to view entropy is as nature's effort to spread energy evenly between systems. Nature likes to lower energy of a system when it is high relative to the energy of the surroundings, but that means that nature likes to raise energy of a system when it is low relative to the energy of the surroundings. A warm object

3-12
Entropy

The second law of thermodynamics is a funny law because it could be violated, but it is so unlikely to be violated that we say it won't be violated no matter what.

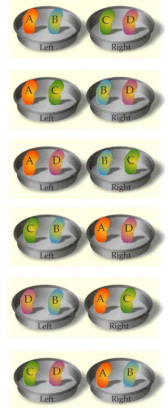

Six possible situations with two beans in one pan.

Only one possible situation with four beans in the left pan.

Copyright © 2005 Examkrackers, Inc.

Entropy, and not energy, dictates the direction of a reaction.

will lose energy to its surroundings when placed in a cool room, but the same object will gain energy when placed in a hot room. This means that it is entropy and not energy that drives reactions in a given direction. The second law of thermodynamics tells us that entropy of the universe is the driving force that dictates whether or not a reaction will proceed. A reaction can be unfavorable in terms of enthalpy, or even energy, and still proceed, but a reaction must increase the entropy of the universe in order to proceed.

Reactions at equilibrium have achieved maximum universal entropy.

Equilibrium is the point in a reaction where the universe has achieved maximum entropy. A thermodynamically reversible reaction is one that remains infinitely close to a state of equilibrium at all times. (Such conditions are called *quasistatic*.) A quasistatic reaction moves infinitely slowly with infinitely small changes being made to the system, each one establishing a new equilibrium.

Entropy increases with number, volume, and temperature.

Entropy is an extensive property. (It increases with amount of substance.) All other factors being equal, entropy increases with number, volume, and temperature. On the MCAT, if a reaction increases the number of gaseous molecules, then that reaction has positive entropy (for the reaction system, not necessarily for the surroundings or the universe). The greater the temperature of a substance the greater its entropy.

The third law of thermodynamics assigns by convention a zero entropy value to any pure substance (either an element or a compound) at absolute zero and in internal equilibrium. At absolute zero, atoms have very little motion. Absolute zero temperature is unattainable.

The units for entropy are J/K. Entropy change is defined mathematically by the infinitesimal change in heat dq_{rev} per kelvin in a reversible process:

$$\Delta S = dq_{rev}/T$$

Since entropy is a state function, the change in entropy for any process will be the same as the change in entropy for a reversible process between the same two states.

Imagine what happens when you slide a box across the floor. The kinetic energy of the box is dissipated into internal energy of the box and floor via molecular collisions collectively called friction. Of course, energy is conserved; the increase in internal energy equals the initial kinetic energy. Now imagine the reverse reaction: the molecules of the floor and the box happen to be moving in a coordinated fashion so as to collide and make the stationary box suddenly start moving. The internal energy of the molecules becomes kinetic energy. Why doesn't this happen in real life? Energy is still conserved in the reverse reaction, so there is no violation of the first law of thermodynamics. The only reason boxes don't spontaneously start sliding across the floor is due to the decrease in entropy which would accompany such a reaction.

Look out, Crouton! Reverse friction could start these boxes moving and crush you like a grape.

But there's no need to fear! Captain Entropy is here.

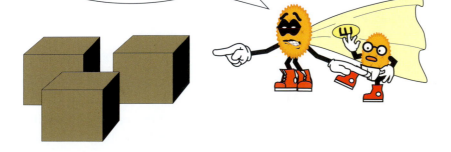

Copyright © 2005 Examkrackers, Inc.

Recall that equilibrium is achieved by maximizing the entropy of the universe. We can restate this relationship in terms of only the system by using the equation: $\Delta S_{surroundings} = dq_{rev}/T$. We know that at constant pressure the change in enthalpy is equal to the heat; thus, $\Delta S_{surroundings} = \Delta H_{surroundings}/T$. Also, since $\Delta H_{surroundings} = -\Delta H_{system}$ under these conditions, we have $\Delta S_{surroundings} = -\Delta H_{system}/T$. Therefore, in a closed system capable of doing only PV work, and at constant temperature and pressure, equilibrium is achieved by maximizing universal entropy via the equation:

$$\Delta S_{universe} = -\Delta H_{system}/T + \Delta S_{system}$$

If we multiply through by $-T$, and substitute ΔG for $-\Delta S_{universe}T$, we have the important MCAT equation for **Gibbs free energy G**:

$$\Delta G = \Delta H - T\Delta S$$

3-13
Gibbs Free Energy

Important MCAT equation!

All variables in this equation refer to the system and not the surroundings. This equation is good only for constant temperature reactions, and loses some significance if pressure is not held constant. Before we multiplied the $\Delta S_{universe}$ equation by $-T$, we wanted to maximize $\Delta S_{universe}$ in order to achieve equilibrium. Since we multiplied by a negative to arrive at the Gibbs function, we must minimize the ΔG in the Gibbs function in order to achieve equilibrium. Thus equilibrium is achieved when the change in the Gibbs free energy is zero (constant temperature and pressure, PV work only, and a reversible process). A reaction where the change in the Gibbs energy is negative indicates an increase in $\Delta S_{universe}$, and such a reaction is said to occur spontaneously. This definition of spontaneity is derived from the Gibbs function, and requires constant temperature and pressure, PV work only, and a reversible process. The true definition of a spontaneous reaction requires only that $\Delta S_{universe}$ be positive under any conditions. For the MCAT however, a negative ΔG from the Gibbs function is good enough for **spontaneity**.

A negative ΔG indicates a spontaneous reation.

Gibbs energy is an extensive property and a state function. It is not conserved in the sense of the conservation of energy law. An isolated system can change its Gibbs energy. The Gibbs energy represents the maximum non-PV work available from a reaction, hence the name 'free energy'. Contracting muscles, transmitting nerves, and batteries are some examples of things that do only non-PV work, making Gibbs energy a useful quantity when analyzing these systems.

You must know the Gibbs function, and, most importantly, that a negative ΔG indicates a spontaneous reaction. Realize that the Gibbs function deals with the change in enthalpy and entropy of a system.

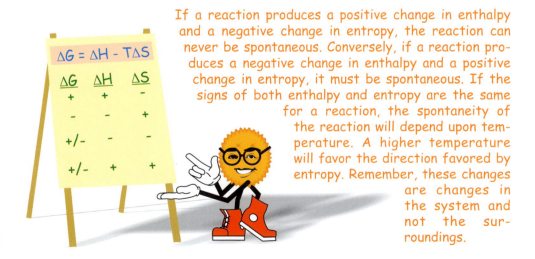

If a reaction produces a positive change in enthalpy and a negative change in entropy, the reaction can never be spontaneous. Conversely, if a reaction produces a negative change in enthalpy and a positive change in entropy, it must be spontaneous. If the signs of both enthalpy and entropy are the same for a reaction, the spontaneity of the reaction will depend upon temperature. A higher temperature will favor the direction favored by entropy. Remember, these changes are changes in the system and not the surroundings.

Copyright © 2005 Examkrackers, Inc.

To finish this lecture, let's summarize the laws of thermodynamics. It's not so important to memorize the laws, as it is to understand them and keep them in mind. The first and second laws are the important ones for the MCAT.

0th law: Two bodies in thermal equilibrium with the same system are in thermal equilibrium with each other. (In other words, temperature exists and is a state function.)

1st law: The energy of an isolated system is conserved for any reaction.

2nd law: The entropy of the universe increases for any reaction.

3rd law: A perfect crystal at zero kelvin is assigned an entropy value of zero. All other substances and all temperatures have a positive entropy value. (Zero kelvin is unattainable.)

Copyright © 2005 Examkrackers, Inc.

65. Which of the following describes a reaction that is always spontaneous?

    A. increasing enthalpy and increasing entropy
    B. decreasing enthalpy and decreasing entropy
    C. increasing enthalpy and decreasing entropy
    D. decreasing enthalpy and increasing entropy

66. Which of the following statements about entropy is false?

    A. The entropy of a system will always increase in a spontaneous reaction.
    B. Entropy is a measure of disorder.
    C. The entropy change of a forward reaction is exactly opposite to the entropy of the reverse reaction.
    D. Entropy increases with temperature.

67. Which of the following is a violation of the law of conservation of energy?

    A. Heat can be changed completely to work in cyclical process.
    B. A system undergoing a reaction with constant enthalpy experiences a temperature change.
    C. After sliding to a stop, a box with initial kinetic energy K has only thermal energy in an amount less than K.
    D. A bond is broken and energy is released.

68. All of the following are examples of processes which increase system entropy EXCEPT:

    A. the expanding universe
    B. aerobic respiration
    C. melting ice
    D. building a bridge

69. Which of the following statements is most likely true concerning the reaction:

$$2A(g) + B(g) \rightarrow 2C(g) + D(s)$$

    A. System entropy is decreasing.
    B. System entropy is increasing.
    C. The reaction is spontaneous.
    D. The reaction is nonspontaneous.

70. The reaction below shows the condensation of water.

$$H_2O(g) \rightarrow H_2O(l)$$

Which of the following will be positive for the water at 25°C and 1 atm?

    A. ΔH
    B. ΔS
    C. ΔG
    D. None of the above.

71.
$$AgCl(s) \rightarrow Ag^+(aq) + Cl^-(aq)$$

During the course of the reaction above, both entropy and enthalpy are increased. If the reaction is not spontaneous at a given temperature and pressure, what can be done to make the reaction occur spontaneously?

    A. Increase the temperature.
    B. Decrease the temperature.
    C. Increase the pressure.
    D. Decrease the pressure.

72. The normal boiling point of benzene (C_6H_6) is 80.1°C. If the partial pressure of benzene gas is 1 atm, which of the following is true of the reaction shown below at 80.1°C?

$$C_6H_6(l) \rightarrow C_6H_6(g)$$

    A. ΔS is negative
    B. ΔS is zero
    C. ΔG is negative
    D. ΔG is zero

Copyright © 2005 Examkrackers, Inc.

STOP.

Lecture 4

Solutions

A **solution** is a homogeneous mixture of two or more compounds in a single phase, such as solid, liquid, or gas. The MCAT will probably test your knowledge of liquid solutions only. However, you should be aware that solutions are possible in other phases as well. Brass is an example of a solid solution of zinc and copper. Generally, in a solution with two compounds, the compound of which there is more is called the **solvent**, and the compound of which there is less is called the **solute**. Sometimes, when neither compound predominates, both compounds are referred to as solvents. Although a compound's behavior does depend upon the molecules around it, the label of 'solvent' or 'solute' does not indicate a particular behavior.

There are *ideal solutions*, *ideally dilute solutions*, and *nonideal solutions*. Ideal solutions are solutions made from compounds that have similar properties. In other words, the compounds can be interchanged within the solution without changing the spatial arrangement of the molecules or the intermolecular attractions. Benzene in toluene is an example of a nearly ideal solution because both compounds have similar bonding properties and similar size. In an ideally dilute solution, the solute molecules are completely separated by solvent molecules so that they have no interaction with each other. Nonideal solutions violate both of these conditions. On the MCAT, you can assume that you are dealing with an ideally dilute solution unless otherwise indicated; however, you should not automatically assume that an MCAT solution is ideal.

Solvent usually indicates the compound that predominates in a solution.

The concepts of an ideal and an ideally dilute solution are not tested directly on the MCAT. They are mentioned here in order to deepen your understanding of solutions and to help explain some apparent paradoxes which result when they are not considered.

In ideally dilute solutions, the mole fraction of the solvent is approximately equal to one.

4-2
Colloids

A colloid is like a solution, only the solute particles are larger. The colloid particles are usually too small to be extracted by filtration but usually large enough or charged enough to be separated by a semipermeable membrane.

Particles larger than small molecules may form mixtures with solvents. If gravity does not cause these particles to settle out of the mixture over time, the mixture is called a *colloidal system*, or *colloid*. (The term 'colloid' can also refer to the colloidal particles.) Colloidal particles are larger than solute particles, and can even be single large molecules such as hemoglobin. A colloidal system can be any combination of phases (except gas in gas). Some examples of colloidal systems are an *aerosol* (liquid or solid particles in a gas like fog or smoke), a *foam* (gas particles in a liquid like whipped cream), an *emulsion* (liquid particles in a liquid or solid like milk or butter), or a *sol* (solid particles in a liquid like paint).

Unlike a true solution, colloidal suspensions will scatter light, a phenomenon known as the *Tyndall effect*. The beam of light in a smoke filled theatre is visible due to the Tyndall effect.

Colloidal particles may be attracted (*lyophilic*) or repelled (*lyophobic*) by their *dispersion medium*. (The dispersion medium in a colloid is analogous to the solvent in a solution.) Lyophobic colloids form when amphipathic or charged particles adsorb to the surface of the colloidal particles stabilizing them in the dispersion medium. Protein in water is an example of a lyophilic colloid; emulsyfied fat in water is an example of a lyophobic colloid.

Colloidal particles are usually too small to be extracted by filtration; however, heating a colloid or adding an electrolyte may cause the particles to *coagulate*. The larger particles produced by coagulation will settle out or can be extracted by filtration. Colloidal systems can also be separated by a semipermeable membrane, a process called *dialysis*.

4-3
More Solutions

Like dissolves like; polar solvents dissolve polar solutes; nonpolar solvents dissolve nonpolar solutes.

When a solute is mixed with a solvent, it is said to dissolve. The general rule for dissolution is **'like dissolves like'**. This rule refers to the polarity of the solute and solvent. Highly polar molecules are held together by strong intermolecular bonds formed by the attraction between their partially charged ends. Nonpolar molecules are held together by weak intermolecular bonds resulting from instantaneous dipole moments. These forces are called **London dispersion forces**. A polar solute interacts strongly with a polar solvent by tearing the solvent-solvent bonds apart and forming solvent-solute bonds. A nonpolar solute does not have enough charge separation to interact effectively with a polar solvent, and thus cannot intersperse itself within the solvent. A nonpolar solute can, however, tear apart the weak bonds of a nonpolar solvent. The bonds of a polar solute are too strong to be broken by the weak forces of a nonpolar solvent.

Ionic compounds are dissolved by polar substances. When ionic compounds dissolve, they break apart into their respective cations and anions and are surrounded by the oppositely charged ends of the polar solvent. This process is called **solvation**. Water acts as a good solvent for ionic substances. The water molecules surround the individual ions pointing their positive hydrogens at the anions and their negative oxygens toward the cations. When several water molecules attach to one side of an ionic compound, they

Come on buddy! I said you can join our club.

We're stickin' together, cracker boy.

Nonpolar Nerd's Club

Nonpolar Salty

The Polar Muscle Club

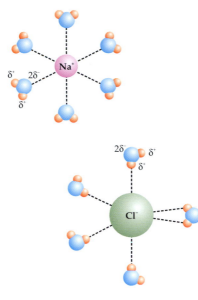

Hydration shell

are able to overcome the strong ionic bond, and break apart the compound. The molecules then surround the ion. In water this process is called **hydration**. Something that is hydrated is said to be in an **aqueous phase**. The number of water molecules needed to surround an ion varies according to the size and charge of the ion. This number is called the *hydration number*. The hydration number is commonly 4 or 6.

For the MCAT you should be aware of common names, formulae, and charges for the polyatomic ions listed on the right.

When ions form in aqueous solution, the solution is able to conduct electricity. A compound which forms ions in aqueous solution is called an **electrolyte**. Strong electrolytes create solutions which conduct electricity well and contain many ions. Weak electrolytes are compounds which form few ions in solution.

Water is a poor conductor of electricity unless it contains electrolytes. Electrolytes are compounds that form ions in aqueous solution.

Name	Formula
nitrite	NO_2^-
nitrate	NO_3^-
sulfite	SO_3^{2-}
sulfate	SO_4^{2-}
hypochlorite	ClO^-
chlorite	ClO_2^-
chlorate	ClO_3^-
perchlorate	ClO_4^-
carbonate	CO_3^{2-}
bicarbonate	HCO_3^-
phosphate	PO_4^{3-}

There are several ways to measure the concentration of a solution, five of which you should know for the MCAT: molarity (*M*), molality (*m*), mole fraction (χ), mass percentage and parts per million (ppm). **Molarity** is the moles of the compound divided by the volume of the solution. Molarity generally has units of mol/L. **Molality** is moles of solute divided by kilograms of solvent. Molality generally has units of mol/kg and is usually used in formulae for colligative properties. The **mole fraction** is the moles of a compound divided by the total moles of all species in solution. Since it is a ratio, mole fraction has no units. **Mass percentage** is 100 times the ratio of the mass of the solute to the total mass of the solution. **Parts per million** is 10^6 times the ratio of the mass of the solute to the total mass of the solution.

4-4 Units of Concentration

$$M = \frac{\text{moles of solute}}{\text{volume of solution}}$$

$$m = \frac{\text{moles of solute}}{\text{kilograms of solvent}}$$

$$\chi = \frac{\text{moles of solute}}{\text{total moles of all solutes and solvent}}$$

$$\text{mass \%} = \frac{\text{mass of solute}}{\text{total mass of solution}} \times 100$$

$$\text{ppm} = \frac{\text{mass of solute}}{\text{total mass of solution}} \times 10^6$$

Notice that parts per million is NOT number of solute molecules per million molecules. It is the mass of the solute per mass of solution times one million.

Copyright © 2005 Examkrackers, Inc.

Remember that solution concentrations are always given in terms of the form of the solute before dissolution. For instance, when 1 mole of NaCl is added to 1 liter of water, it is approximately a 1 molar solution and NOT a 2 molar solution even though each NaCl dissociates into two ions.

Normality measures the number of *equivalents* per liter of solution. The definition of an equivalent will depend upon the type of reaction taking place in the solution. The only time normality is likely to appear on the MCAT is with an acid-base reaction. In an acid-base reaction an equivalent is defined as the mass of acid or base that can furnish or accept one mole of protons. For instance, a 1 molar solution of H_2SO_4 would be called a 2 normal solution because it can donate 2 protons for each H_2SO_4.

Copyright © 2005 Examkrackers, Inc.

Questions 73 through 80 are **NOT** based on a descriptive passage.

73. What is the approximate molarity of a NaCl solution with a specific gravity of 1.006?

    A. 0.05 M
    B. 0.06 M
    C. 0.1 M
    D. 0.2 M

74. Which of the following substances is least soluble in water?

    A. NH_3
    B. NaCl
    C. HSO_4^-
    D. CCl_4

75. Which of the following solutions is the most concentrated? (Assume 1 L of water has a mass of 1 kg.)

    A. 1 M NaCl
    B. 1 m NaCl
    C. A aqueous solution with a NaCl mole fraction of 0.01
    D. 55 grams of NaCl mixed with one liter of water.

76. The air we breathe is approximately 21% O_2 and 79% N_2. If the partial pressure of nitrogen in air is 600 torr, then all of the following are true EXCEPT:

    A. The mole fraction of nitrogen in air is 0.79.
    B. The mass of nitrogen in a 22.4 L sample of air is 22.1 grams at 0°C.
    C. The partial pressure of oxygen is approximately 160 torr.
    D. For every 21 grams of oxygen in an air sample, there are 79 grams of nitrogen.

77. A polar solute is poured into a container with a nonpolar solvent. Which of the following statements best explains the reaction?

    A. The strong dipoles of the polar molecules separate the weak bonds between the nonpolar molecules.
    B. The dipoles of the polar molecules are too weak to break the bonds between the nonpolar molecules.
    C. The instantaneous dipoles of the nonpolar molecules are too weak to separate the bonds between the polar molecules.
    D. The instantaneous dipoles of the nonpolar molecules separate the bonds between the polar molecules.

78. A solution contains 19 grams of $MgCl_2$ in 0.5 liters of distilled water. If $MgCl_2$ totally dissociates, what is the concentration of chloride ions in the solution?

    A. 0.1 M
    B. 0.2 M
    C. 0.4 M
    D. 0.8 M

79. A student has 0.8 liters of a 3 molar HCl solution. How many liters of distilled water must she mix with the 3 molar solution in order to create a 1 molar HCl solution?

    A. 0.8 L
    B. 1.6 L
    C. 2.4 L
    D. 3.2 L

80. All of the following substances are strong electrolytes EXCEPT:

    A. HNO_3
    B. CO_2
    C. NaCl
    D. KOH

_____

4-5

Solution Formation

The formation of a solution is a physical reaction. It involves three steps:

Step 1: the breaking of the intermolecular bonds between solute molecules;

Step 2: the breaking of the intermolecular bonds between solvent molecules;

Step 3: the formation of intermolecular bonds between the solvent and the solute molecules.

Energy is required in order to break a bond. Recall from Chemistry Lecture 3 that at constant pressure the enthalpy change of a reaction equals the heat: $\Delta H = q$, and that for condensed phases not at high pressure (for instance the formation of most MCAT solutions) enthalpy change approximately equals internal energy change: $\Delta H \approx \Delta U$. For solution chemistry we shall use these approximations. Thus the heat of solution is given by:

$$\Delta H_{sol} = \Delta H_1 + \Delta H_2 + \Delta H_3$$

Since energy is required to break a bond, the first two steps in dissolution are endothermic while the third step is exothermic.

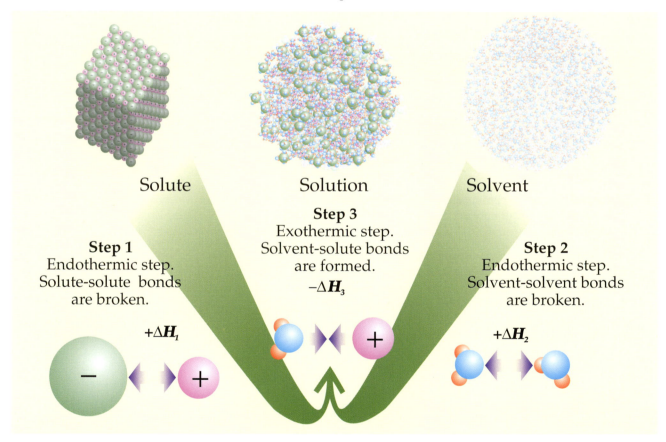

Solute

Solution

Solvent

Step 1
Endothermic step.
Solute-solute bonds
are broken.

$+\Delta \boldsymbol{H_1}$

Step 3
Exothermic step.
Solvent-solute bonds
are formed.
$-\Delta \boldsymbol{H_3}$

Step 2
Endothermic step.
Solvent-solvent bonds
are broken.

$+\Delta \boldsymbol{H_2}$

You must recognize that breaking a bond always requires energy input. Since enthalpy and heat are equal at constant pressure, a solution with a negative enthalpy will give off heat when it forms. Thus, a solution that gives off heat when it forms is creating stronger bonds within the solution.

If the overall reaction releases energy (is exothermic), the new intermolecular bonds are more stable than the old, and, in general, the intermolecular attractions within the solution are stronger than the intermolecular attractions within the pure substances. (Remember, less energy in the system usually means a more stable system.) If the overall reaction absorbs energy (is endothermic), the reverse is true. Using the approximations mentioned above, the overall change in energy of the reaction is equal to the change in enthalpy and is called the heat of solution ΔH_{sol}. A negative heat of solution results in stronger intermolecular bonds, while a positive **heat of solution** results in weaker intermolecular bonds. (Some books combine steps 2 and 3 of solution formation for aqueous solutions calling the sum of their enthalpy changes the *heat of hydration*.)

Copyright © 2005 Examkrackers, Inc.

Since the combined mixture is more disordered than the separated pure substances, most of the time, the formation of a solution involves an increase in entropy. In fact, positional entropy always increases in the formation of a solution, so, on the MCAT, solution formation has positive entropy.

When solutions form, entropy increases.

Imagine a pure liquid in a vacuum-sealed container. If we were to examine the space inside the container, above the liquid, we would find that it is not really a vacuum. Instead it would contain vapor molecules from the liquid. The liquid molecules are held in the liquid by intermolecular bonds. However, they contain a certain amount of kinetic energy, which depends upon the temperature. Some of the liquid molecules at the surface contain enough kinetic energy to break the intermolecular bonds that hold them in the liquid. These molecules launch themselves into the open space above the liquid. As the space fills with molecules, some of the molecules crash back into the liquid. When the rate of molecules leaving the liquid equals the rate of molecules entering the liquid, equilibrium has been established. At this point, the pressure created by the molecules in the open space is called the **vapor pressure** of the liquid.

4-6
Vapor Pressure

Equilibrium between the liquid and gas phases of a compound occurs when the molecules move from liquid to gas as quickl;y as they move from gas to liquid. The vapor pressure necessary to bring the liquid and gas phases of a compound to equilibrium is called the vapor pressure of the compound.

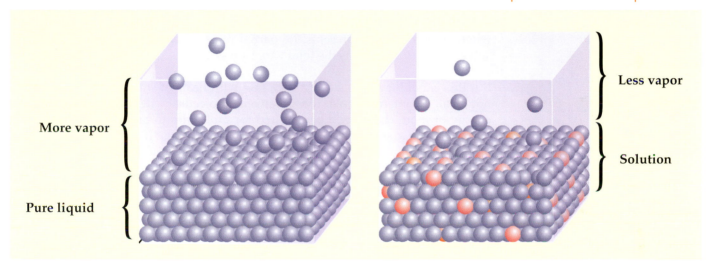

Since vapor pressure is related to the kinetic energy of the molecules, vapor pressure is a function of temperature. A derivation of the Clausius-Clapeyron equation relates vapor pressure and temperature to the heat of vaporization:

$$\ln(P_v) = -\frac{\Delta H_{vap}}{R}\left(\frac{1}{T}\right) + C$$

where ΔH_{vap} is the heat of vaporization, and C is a constant specific to the compound. Vaporization is an endothermic process, so the equation indicates that vapor pressure increases with temperature.

Vapor pressure increases with temperature.

When vapor pressure equals local atmospheric pressure, a compound boils. Solids also have a vapor presssure. The melting point is the temperature at which the vapor pressures of the solid is equal to the vapor pressure of the liquid. Above the melting point the liquid vapor pressure is greater than that of the solid; below the melting point the liquid vapor pressure is less than that of the solid.

Boiling occurs when the vapor pressure of a liquid equals the atmospheric pressure. Melting occurs when the vapor pressure of the solid phase equals the vapor pressure of the liquid phase.

When a **nonvolatile solute** (a solute with no vapor pressure) is added to a liquid, some of those solute molecules will reach the surface of the solution, and reduce the

Copyright © 2005 Examkrackers, Inc.

amount of surface area available for the liquid molecules. Since the solute molecules don't break free of the solution but do take up surface area, the number of molecules breaking free from the liquid is decreased while the surface area of the solution and the volume of open space above the solution remain the same. From the ideal gas law, $PV = nRT$, we know that a decrease in n at constant volume and temperature is proportional to a decrease in P. The vapor pressure of the solution P_v is given by **Raoult's law**, and is proportional to the mole fraction of the liquid a and the vapor pressure of the pure liquid P_a.

$$P_v = \chi_a P_a$$

If the solute is a **volatile solute** (a solute with a vapor pressure), the situation is a little more complicated. A volatile solute will also compete for the surface area of a liquid. However, some of the molecules of a volatile solute will escape from solution and contribute to the vapor pressure. If the solution is an ideal solution (solute and solvent have similar properties), the partial pressures contributed by the solvent and solute can be found by applying Raoult's law separately. The sum of the partial pressures gives the total vapor pressure of the solution, and we arrive at a modified form of Raoult's law:

$$P_v = \chi_a P_a + \chi_b P_b$$

where each χP term represents the partial pressure contributed by the respective solvent, and P_v represents the total vapor pressure.

But this is not the entire story. As we saw with heats of solution, if the solution is not ideal, the intermolecular forces between molecules will be changed. Either less energy or more energy will be required for molecules to break the intermolecular bonds and leave the surface of the solution. This means that the vapor pressure of a nonideal solution will deviate from the predictions made by Raoult's law. We can make a general prediction of the direction of the deviation based upon heats of solution. If the heat of solution is negative, stronger bonds are formed, fewer molecules are able to break free from the surface and there will be a negative deviation of the vapor pressure from Raoult's law. The opposite will occur for a positive heat of solution.

Raoult's law for nonvolatile solutes: If 97% of the solution is solvent, then the vapor pressure will be 97% of the vapor pressure of the pure solvent.

Raoult's law for volatile solutes: If 97% of the solution is solvent, then the vapor pressure will be 97% of the vapor pressure of the pure solvent PLUS 3% of the vapor pressure of the pure solute.

Negative heats of solution form stronger bonds and lower vapor pressure; positive heats of solution form weaker bonds and raise vapor pressure.

Copyright © 2005 Examkrackers, Inc.

The deviation of vapor pressure from Raoult's law can be represented graphically by comparing the mole fractions of solvents with their vapor pressures. Graph 1 below shows only the partial pressure of the solvent as its mole fraction increases. As predicted by Raoult's law, the relationship is linear. Graph 2 shows the vapor pressure of an ideal solution and the individual partial pressures of each solvent. Notice that the partial pressures add at every point to equal the total pressure. This must be true for any solution. Graph 3 and 4 show the deviations of nonideal solutions. The straight lines are the Raoult's law predictions and the curved lines are the actual pressures. Notice that the partial pressures still add at every point to equal the total pressure. Notice also that a positive heat of solution leads to an increase in vapor pressure, and a negative heat of solution, to a decrease in vapor pressure.

In order to really understand this section you must have a thorough understanding of many of the physics and chemistry concepts that we've studied so far (i.e. bond energy, thermodynamics, pressure, and solutions). I suggest that you re-read this section and be sure that you thoroughly understand the concepts.

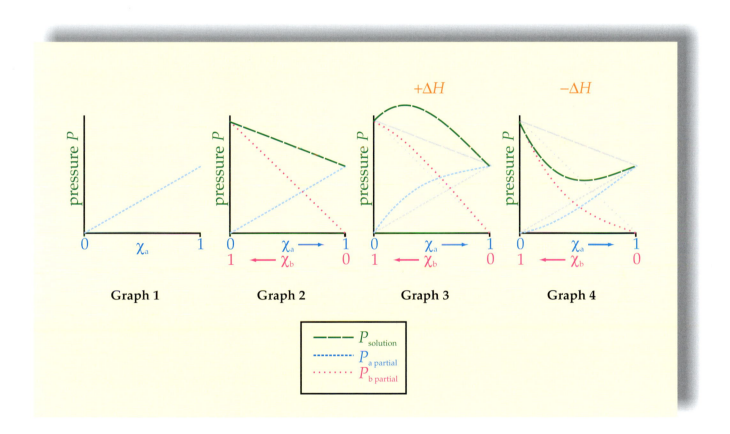

81. NaCl dissolves spontaneously in water. Based upon the following reaction:

$$NaCl(s) \rightarrow Na^+(g) + Cl^-(g) \quad \Delta H = 786 \text{ kJ/mol}$$

the heat of hydration for NaCl must be:

   A.   negative with a magnitude less than 786.
   B.   negative with a magnitude greater than 786.
   C.   positive with a magnitude greater than 786.
   D.   Nothing can be determined about the heat of hydration without more information.

82. Which of the following indicates an exothermic heat of solution?

   A.   Heat is evolved.
   B.   The final solution is acidic.
   C.   A precipitate is formed.
   D.   The reaction is spontaneous.

83. When two pure liquids, *A* and *B*, are mixed, the temperature of the solution increases. All of the following must be true EXCEPT:

   A.   The intermolecular bond strength in at least one of the liquids is less than the intermolecular bond strength between *A* and *B* in solution.
   B.   The reaction is exothermic.
   C.   The vapor pressure of the solution is less than both the vapor pressure of pure *A* and pure *B*.
   D.   The rms velocity of the molecules increases when the solution is formed.

84. Which of the following will increase the vapor pressure of a liquid?

   A.   increasing the surface area of the liquid by pouring it into a wider container
   B.   increasing the kinetic energy of the molecules of the liquid
   C.   decreasing the temperature of the liquid
   D.   adding a nonvolatile solute

85. When two volatile solvents are mixed, the vapor pressure drops below the vapor pressure of either solvent in its pure form. What else can be predicted about the solution of these solvents?

   A.   The solution is ideal.
   B.   The mole fraction of the more volatile solvent is greater than the mole fraction of the less volatile solvent.
   C.   The heat of solution is exothermic.
   D.   The heat of solution is endothermic.

86. A solution composed of ethanol and methanol can be thought of as ideal. At room temperature, the vapor pressure of ethanol is 45 mmHg and the vapor pressure of methanol is 95 mmHg. Which of the following will be true regarding the vapor pressure of a solution containing only ethanol and methanol?

   A.   It will be less than 45 mmHg.
   B.   It will be greater than 45 mmHg and less than 95 mmHg.
   C.   It will be greater than 95 mmHg and less than 140 mmHg.
   D.   It will be greater than 140 mmHg.

87. Benzene and toluene combine to form an ideal solution. At 80°C, vapor pressure of pure benzene is 800 mmHg and the vapor pressure of pure toluene is 300 mmHg. If the vapor pressure of the solution is 400 mmHg, what are the mole fractions of benzene and toluene?

   A.   60% benzene and 40% toluene
   B.   50% benzene and 50% toluene
   C.   40% benzene and 60% toluene
   D.   20% benzene and 80% toluene

88. When solute *A* is added to solvent *B*, heat is released. Which of the following must be true of the solvation process?

   A.   The bonds broken in solute *A* must be stronger than the bonds broken in solvent *B*.
   B.   The bonds broken in solute *A* must be weaker than the bonds broken in solvent *B*.
   C.   The bonds formed in the solution must be stronger than the bonds broken in solute *A* and solvent *B*.
   D.   The bonds formed in the solution must be weaker than the bonds broken in solute *A* and solvent *B*.

Solubility is a solute's tendency to dissolve in a solvent. On the MCAT, the solute will usually be a salt, and the solvent will most often be water. Dissolution of a salt is reversible on a molecular scale; dissolved molecules of the salt reattach to the surface of the salt crystal. For a dissolving salt, the reverse reaction, called **precipitation**, takes place initially at a slower rate than dissolution. As the salt dissolves and the concentration of dissolved salt builds, the rate of dissolution and precipitation equilibrate. When the rate of dissolution and precipitation are equal, the solution is said to be **saturated**; the concentration of dissolved salt has reached a maximum in a saturated solution. Just like any other reaction, the equilibrium established at the saturation point is dynamic; the concentrations of products and reactants remain constant, but the forward and reverse reactions continue at the same rate.

The equilibrium of a solvation reaction has its own equilibrium constant called the **solubility product K_{sp}**. Use K_{sp} the same way you would use any other equilibrium constant. Remember that solids and pure liquids have an approximate mole fraction of one and can be excluded from the equilibrium expression. Thus, solids are left out of the solubility product expression as in the example of the K_{sp} for barium hydroxide shown below.

$$Ba(OH)_2(s) \rightleftharpoons Ba^{2+}(aq) + 2OH^-(aq)$$

$$K_{sp} = [Ba^{2+}][OH^-]^2$$

Solubility and the solubility product are not the same thing. The solubility of a substance in a given solvent is found from the solubility product. The solubility is the number of moles of solute per liter of a solution that can be dissolved in a given solvent. Solubility depends upon the common ions in the solution. The solubility constant is independent of the common ions, and can be found in a reference book.

For most salts, crystallization is exothermic.

We can write an equation for the solvation of BaF_2 in water as follows:

$$BaF_2(s) \rightleftharpoons Ba^{2+}(aq) + 2F^-(aq)$$

The solubility product for BaF_2 is:

$$K_{sp} = [Ba^{2+}][F^-]^2$$

If we look in a book, we find that the K_{sp} for BaF_2 has a value of 2.4×10^{-5} at 25°C. Like any equilibrium constant, the K_{sp} is unitless. From the K_{sp} we can find the solubility of BaF_2 in any solution at 25°C. For instance, to find the solubility of BaF_2 in one liter of water, we simply saturate one liter of water with BaF_2. The solubility is the maximum number of moles per liter that can dissolve in the solution. We call the solubility 'x', since it is unknown. If x moles per liter of BaF_2 dissolve, then there will be x moles per liter of Ba^{2+} in solution and twice as many, or $2x$ moles per liter, of F^-. We plug these values into the K_{sp} equation and solve.

$$2.4 \times 10^{-5} = (x)(2x)^2$$

$$x \approx 1.8 \times 10^{-2}$$

1.8×10^{-2} mol/L is the solubility of BaF_2 in one liter of water at 25°C.

What would happen if we added 1 mole of F^- to our solution in the form of NaF? The solubility of BaF_2 would change. The NaF would completely dissociate forming 1 mole of F^- and 1 mole of Na^+. The Na^+ ions are not in the equilibrium expression and (ideally) would have no effect on the equilibrium. Because they

4-7
Solubility

Use K_{sp} like any other equilibrium constant to create an equilibrium expression. Set the K_{sp} equal to products over reactants raised to the power of their coefficients in the balanced equation. As always, leave out pure solids and liquids.

Solubility and the solubility product are not the same thing. Solubility product or K_{sp} is a constant found in a book. Solubility is the maximum number of moles of the solute that can dissolve in solution.

The solubility product changes only with temperature. The solubility depends upon the temperature and the ions in solution.

Copyright © 2005 Examkrackers, Inc.

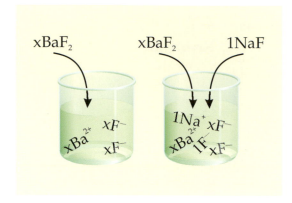

have no effect, the Na^+ ions are called __spectator ions__. The F^- ions, however, do affect the equilibrium. Their disturbance of the equilibrium is called __the common ion effect__ because it involves an ion common to an ion in the equilibrium expression. By Le Chatâlier's principle, the addition of a common ion will push the equilibrium in a direction which tends to reduce the concentration of that ion. In this case, the equilibrium will move to the left, and the solubility of BaF_2 will be reduced. To find out by exactly how much the solubility will be reduced, we go back to the equilibrium expression. One key to solving solubility problems is realizing that the order in which you mix the solution is irrelevant, so you should mix them in the order that is most convenient to you. In this case it is easiest to add the NaF first, since it completely dissociates. Now we add BaF_2 to a solution of 1 liter of water and 1 mole of F^-. Again, x moles will dissolve leaving x moles of Ba^{2+}. But this time, since there is already 1 mole of F^-, $2x + 1$ moles of F^- will be in solution at equilibrium.

> *A common ion added to a saturated solution will shift the equilibrium increasing precipitate. It does not affect the K_{sp}.*

> *A common ion added to a solution that is not saturated will NOT shift the equilibrium, because in an unsaturated solution, there is no equilibrium to shift.*

$$2.4 \times 10^{-5} = (x)(2x + 1)^2$$

Now here's a trick to simplify the math. We know that the equilibrium is shifting to the left, so x will be smaller than our earlier calculations of 1.8×10^{-2}. Even $2x$ will be much smaller than 1. Thus, $2x + 1$ is going to be very close to 1. Therefore, we drop the $2x$ and solve:

$$2.4 \times 10^{-5} \approx (x)(1)^2$$

$$x \approx 2.4 \times 10^{-5}$$

Just to be sure that we were correct in our estimation of $2x$, we plug our estimated value of x into the term that we deleted ($2x$), and we see if it is truly much smaller than the term to which we added it (in this case 1).

$$2x = 4.8 \times 10^{-5} \ll 1$$

Our assumption was valid. Thus our new solubility of BaF_2 is 2.4×10^{-5} mol/L.

4-8
Solubility Guidelines

Compounds with water solubilities of less than 0.01 mol L^{-1} are generally considered insoluble. MCAT will not require you to memorize the solubilities of different compounds. Nevertheless, here are a few solubility guidelines for compounds in water:

Nearly all ionic compounds containing nitrate (NO_3^-), ammonium (NH_4^+), and alkali metals (Li^+, Na^+, K^+...) are *soluble*.

> *It is very unlikely that an MCAT question would require that you know these solubilities. However, knowing them will make solution chemistry easier.*

Ionic compounds containing halogens (Cl^-, Br^-, I^-) are *soluble*, EXCEPT for silver, mercury, and lead compounds (Ag^+, Hg_2^{2+}, Pb^{2+}).

Sulfate compounds (SO_4^{2-}) are *soluble*, EXCEPT for mercury, lead, and the heavier alkaline metals (Hg_2^{2+}, Pb^{2+}, Ca^{2+}, Sr^{2+}, Ba^{2+}).

Compounds containing the heavier alkaline metals (Ca^{2+}, Sr^{2+}, Ba^{2+}) are *soluble* when paired with sulfides (S^{2-}) and hydroxides (OH^-).

Carbonates, phosphates, sulfides, and hydroxides (CO_3^{2-}, PO_4^{3-}, S^{2-}, OH^-) are generally *insoluble* other than in the cases mentioned above.

Copyright © 2005 Examkrackers, Inc.

Pressure and temperature affect solubilities. Pressure on liquids and solids has little effect, but pressure on a gas increases its solubility. For an ideally dilute solution, the increase in pressure of gas a over a solution is directly proportional to the solubility of gas a, if the gas does not react with, or dissociate in, the solvent. This relationship is given by *Henry's law*:

$$C = k_{a1}P_v$$

where C is the solubility of the gas a (typically in moles per liter), k_{a1} is Henry's law constant, which varies with each solute-solvent pair, and P_v is the vapor partial pressure of gas a above the solution. Strangely, Henry's law can also be written as:

$$P_v = \chi_a k_{a2}$$

where χ_a is the mole fraction of a in solution, P_v is the vapor partial pressure of gas a, and k_{a2} is Henry's law constant. Although both equations show that the concentration of a gas in solution is proportional to the vapor partial pressure of the gas above the solution, the Henry's law constant in the second equation has a different value than the Henry's law constant in the first equation. If we compare the second equation with Raoult's law ($P_v = \chi_a P_a$), they appear to conflict unless P_a has the same value as k_{a2}. In fact, they do NOT agree. Both are approximations. Rault's law is most accurate when looking at the vapor partial pressure of a solvent with high concentration. Henry's law is more accurate when looking at the vapor partial pressure of a volatile solute where the solute has a low concentration. In other words, in an ideally dilute solution, the solvent obeys Raoult's law and the solute obeys Henry's law. One way to remember this is when the solvent concentration is high, each solvent molecule is surrounded by other solvent molecules, so it behaves more like a pure solvent. Thus the solvent vapor partial pressure is proportional to its vapor pressure as a pure liquid; Raoult's law. When the volatile solute concentration is low, each molecule is surrounded by solvent molecules creating a deviation from the behavior of the pure volatile solute. Thus its vapor partial pressure is not proportional to its pressure as a pure substance (Raoult's law doesn't work in this case.), but is proportional to some constant; Henry's law.

Le Chatâlier's principle, when applied to solutions, should be used with caution. Because heat energy is a product of a reaction with a negative heat of solution, Le Chatâlier's principle predicts that a temperature increase will push such a reaction to the left decreasing the solubility of the solute. However, entropy increase is large in solution formation. From the equation $\Delta G = \Delta H - T\Delta S$, we see that a temperature increase emphasizes the ΔS term tending to result in a more negative ΔG and thus a more spontaneous reaction. Due to the large increase in entropy, the water solubility of many solids increases with increasing temperature regardless of the enthalpy change. To be absolutely certain, the change in solubility due to temperature must be found by experiment, but the solubility of most salts increases with temperature.

The solubility of gases, on the other hand, typically decreases with increasing temperature. You can remember this by understanding why hot waste water from factories that is dumped into streams is hazardous to aquatic life. The hot water has a double effect. First, it holds less oxygen than cold water. Second, it floats on the cold water and seals it off from the oxygen in the air above.

Other factors that affect the solubility of a gas are its size, and reactivity with the solvent. Heavier, larger gases experience greater van der Waals forces and tend to be more soluble. Gases that chemically react with a solvent have greater solubility.

4-9
Solubility Factors

As shown by Rault's law and Henry's law, the partial vapor pressure of a solution component is always proportional to its mole fraction. If the component predominates as the solvent, Rault's law says that the partial vapor pressure is proportional to the pure vapor pressure. If the component represents a tiny amount of solution, Henry's law says that the vapor partial pressure is proportional to Henry's law constant.

The most important thing to remember about Henry's law is that it demonstrates that the solubility of a gas is proportional to its vapor partial pressure. We can remember this by thinking of a can of soda. When we open the can and release the pressure, the solubility of the gas decreases causing some gas to rise out of the solution and create the familiar hiss and foam.

As the temperature increases, the solubility of salts generally increases.

Gases behave in the opposite fashion. As temperature increases, the solubility of gases decreases. The can of soda is useful here as well. If we place a can of soda on the stove, the gas escapes the solution and expands in the can causing it to explode. (This is not the only reason that the can explodes, but it is a good memory aid.)

Copyright © 2005 Examkrackers, Inc.

Questions 89 through 96 are **NOT** based on a descriptive passage.

89. When a solution is saturated:

A. the solvent changes to solute, and the solute changes to solvent at an equal rate.
B. the vapor pressure of the solution is equal to atmospheric pressure.
C. the concentration of solvent is at a maximum.
D. the concentration of solvent is at a minimum.

90. The addition of a strong base to a saturated solution of $Ca(OH)_2$ would:

A. decrease the number of OH^- ions in solution.
B. increase the number of Ca^{2+} ions in solution.
C. cause $Ca(OH)_2$ to precipitate.
D. decrease the pH.

91. Na_2SO_4 dissociates completely in water. From the information given in the table below, if Na_2SO_4 were added to a solution containing equal concentrations of aqueous Ca^{2+}, Ag^+, Pb^{2+}, and Ba^{2+} ions, which of the following solids would precipitate first?

Compound	K_{sp}
$CaSO_4$	6.1×10^{-5}
Ag_2SO_4	1.2×10^{-5}
$PbSO_4$	1.3×10^{-8}
$BaSO_4$	1.5×10^{-9}

A. $CaSO_4$
B. Ag_2SO_4
C. $PbSO_4$
D. $BaSO_4$

92. A sealed container holds gaseous oxygen and liquid water. Which of the following would increase the amount of oxygen dissolved in the water?

A. expanding the size of the container
B. adding an inert gas to the container
C. decreasing the temperature of the container.
D. shaking the container

93. The K_{sp} of $BaCO_3$ is 1.6×10^{-9}. How many moles of barium carbonate can be dissolved in 3 liters of water?

A. 4×10^{-5} moles
B. 6.9×10^{-5} moles
C. 1.2×10^{-4} moles
D. 2.1×10^{-4} moles

94. Which of the following expressions represents the solubility product for $Cu(OH)_2$?

A. $K_{sp} = [Cu^{2+}][OH^-]^2$
B. $K_{sp} = [Cu^{2+}]^2[OH^-]$
C. $K_{sp} = [Cu^{2+}]^2[OH^-]^2$
D. $K_{sp} = [Cu^{2+}][OH^-]$

95. If the solubility of $PbCl_2$ is equal to x, which of the following expressions will be equal to the solubility product for $PbCl_2$?

A. $4x^3$
B. $2x^3$
C. x^3
D. x^2

96. A beaker contains a saturated solution of CaF_2 ($K_{sp} = 4 \times 10^{-11}$). There are some Na^+ ions in the solution. If NaF is added to the beaker, which of the following will occur?

A. The concentration of Na^+ will decrease.
B. The concentration of Ca^{2+} will decrease.
C. The concentration of F^- will decrease.
D. All concentrations will remain constant.

Copyright © 2005 Examkrackers, Inc.

STOP.

Lecture 5

Heat Capacity, Phase Change, and Colligative Properties

5-1

If all the intensive macroscopic properties of a system are constant, that system is said to be *homogeneous*. Any part of a system that is homogeneous is called a phase. A phase is uniform throughout with respect to chemical composition and physical state. Some examples of different phases are crystalline solid, amorphous solid, aqueous, pure liquid, and vapor. A system may have a number of solid and liquid phases, but it will usually have only one gaseous phase. Pure substances have only one gaseous phase and usually have only one liquid phase.

Phases

Most of the time, you can think of phases as solid, liquid, and gas. Just be aware that this is not the technical definition. And when we discuss things like solutions, remember that pure water is a different phase than aqueous Na^+ ions. Another common example is rhombic sulfur and monoclinic sulfur; these are two different solid phases of the same element.

5-2
Heat Capacity

Phase changes arise through changes in the manner in which internal energy is distributed over molecules and space. In other words, a phase change may result when the energy of each molecule is decreased or increased, or when the space around each molecule is reduced or enlarged. Such changes are accomplished via heat or work. In order to understand phase changes then, we must understand how substances react to heat and PV work.

Heat capacity C is a measure of the energy change needed to change the temperature of a substance. The heat capacity is defined as:

$$C = \frac{q}{\Delta T}$$

Don't let the name 'heat capacity' fool you. Recall that heat is a process of energy transfer, and cannot be stored. Heat capacity was given its name before heat was fully understood. 'Internal energy capacity' would be a better, but not perfect, name. Not perfect because we can change the temperature of a substance at constant internal energy by changing only the volume. Likewise, in an isothermal expansion of a gas, we can expand a gas at constant temperature by adding heat during the expansion.

If, while being heated, no PV work is done by a system at rest, nearly all the heat energy goes into increasing the temperature. When the system is allowed to expand at constant pressure, some energy leaves the system as work and the temperature increase is diminished. Thus constant pressure heat capacities are greater than constant volume heat capacities.

There are two heat capacities for any substance: a constant volume heat capacity C_V and a constant pressure heat capacity C_P. If we recall the first law of thermodynamics for a system at rest, $\Delta U = q + w$, and remember the relationship between temperature and internal energy, we can understand why the same substance can have different responses to the same amount of energy change. For instance, if the volume of a system is held constant, then the system can do no PV work; all energy change must be in the form of heat. This means that none of the energy going into the system can escape as work done by the system. Most of the energy must contribute to a temperature change. On the other hand, when pressure is held constant and the substance is allowed to expand, some of the energy can leave the system as PV work done on the surroundings as the volume changes. Thus, at constant pressure, a substance can absorb energy with less change in temperature by expelling some of the energy to the surroundings as work. C_P is greater than C_V.

$$C_V = \frac{q}{\Delta T} \text{ constant volume}$$

$$C_P = \frac{q}{\Delta T} \text{ constant pressure}$$

Just think about the heat capacity of a substance as the amount of energy a substance can absorb per unit of temperature change. Don't worry too much about the difference between constant pressure and constant volume heat capacities. The MCAT might even ignore this fact completely. Use units to help you solve heat capacity problems. For instance, if a heat capacity is given in cal g^{-1} $°C^{-1}$, then you know that to find the heat (measured in calories) you simply multiply by grams and degrees Celsius. This gives you the equation $q = mc\Delta T$. Most of the time you don't have to know the formula, if you look at the units. Also with heat capacity problems, follow the energy flow, remembering that energy is always conserved: $\Delta E = q + w$.

For a solid or a liquid, both of which experience very little change in volume, there is a more important reason why constant volume and pressure heat capacities differ. The intermolecular forces of a solid or liquid are much stronger than those of a gas. Small changes in the intermolecular distances of noncompressible phases result in large changes in intermolecular potential energy. Intermolecular potential energy does not affect temperature, and thus heat is absorbed at constant pressure with less change in temperature than when heat is absorbed at constant volume. Again: C_P is greater than C_V.

Heat capacity is always positive on the MCAT; the temperature will always increase when energy is added to a substance at constant volume or pressure. In the real world, heat capacity also changes with temperature; the amount of energy that a substance can absorb per change in temperature varies with the temperature. However, unless otherwise indicated, for the MCAT, assume that heat capacity does not change with temperature.

Sometimes the MCAT will give you the heat capacity of an entire system. For instance, a thermometer may be made from several substances each with its own heat

Copyright © 2005 Examkrackers, Inc.

capacity. The thermometer may be immersed in a bath of oil. The oil has its own heat capacity. On the MCAT, the heat capacity of the thermometer-oil system may be precalculated and given in units of energy divided by units of temperature: i.e. J/K or cal/°C. For such a situation, we would use the following equation:

$$q = C\Delta T$$

Sometimes the MCAT will give a specific heat capacity *c*. *Specific* means divided by mass, so the **specific heat capacity** is simply the heat capacity per unit mass. A specific heat usually has units of $J\ kg^{-1}\ K^{-1}$ or $cal\ g^{-1}\ °C^{-1}$. When a specific heat is given, use the following equation:

$$q = mc\Delta T$$

The '*m*' in this equation is for mass, not molality. This equation is easy to remember because it looks like *q* = MCAT. Notice that the symbol for specific heat is usually a lower case '*c*' while the symbol for heat capacity is usually an upper case '*C*'.

For the MCAT you must know that water has a specific heat of $1\ cal\ g^{-1}\ °C^{-1}$. This was once the definition of a calorie.

$$c_{water} = 1\ cal\ g^{-1}\ °C^{-1}$$

> By the way, don't be surprised if you see molar heat capacity or something similar. Heat capacities can be given per mole, per volume, per gram, or per whatever. Just use the equation $q = mc\Delta T$ and rely on the units of c to find the units of m. For instance, if c is given as the molar heat capacity, m would be in moles.

5-3
Calorimeters

A calorimeter is a device which measures energy change. There are both constant pressure and constant volume calorimeters. A **coffee cup calorimeter** is an example of a constant pressure calorimeter because it measures energy change at atmospheric pressure. In a coffee cup calorimeter, two coffee cups are used to insulate the solution. A stirrer maintains equal distribution of energy throughout, and a thermometer measures the change in temperature. Obviously, a coffee cup calorimeter cannot contain expanding gases. Reactions that take place inside a coffee cup calorimeter occur at the constant pressure of the local atmosphere. A coffee cup calorimeter is used to measure **heats of reaction**. (Recall that at constant pressure $q = \Delta H$.) For instance, if we mix HCl and NaOH in a coffee cup calorimeter, the net ionic reaction is:

$$H^+ + OH^- \rightarrow H_2O$$

Using the specific heat of water, the mass of water, and the measured change in temperature, we can solve for *q* in the equation: $q = mc\Delta T$. Since $q = \Delta H$ at constant pressure, we have the heat of reaction.

A **bomb calorimeter** measures energy change at constant volume. A bomb calorimeter tells us the internal energy change in a reaction. (Recall that at constant volume $q = \Delta U$.) In a bomb calorimeter, a steel container full of reactants is placed inside another rigid, thermally insulated container. When the reaction occurs, heat is transferred to the surrounding water (shown in the diagram). Using the known heat capacity of the container and the equation: $q = C\Delta T$, we can deduce the heat of the reaction, and thus the internal energy change in the reaction.

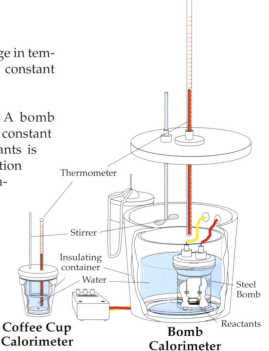

Thermometer

Stirrer

Insulating container

Water

Steel Bomb

Reactants

Coffee Cup Calorimeter

Bomb Calorimeter

Copyright © 2005 Examkrackers, Inc.

97. 20 grams of NaCl is poured into a coffee cup calorimeter containing 250 ml of water. If the temperature inside the calorimeter drops 1°C by the time the NaCl is totally dissolved, what is the heat of solution for NaCl and water? (specific heat of water is 4.18 J/g °C.)

    A.   −3 kJ/mol
    B.   −1 kJ/mol
    C.   1 kJ/mol
    D.   3 kJ/mol

98. Using a bomb calorimeter, the change in energy for the combustion of one mole of octane is calculated to be -5.5×10^3 kJ. Which of the following is true concerning this process?

    A.   Since no work is done, the change in energy is equal to the heat.
    B.   Since there is no work, the change in energy is equal to the enthalpy.
    C.   Since work is done, the change in energy is equal to the heat.
    D.   The work done can be added to the change in energy to find the enthalpy.

99. Which of the following are true statements?

    I.   The heat capacity of a substance is the amount of heat that substance can hold per unit of temperature.
    II.   The specific heat for a single substance is the same for all phases of that substance.
    III.   When heat is added to a fluid, its temperature will change less if it is allowed to expand.

    A.   I only
    B.   III only
    C.   I and III only
    D.   I, II, and III

100. Substance A has a greater heat capacity than substance B. Which of the following is most likely true concerning substances A and B?

    A.   Substance A has larger molecules than substance B.
    B.   Substance B has a lower boiling point than substance A.
    C.   At the same temperature, the molecules of substance B move faster than those of substance A.
    D.   Substance A has more methods of absorbing energy than substance B.

101. In a free adiabatic expansion, a real gas is allowed to spread to twice its original volume with no energy transfer from the surroundings. All of the following are true concerning this process EXCEPT:

    A.   No work is done.
    B.   Increased potential energy between molecules results in decreased kinetic energy and the gas cools.
    C.   Entropy increases.
    D.   The gas loses heat.

Questions 102 through 104 refer to the table below, which lists several common metals and their specific heats.

Metal	Specific Heat c (J/g-°C)
Fe	0.44
Au	0.13
Al	0.90
Cu	0.39

102. If samples of equal mass of all of the metals listed are subjected to the same heat source, which metal would be expected to show the LEAST change in temperature?

    A.   Iron
    B.   Gold
    C.   Aluminum
    D.   Copper

103. In an experiment, it was found that 6 kJ of heat were required to raise the temperature of a sample of copper by 15°C. If the experiment was repeated with a gold sample of the same mass, how much heat would be required achieve the same temperature change?

    A.   2 kJ
    B.   4 kJ
    C.   12 kJ
    D.   18 kJ

104. When a sample of aluminum of unknown mass was subjected to 1.8 kJ of heat, the temperature of the aluminum sample increased from 26°C to 31°C. What was the mass of the sample?

    A.   200 g
    B.   400 g
    C.   600 g
    D.   800 g

Copyright © 2005 Examkrackers, Inc.

STOP.

To understand the phase change process, we shall examine H_2O at constant pressure of 1 atm. If we start with ice at –10°C and begin heating uniformly at a constant rate, initially, the energy going into the ice increases the vibration of its molecules and raises its temperature. When the ice reaches 0°C, the temperature stops increasing. Energy now goes into breaking and weakening hydrogen bonds. This results in a phase change; the ice becomes liquid water. When all of the ice has changed to water, the temperature begins to rise again; the heat goes into increased movement of the molecules. When the water reaches 100°C, the temperature stops rising. The energy once again goes into breaking hydrogen bonds. This process results in a second phase change: liquid water to steam. Once all the hydrogen bonds are broken, the heat increases the speed of the molecules and the temperature rises again. This simplified explanation of phase change is diagrammed below in a heating curve.

5-4
Phase Changes

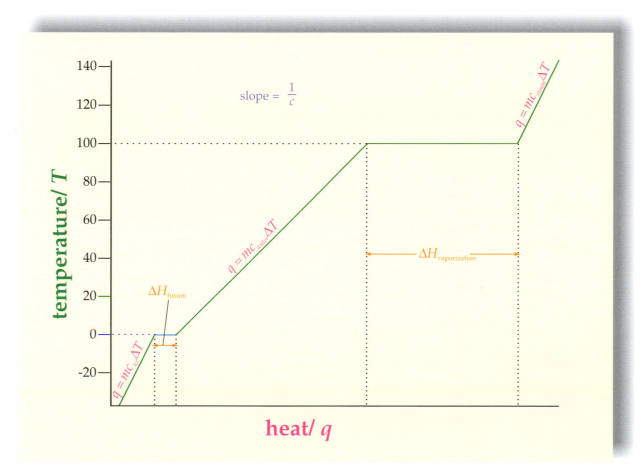

Notice that at 0°C and 100°C the heat stops changing the temperature until the phase change is complete. At these temperatures, the heat capacity is infinite. These points are called the **normal melting point** and **normal boiling point** for water. The word 'normal' indicates a constant pressure of 1 atm. Since the pressure is constant, heat equals the enthalpy change ($q = \Delta H$). The enthalpy change associated with melting is called **the heat of fusion**; the enthalpy change associated with boiling, **the heat of vaporization**. Since enthalpy change is a state function, exactly the same amount of heat absorbed during melting is released during freezing. This is also true for vaporization and condensation, and sublimation and deposition.

The slope of the heating curve, where not zero, is the reciprocal of the specific heat. Notice that each phase of a substance has a unique slope, and therefore a unique specific heat.

The flat line segments of the heating curve represent a phase change.

You need to know the names of the types of phase changes: melting-freezing; vaporization-condensation; sublimation-deposition.

Each phase of a substance has its own specific heat.

Copyright © 2005 Examkrackers, Inc.

Evaporation occurs when the partial pressure above a liquid is less than the liquid's vapor pressure, but the atmospheric pressure is greater than the vapor pressure. Under these conditions, the liquid evaporates rather than boils.

The heating curve shows that melting and boiling are endothermic processes; heat is added. You should also know that melting and boiling normally increase volume and molecular movement, and therefore result in increased system entropy, so entropy and enthalpy are both positive for the processes of melting and vaporizing, and both negative for the processes of freezing and condensing. From the equation, $\Delta G = \Delta H - T\Delta S$, we see that when enthalpy and entropy have the same sign, temperature will dictate in which direction the reaction will move. So phase changes at constant pressure are governed by temperature.

5-5 Phase Diagrams

Pressure and temperature are two important intensive properties that help determine the phase of a substance. A **phase diagram** indicates the phases of a substance at different pressures and temperatures. Each section of a phase diagram represents a different phase. The lines marking the boundaries of each section represent temperatures and pressures where the corresponding phases are in equilibrium with each other. Like other equilibriums in chemistry, this equilibrium is a dynamic equilibrium. For instance, when water and steam are in equilibrium, water molecules are escaping from the liquid phase at the same rate that they are returning. Notice that there is only one point where a substance can exist in equilibrium as a solid, liquid, and gas. This point is called the **triple point**.

There is also a temperature above which a substance cannot be liquefied regardless of the pressure applied. This temperature is called the **critical temperature**. The pressure required to produce liquefaction while the substance is at the critical temperature is called the **critical pressure**. Together, the critical temperature and critical pressure define the **critical point**. Fluid beyond the critical point has characteristics of both gas and liquid, and is called *supercritical fluid*.

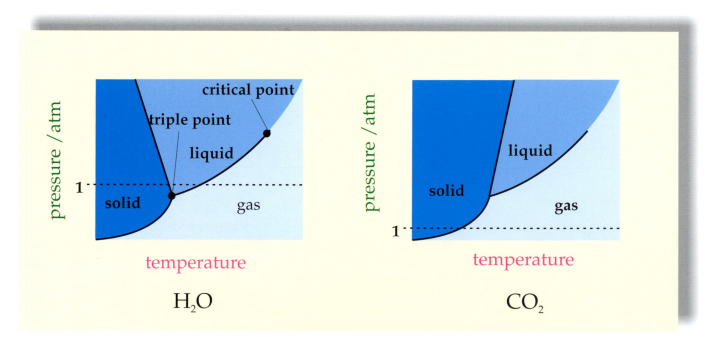

Comparing the phase diagrams for water and carbon dioxide, we notice some interesting things. Even if it were not labeled, we could approximate the location of the 1 atm mark for either diagram. We know that at atmospheric pressure, water exists in all three phases at different temperatures. Thus, we know that the 1 atmosphere mark must be above the triple point. Since carbon dioxide (dry ice) sublimes (changes from solid to gas) at one atmosphere, we know that the triple point must be above the 1 atm mark.

Copyright © 2005 Examkrackers, Inc.

Compare the equilibrium line separating the liquid and solid phases on each diagram shown. For water, the line has a negative slope; for carbon dioxide, a positive slope. Most phase diagrams resemble carbon dioxide in this respect. The negative slope of water explains why ice floats. Since volume decreases with increasing pressure, as we move upward on the phase diagram from ice to liquid water, the volume occupied by H_2O must be decreasing and thus the water must be increasing in density. Therefore, water must be denser than ice. The reason for this is that the crystal structure formed by ice requires more space than the random arrangement of water molecules.

For phase changes you must know where the energy goes. It enters the substance as heat or *PV* work, but what then? During a phase change, it breaks bonds and doesn't change the temperature. When the phase is NOT changing, energy increases molecular movement, which increases the temperature.

Think about this: for a single sample of a substance, *P*, *V*, *n*, and *T* are interrelated in such a way that if you know three of them, you can derive the other. This means that a phase diagram can also be given as a comparison between volume and pressure, or volume and temperature. What would that look like? See the problems on the next page for the answer.

Copyright © 2005 Examkrackers, Inc.

Questions 105 through 112 are **NOT** based on a descriptive passage.

105. What is the total heat needed to change 1 gram of water from –10°C to 110°C at 1 atm? (ΔH_{fusion} = 80 cal/g, $\Delta H_{vaporization}$ = 540 cal/g, specific heat of ice and steam are 0.5 cal/g °C)

   A.   –730 cal
   B.   –630 cal
   C.   630 cal
   D.   730 cal

106. When heat energy is added evenly throughout a block of ice at 0°C and 1 atm, all of the following are true EXCEPT:

   A.   The temperature remains constant until all the ice is melted.
   B.   The added energy increases the kinetic energy of the molecules.
   C.   Entropy increases.
   D.   Hydrogen bonds are broken.

107. Below is a phase diagram for carbon dioxide.

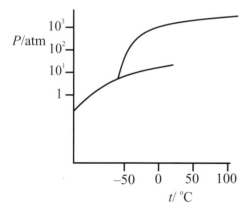

What is the critical temperature for carbon dioxide?

   A.   –57°C
   B.   0°C
   C.   31°C
   D.   103°C

108. The diagram below compares the density of water in the liquid phase with its vapor phase.

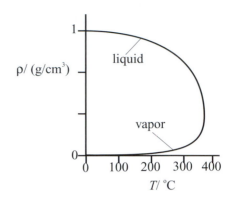

What is the critical temperature of water?

   A.   0°C
   B.   135°C
   C.   374°C
   D.   506°C

109. In graph (*a*) below, isotherms for water are plotted against pressure and volume. Graph (*b*) is a phase diagram of water with pressure vs. temperature.

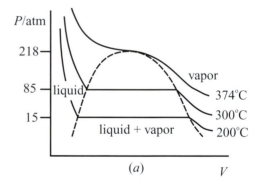

(a)

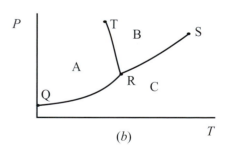

(b)

The area inside the dashed line on graph (*a*) is represented on graph (*b*) by:

   A.   the line between points *R* and *S*.
   B.   the area *B*.
   C.   the area *C*.
   D.   parts of both area *B* and *C*.

Copyright © 2005 Examkrackers, Inc.
GO TO THE NEXT PAGE.

110. A solid 78 gram sample of benzene (C_6H_6) was gradually heated until it was melted completely. The heating curve for the sample is shown below.

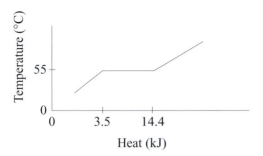

What is the heat of fusion of benzene?

A. 3.5 kJ/mole
B. 10.9 kJ/mole
C. 14.4 kJ/mole
D. 17.9 kJ/mole

111. At atmospheric pressure, the temperature of a pot of boiling water remains at 100°C, when heat is added. The best explanation as to why the added energy does not raise the temperature is that:

A. at the boiling point, the large heat capacity of water allows water to absorb the added energy.
B. the hydrogen bonds of water are strong enough to absorb the added energy without breaking.
C. as the water becomes steam, the added energy becomes kinetic energy of the gas molecules.
D. the added energy is used to break bonds between water molecules.

112. A student has a block of an unknown solid in the laboratory. Which of the following will most likely melt the block?

I. Heating the solid at constant pressure
II. Compressing the solid at constant temperature
III. Accelerating the solid to high speeds to increase its kinetic energy.

A. I only
B. I and II only
C. I and III only
D. I, II, and III

Copyright © 2005 Examkrackers, Inc.

STOP.

5-6
Colligative Properties

Some properties in chemistry depend solely on the number of particles, irrespective of the type of particle. Such properties are called **colligative**. There are four colligative properties of solutions: vapor pressure, boiling point, freezing point, and osmotic pressure.

Colligative properties depend upon number, not kind.

In Chemistry Lecture 4, we saw that the addition of a nonvolatile solute will lower the vapor pressure of the solution in direct proportion to the number of particles added, as per Raoult's law. The vapor pressure has an important relationship to the normal boiling point. When the vapor pressure of a solution reaches the local atmospheric pressure, boiling occurs. Thus, the boiling point of a substance is also changed by the addition of a solute. The addition of a nonvolatile solute lowers the the vapor pressure and elevates the boiling point. The equation for the **boiling point elevation** of an ideally dilute solution due to the addition of a nonvolatile solute is:

A substance boils when its vapor pressure equals the local atmospheric pressure.

$$\Delta T = k_b mi$$

where k_b is a specific constant of the substance being boiled, m is the molality of the solution, and i, called the **van't Hoff factor**, is the number of particles into which a single solute particle will dissociate when added to solution.

When using the nonvolatile solute equations, be sure to consider the number of particles after dissociation.

The van't Hoff factor has two possible values: the expected value and the observed value. For an ionic compound, the *expected value* of the van't Hoff factor is the number of ions created upon complete dissociation. For instance, the expected value of i for NaCl is 2, and for $MgCl_2$ is 3. These values are for an ideally dilute solution. It turns out that, in a nonideal solution consisting of ions, there is *ion pairing*. Ion pairing is the momentary aggregation of two or more ions into a single particle. Ion pairing is not the solute incompletely dissolving; ion pairs are still in the aqueous phase. Ion pairs occur due to the strong attraction between positive and negative ions. The *observed value* of the van't Hoff factor will take into account ion pairing. Ion pairing increases with solution concentration, and decreases with increasing temperature. In a dilute solution, the observed value will be only slightly less than the expected value. On the MCAT, use the expected value unless otherwise instructed.

For boiling point and freezing point calculations molality is used instead of molarity because molality doesn't change with temperature while molarity does.

You cannot apply the boiling point elevation equation to volatile solutes. As shown in Chemistry Lecture 4, a volatile solute can actually decrease the boiling point by increasing the vapor pressure. If you know the heat of solution, you can make qualitative predictions about the boiling point change when a volatile solute is added. For instance, since you know that an endothermic heat of solution indicates weaker bonds, which lead to higher vapor pressure, you can predict that the boiling point will go down.

Boiling point — Boling point elevation with addition of nonvolatile solute

Melting point — Freezing point depression with addition of nonvolatile solute

Melting point also changes when a solute is added, but it is not related to the vapor pressure. Instead, it is a factor of crystallization. Impurities (the solute) interrupt the crystal lattice and lower the freezing point. **Freezing point depression** for an ideally dilute solution is given by the equation:

$$\Delta T = k_f mi$$

Again, the constant k_f is specific for the substance being frozen.

Be careful with freezing point depression. If you add a liquid solute, the impurities will initially lower the melting point; however, as the mole fraction of the solute increases, you will come to a point where the solvent becomes the impurity preventing the solute from freezing. At this point, additional solute acts to reduce the impurities creating a more pure solute, and the freezing point of the solution will rise as solute is added.

Copyright © 2005 Examkrackers, Inc.

The fourth colligative property is **osmotic pressure**. Osmotic pressure is a measure of the tendency of water (or some other solvent) to move into a solution via osmosis. To demonstrate osmotic pressure, we divide a pure liquid by a membrane that is permeable to the liquid but not to the solute. We then add solute to one side. Due to entropy, nature wants to make both sides equally dilute. Since the solute cannot pass through the barrier to equalize the concentrations, the pure liquid begins to move to the solution side. As it does so, the solution level rises and the pressure increases. Eventually a balance between the forces of entropy and pressure is achieved. The extra pressure on the solution side is called osmotic pressure. Osmotic pressure Π is given by:

$$\Pi = iMRT$$

where M is the molarity of the solution.

Related to osmotic pressure is *osmotic potential*. Osmotic potential is a partial measure of a system's free energy. Pure water is arbitrarily assigned an osmotic potential of zero. When a solute is added, the osmotic potential becomes negative. At constant temperature and pressure, water flows from higher osmotic potential to lower osmotic potential. *Water potential*, another related term, is similar to osmotic potential but takes into account temperature and pressure. Water potential is essentially the same as free energy. When water and the solution in the diagram below have come to equilibrium, points A and B have the same water potential, but the osmotic potential of point B is less than that of point A.

Osmotic pressure is a funny thing. It is not really pressure at all. For instance, the total pressure at the bottom of a 10 meter swimming pool filled with pure water is about 1 atm. The osmotic pressure is zero. If you dump a couple of wheel barrows full of salt into the pool, the osmotic pressure increases significantly, but the total pressure barely changes.

Osmotic pressure is only relevant when comparing one solution with another.

Students often think about osmotic pressure as the pressure pulling into a solution, and hydrostatic pressure as the pressure pushing out of a solution. Although this is technically incorrect because pressure is a scalar and has no direction, thinking about osmotic pressure in this way may give you some intuition about it.

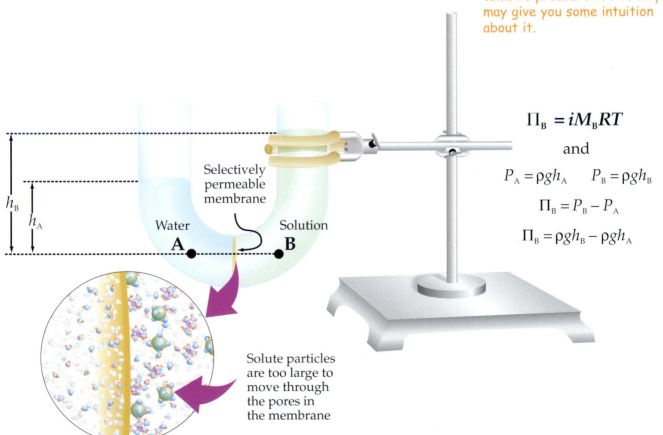

Selectively permeable membrane

Water

Solution

A

B

h_B

h_A

$$\Pi_B = iM_BRT$$

and

$$P_A = \rho g h_A \qquad P_B = \rho g h_B$$

$$\Pi_B = P_B - P_A$$

$$\Pi_B = \rho g h_B - \rho g h_A$$

Solute particles are too large to move through the pores in the membrane

Copyright © 2005 Examkrackers, Inc.

Questions 113 through 120 are **NOT** based on a descriptive passage.

113. Which of the following aqueous solutions will have the lowest boiling point?

    A.   0.5 M glucose
    B.   1 M glucose
    C.   0.5 M NaCl
    D.   0.6 M NaCl

114. An object experiences a greater buoyant force in seawater than in fresh water. The most likely reason for this is:

    A.   Seawater has greater osmotic pressure making the pressure difference greater at different depths.
    B.   Fresh water has greater osmotic pressure making the pressure difference greater at different depths.
    C.   Seawater has greater density.
    D.   Fresh water has greater density.

115. Glycol ($C_2H_6O_2$) is the main component in antifreeze. What mass of glycol must be added to 10 liters of water to prevent freezing down to $-18.6°C$? (The molal freezing point depression constant for water is $1.86°C$ kg/mol.)

    A.   3.1 kg
    B.   6.2 kg
    C.   10 kg
    D.   12.4 kg

116. A student holds a beaker of pure liquid A in one hand and pure liquid B in the other. Liquid A has a higher boiling point than liquid B. When the student pours a small amount of liquid B into liquid A, the temperature of the solution increases. Which of the following statements is true?

    A.   The boiling point of the solution is lower than either pure liquid A or B.
    B.   The boiling point of the solution is higher than either pure liquid A or B.
    C.   The freezing point of the solution is higher than either pure liquid A or B.
    D.   The vapor pressure of the solution is higher than pure liquid B.

117. 500 ml of an aqueous solution having a mass of 503 grams and containing 20 grams of an unknown protein was placed into a bulb and lowered into pure water as shown. A membrane permeable to water but not to the solute separated the solution from the water.

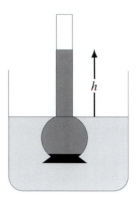

The height of the column of solution was found to be 'h'. Which of the following statements is true concerning this procedure?

    A.   A large value for h indicates a low osmotic pressure in the solution.
    B.   A large value for h indicates a high osmotic pressure in the pure water.
    C.   A large value for h indicates that the protein has a low molecular weight.
    D.   A large value for h indicates that the protein has a high molecular weight.

118. Calcium chloride is sometimes sprinkled on winter sidewalks to melt snow and ice. If 333 grams of calcium chloride is dissolved completely in 1.00 kg of water, what will be the freezing point of the solution? (The molal freezing point depression constant for water is $1.86°C$ kg/mol)

    A. $-5.58°C$
    B. $-9.30°C$
    C. $-11.7°C$
    D. $-16.7°C$

119. A popular experiment uses freezing point depression to find the molar mass of an unknown solute. If a known mass of an unknown non-polar solute is placed into a known mass of a known non-polar solvent and the freezing point depression is measured, which of the following expressions will be equal to the molar mass of the unknown solute?

A. $\dfrac{(k_f)(\text{grams of solute})}{(\Delta T)(\text{kg of solvent})}$

B. $\dfrac{(k_f)(\text{kg of solvent})}{(\Delta T)(\text{grams of solute})}$

C. $\dfrac{(\Delta T)(\text{grams of solute})}{(k_f)(\text{kg of solvent})}$

D. $\dfrac{(\Delta T)(\text{kg of solvent})}{(k_f)(\text{grams of solute})}$

120. A student prepared two solutions in separate flasks. Solution A consisted of 0.1 mole of sodium fluoride in 1 liter of water. Solution B consisted of 0.1 mole of potassium chloride in 1 liter of water. The student then heated both flasks and measured the boiling point of each solution. Which of the solutions would be expected to have the higher boiling point?

A. Solution A, because sodium fluoride has a lower molar mass than potassium chloride.

B. Solution B, because potassium chloride is less volatile than sodium fluoride.

C. Solution A, because potassium chloride will not dissociate completely in water.

D. Both solutions will have the same boiling point.

Copyright © 2005 Examkrackers, Inc.

STOP.

Lecture 6

Acids and Bases

There are three definitions of an acid that you must know for the MCAT: Arrhenius, Bronsted-Lowry, and Lewis. These definitions are given here in the order in which they were created. An **Arrhenius acid** is anything that produces hydrogen ions in aqueous solution, and an Arrhenius base is anything that produces hydroxide ions in aqueous solution. This definition covers only aqueous solutions. **Bronsted and Lowry** redefined acids as anything that donates a proton, and bases as anything that accepts a proton. Finally, the **Lewis** definition is the most general, defining an acid as anything that accepts a pair of electrons, and a base as anything that donates a pair of electrons. The Lewis definition includes all the acids and bases in the Bronsted-Lowry and more. Lewis acids include molecules that have an incomplete octet of electrons around the central atom, like $AlCl_3$ and BF_3. They also include all simple cations except the alkali and the heavier alkaline earth metal cations. The smaller the cation and the higher the charge, the stronger the acid strength. Fe^{3+} is a common example of a Lewis acid. Molecules that are acidic only in the Lewis sense are not generally called acids unless they are referred to explicitly as Lewis acids.

$$H^+ \qquad OH^-$$
$$\textbf{acid} \qquad \textbf{base}$$

One measure of the hydrogen ion concentration is called the pH, where p(x) is a function in which, given any x, p(x) = −log(x). If we measure the hydrogen ion concentration in moles per liter ($[H^+]$ the brackets always indicate concentration), pH is given by:

$$\textbf{pH} = -\log[H^+]$$

Notice that in the Bronsted definition, the acid 'donates', and in the Lewis definition the acid 'accepts'.

Although you must memorize the definitions, it is usually convenient to think of an acid as H^+ and a base as OH^-. In fact, aqueous solutions always contain both H^+ and OH^-. An aqueous solution containing a greater concentration of H^+ than OH^- is acidic, while an aqueous solution containing a greater concentration of OH^- than H^+ is basic. An aqueous solution with equal amounts of H^+ and OH^- is neutral.

Beware of Acid Rain

You must understand some very basic ideas about logarithms for the MCAT. pH uses the base 10 logarithm. The base 10 logarithm is used to solve a problem like:

$$10^x = 3.16$$

The answer is: $x = \log(3.16)$. Luckily on the MCAT we don't have to do calculations; instead we estimate. Since 10^0 equals 1, and 10^1 equals 10, in the problem above x must be between 0 and 1. The answer is: $x = 0.5$. Applying this to acids, if we have a hydrogen ion concentration of 10^{-3}, the log of 10^{-3} is -3, and the negative log of 10^{-3} is positive 3. Thus the pH is 3. If we have a hydrogen ion concentration of a little more than 10^{-3}, say 4×10^{-3}, then the solution is a little more acidic and the pH is slightly lower than 3: say 2.4. Notice that 4×10^{-3} is not as large a number as 10^{-2}, so the pH is lower than 3 but not quite 2. On the MCAT you **must** be able to estimate pH values as shown in this paragraph.

The second and last thing you should know about logarithms is:

$$\log(AB) = \log(A) + \log(B)$$

This is easily verifiable:

$$\log(10^2) = 2; \quad \log(10^3) = 3;$$
$$\log(10^2 \times 10^3) = 5.$$

One more thing; many reactions in living cells involve the transfer of a proton. The rate of such reactions depends upon the concentration of H^+ ions or the pH.

Acids taste sour or tart; bases taste bitter. Bases are slippery when wet.

The scale for pH generally runs from 0 to 14, but since any H^+ concentration is possible, any pH value is possible. At 25°C, a pH of 7 is neutral; a lower pH is acidic and a higher pH is basic. Each point on the pH scale corresponds to a tenfold difference in hydrogen ion concentration. An acid with a pH of 2 produces 10 times as many hydrogen ions as an acid with a pH of 3, and 100 times as many hydrogen ions as an acid with a pH of 4.

From the definitions of an acid, it must be clear that, if there is an acid in a reaction, there must also be a base; you can't have a proton donated without something to accept it. We can write a hypothetical acid-base reaction in aqueous solution as follows:

$$HA + H_2O \rightarrow A^- + H_3O^+$$

Here, HA is the acid, and, since water accepts the proton, water is the base. If we look at the reverse reaction, the hydronium ion donates a proton to A^-, making the hydronium ion the acid and A^- the base. To avoid confusion, we refer to the reactants as the acid and base, and the products as the **conjugate acid** and **conjugate base**. Thus, in every reaction the acid has its conjugate base, and the base has its conjugate acid. Deciding which form is the conjugate simply depends upon in which direction you happen to be viewing the reaction.

In other words, it is correct to say either: "HA is the conjugate acid of base A^-"; or "A^- is the conjugate base of acid HA." You must be able to identify conjugates on the MCAT.

You should also know that the stronger the acid, the weaker its conjugate base, and the stronger the base, the weaker its conjugate acid. Warning: Many students and even some prep books translate this into "Strong acids have weak conjugate bases, and weak acids have strong conjugate bases." The second part of this statement is incorrect! Acid strength is on the logarithmic scale and a weak acid may have a strong or weak conjugate base.

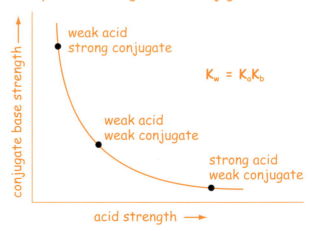

Some substances act as either an acid or a base, depending upon their environment. They are called **amphoteric**. Water is a good example. In the reaction above, water acts as a base accepting a proton. Water can also act like an acid by donating a proton.

$$\log(10^1) = \log(10) = 1$$

$$\log(3.16) = .5$$

$$\log(10^0) = \log(1) = 0$$

Copyright © 2005 Examkrackers, Inc.

For the MCAT, you need to recognize the strong acids and bases in Table 6-1.

Strong Acids		Strong Bases	
hydroiodic acid	HI	sodium hydroxide	NaOH
hydrobromic acid	HBr	potassium hydroxide	KOH
hydrochloric acid	HCl	amide ion	NH_2^-
nitric acid	HNO_3	hydride ion	H^-
perchloric acid	$HClO_4$	calcium hydroxide	$Ca(OH)_2$
chloric acid	$HClO_3$	sodium oxide	Na_2O
sulfuric acid	H_2SO_4	calcium oxide	CaO

Table 6-1

You should recognize a **hydronium ion H_3O^+.** The hydronium ion is simply a hydrated proton. For MCAT acid and base reactions, a hydronium ion and a proton are the same thing.

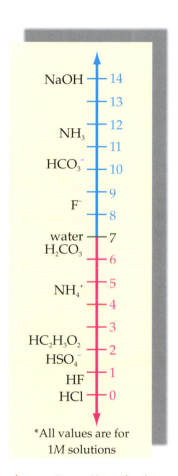

NaOH — 14
— 13
NH_3 — 12
— 11
HCO_3^- — 10
— 9
F^- — 8
water — 7
H_2CO_3
— 6
NH_4^+ — 5
— 4
— 3
$HC_2H_3O_2$ — 2
HSO_4^-
HF — 1
HCl — 0

*All values are for 1M solutions

Some acids can donate more than one proton. These acids are called **polyprotic** acids. An acid that can donate just two protons can be called a **diprotic** acid as well as a polyprotic acid. The second proton donated by a polyprotic acid is usually so weak that its effect on the pH is negligible. On the MCAT the second proton can almost always be ignored. (The rule of thumb is that if the K_a values differ by more than 10^3, the second proton can be ignored.) For instance, the second proton from H_2SO_4 is a strong acid; yet, except with dilute concentrations (concentrations less than 1 M), it has a negligible effect on the pH of H_2SO_4 solution. This is because H_2SO_4 is so much stronger than HSO_4^-. Notice here that the percent dissociation of an acid decreases with acidity. This means that acids dissociate less in more concentrated solutions. It does not mean that concentrated solutions are less acidic.

By the way, when we say "strong acid" in inorganic chemistry, we mean an acid that is stronger than H_3O^+. A strong base is stronger than OH^-. With bases, we often call something as strong as OH^-, like NaOH, a strong base. For MCAT purposes, we assume that a strong acid or base completely dissociates in water.

Acid dissociation decreases with acid concentration but acid strength increases with acid concentration. Imagine the following: I have 100 acid molecules in water and 50 dissociate, so that I have 50% dissociation and 50 hydrogen ions. If I have 1000 acid molecules in the same amount of water, now only 400 dissociate so that I have 40% dissociation and 400 hydrogen ions. More hydrogen ions in the same amount of water means more acid strength. Notice that this means that increasing the concentration of a weak acid by a factor of ten does NOT result in a ten fold increase in hydrogen ion concentration.

Copyright © 2005 Examkrackers, Inc.

6-2
How Molecular Structure Affects Acid Strength

There are three factors in molecular structure that determine whether or not a molecule containing a hydrogen will release its hydrogen into solution, and thus act as an acid: 1) the strength of the bond holding the hydrogen to the molecule; 2) the polarity of the bond; and 3) the stability of the conjugate base. If we examine the C–H bond in methane, which has extremely low acidity, it is nearly the same strength as the H–Cl bond in hydrochloric acid. However, the H–Cl bond is much more polar, and therefore the proton is more easily removed in aqueous solution. HCl is more acidic than methane. On the other hand, a comparison of the bond strengths and polarities of the hydrogen halides shows that, although the H–F bond is the most polar, it is also the strongest bond. In addition, the small size of the fluorine ion concentrates the negative charge and adds to its instability. In this case, the bond strength and conjugate instability outweigh the polarity, and HF is the weakest of the hydrogen halide acids.

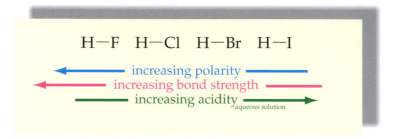

In a series of oxyacids, more oxygens means a stronger acid.

Keeping conjugate stability in mind, if we examine the oxyacids, we see that the electronegative oxygens draw electrons to one side of the bond, increasing polarity. The oxygens in the conjugate of an oxyacid can share the negative charge spreading it over a larger area and stabilizing the conjugate base. In similar oxyacids, the molecule with the most oxygens makes the strongest acid. Another way to look at this phenomenon is that the acidity increases with the oxidation number of the central atom.

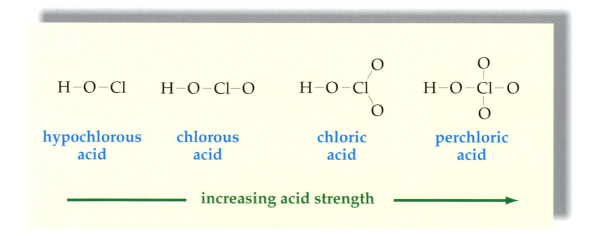

Binary compounds (compounds with only two elements) containing hydrogen are called hydrides. Hydrides can be basic, acidic, or neutral. On the periodic table, the basic hydrides are to the left, and the acidic hydrides are to the right. For instance, NaH is basic; H_2S is acidic. Following this trend, metal hydrides are either basic or neutral, while nonmetal hydrides are acidic or neutral. (Ammonia, NH_3, is an exception to this rule.) The acidity of nonmetal hydrides tends to increase going down the periodic table. $H_2O < H_2S < H_2Se < H_2Te$

6-3
Hydrides

Group			
4A	**5A**	**6A**	**6A**
CH_4	NH_3	H_2O	HF
Neither acidic nor basic	Weakly basic	--------	Weakly acidic
SiH_4	NH_3	H_2S	HCl
Neither acidic nor basic	Weakly basic	Weakly acidic	Strongly acidic

Period 2 / Period 3 (row labels)

Increasing Acidity (vertical arrow)

Increasing Acidity (horizontal arrow)

Copyright © 2005 Examkrackers, Inc.

121. Ammonia reacts with water to form the ammonium ion and hydroxide ion.

$$NH_3 + H_2O \rightarrow NH_4^+ + OH^-$$

According to the Bronsted-Lowry definition of acids and bases, what is the conjugate acid of ammonia?

A. NH_3
B. NH_4^+
C. OH^-
D. H^+

122. By definition, a Lewis base:

A. donates a proton.
B. accepts a proton.
C. donates a pair of electrons.
D. accepts a pair of electrons.

123. Which of the following is the strongest base in aqueous solution?

A. Cl^-
B. NH_4^+
C. F^-
D. Br^-

124. Which of the following is amphoteric?

A. an amino acid
B. H_2SO_4
C. NaOH
D. HF

125. The addition of an electron withdrawing group to the alpha carbon of a carboxylic acid will:

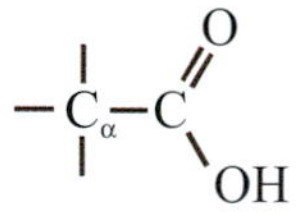

$$-\overset{|}{\underset{|}{C}}_\alpha-C\overset{O}{\underset{OH}{\diagup\diagdown}}$$

A. increase the acidity of the proton by making the O–H bond more polar.
B. increase the acidity of the proton by making the O–H bond stronger.
C. decrease the acidity of the proton by making the O–H bond more polar.
D. decrease the acidity of the proton by stabilizing the conjugate base.

126. A student prepared two acid solutions. Solution A has a hydrogen ion concentration of 6.0×10^{-5} mole L^{-1}. Solution B has a hydrogen ion concentration of 1×10^{-7} mole L^{-1}. The pH of solution A differs from that of solution B by:

A. 1.3
B. 2.8
C. 3.7
D. 5.0

127. In the reaction above, ammonia and boron trifluoride combine when a coordinate covalent bond is formed between nitrogen and boron. In this reaction, ammonia acts as a:

$$NH_3 + BF_3 \rightarrow H_3NBF_3$$

A. Lewis acid
B. Lewis base
C. Bronsted-Lowry acid
D. Brondted-Lowry base

128. Two chemical reactions involving water are shown below.

$$NH_4^+ + H_2O \rightarrow NH_3 + H_3O^+$$
Reaction 1

$$NaH + H_2O \rightarrow Na^+ + OH^- + H_2$$
Reaction 2

Which of the following is true?

A. Water acts as a base in Reaction 1 and an acid in Reaction 2.
B. Water acts as an acid in Reaction 1 and a base in Reaction 2.
C. Water acts as a base in both reactions.
D. Water acts as neither an acid nor a base.

Copyright © 2005Examkrackers, Inc.

98

STOP.

Pure water reacts with itself to form hydronium and hydroxide ions as follows:

$$H_2O + H_2O \rightarrow H_3O^+ + OH^-$$

This is called the **autoionization of water**. K_w is the equilibrium constant for this re-action.

$$K_w = [H^+][OH^-]$$

(For convenience, we have substituted H^+ for H_3O^+.) At 25°C the equilibrium of this reaction lies far to the left:

$$K_w = 10^{-14}$$

In a neutral aqueous solutions at 25°C, the H^+ concentration and the OH^- concentration are equal at 10^{-7} mol L^{-1}. The pH of the solution is found by taking the negative log of the hydrogen ion concentration, which is: $-\log[10^{-7}] = 7$. An acid or base added to an aqueous solution will change the concentrations of both H^+ and OH^-, but K_w will remain 10^{-14} at 25°C. For example, in a solution with a pH of 2, the ion concentrations will be: $[H^+] = 10^{-2}$ mol L^{-1} and $[OH^-] = 10^{-12}$ mol L^{-1}. Using the $p(x)$ function and the rule: $\log(AB) = \log(A) + \log(B)$, we can put this relationship into a simple equation:

$$pH + pOH = pK_w$$

For an aqueous solution at 25°C:

$$pH + pOH = 14$$

An acid will have its own equilibrium constant in water, called the **acid dissociation constant K_a**. If we use our hypothetical acid-base reaction: $HA + H_2O \rightarrow H_3O^+ + A^-$, then the acid dissociation constant for the acid HA is:

$$K_a = \frac{[H^+][A^-]}{[HA]}$$

Corresponding to every K_a, there is a **K_b**. The K_b is the equilibrium constant for the reaction of the conjugate base with water. For the conjugate base A^-, the reaction is:

$$A^- + H_2O \rightarrow OH^- + HA$$

and the K_b is:

$$K_b = \frac{[OH^-][HA]}{[A^-]}$$

Notice that the reaction for K_b is the reaction of the conjugate base and water, and it is not the reverse of the reaction for K_a. Notice also that the product of the two constants is K_w.

$$K_a K_b = \frac{[H^+][A^-]}{[HA]} \times \frac{[OH^-][HA]}{[A^-]} = [H^+][OH^-] = K_w$$

$$K_a K_b = K_w$$

Using the $p(x)$ function and the rule: $\log(AB) = \log(A) + \log(B)$, this formula can also be written as:

$$pK_a + pK_b = pK_w$$

At 25°C:

$$pK_a + pK_b = 14$$

6-4

Equilibrium Constants for Acid-Base Reactions

It may seem like there are a lot of equations to memorize here, but it is really very simple. **First**, all equilibrium constants are derived from the law of mass action. They are all products over reactants, where pure solids and liquids are given a concentration of one. Once you know how to find one K, you should know how to find any K. The subscript on the constant is supposed to make things less complicated, not more complicated.

Second, memorize that: $K_w = 10^{-14}$ at 25°C.

Third, remember the log rule, $\log(AB) = \log(A) + \log(B)$, and you can derive any of the equations.

Notice that the larger the K_a and the smaller the pK_a, the stronger the acid. A K_a greater than 1 or a pK_a less than zero indicates a strong acid. The same is true of the K_b and pK_b of a base.

Copyright © 2005 Examkrackers, Inc.

6-5
Finding the pH

Very strong acids and bases will dissociate almost completely. This means that the HA or BOH concentration (for the acid and base respectively) will be nearly zero. Since division by zero is impossible, for such acids and bases, there is no K_a or K_b. Surprisingly, this fact makes it easier to find the pH of strong acid and strong base solutions. Since the entire concentration of acid or base is assumed to dissociate, the concentration of H^+ or OH^- is the same as the original concentration of acid or base. For instance, a 0.01 molar solution of HCl will have 0.01 mol L^{-1} of H^+ ions. Since $0.01 = 10^{-2}$, and $-\log(10^{-2}) = 2$, the pH of the solution will be 2. Likewise, in a 0.01 molar solution of NaOH, we will have 0.01 mol L^{-1} of OH^- ions. (Be careful here!) The pOH will equal 2 so the pH will equal 12. You can avoid a mistake here by remembering that an acid has a pH below 7 and a base has a pH above 7.

Weak acids and bases can be a little trickier. Doing a sample problem is the best way to learn. For example, in order to find the pH of a 0.01 molar solution of HCN, we do the following:

1. Set up the equilibrium equation:

$$K_a = \frac{[H^+][CN]}{[HCN]} = 6.2 \times 10^{-10}$$

2. If we add 0.01 moles of HCN to one liter of pure water, then 'x' amount of that HCN will dissociate. Thus, we will have 'x' mol L^{-1} of H^+ ions and 'x' mol L^{-1} of CN^- ions. The concentration of undissociated HCN will be whatever is left, or '$0.01 - x$'. Plugging these values into the equation above, we have:

$$\frac{[x][x]}{[0.01 - x]} = 6.2 \times 10^{-10}$$

3. If we solve for x, we have a quadratic equation. Forget it! You don't need this for the MCAT. We make an assumption that x is less than 5% of 0.01, and we will check it when we are done. Throwing out the x in the denominator, we have:

$$\frac{[x][x]}{[0.01]} \approx 6.2 \times 10^{-10}$$

Thus, x is approximately 2.5×10^{-6}. This is much smaller than 0.01, so our assumption was valid. 'x' is the concentration of H^+ ions. The pH of the solution is between 5 and 6. This is close enough for the MCAT. [$-\log(2.5 \times 10^{-6}) = 5.6$] Just to make sure, we ask ourselves, "Is 5.6 a reasonable pH for a dilute weak acid?" The answer is yes.

For a weak base, the process is the same, except that we use K_b, and we arrive at the pOH. Subtract the pOH from 14 to find the pH. This step is often forgotten. If we ask ourselves, "Is this pH reasonable for a weak base?", we won't forget this step.

Copyright © 2005 Examkrackers, Inc.

Salts are ionic compounds that dissociate in water. Often, when salts dissociate, they create acidic or basic conditions. The pH of a salt solution can be predicted qualitatively by comparing the conjugates of the respective ions. Just keep in mind that strong acids have weak conjugate bases and strong bases have weak conjugate acids.

Na^+ and Cl^- are the conjugates of NaOH and HCl respectively, so, as a salt, NaCl produces a neutral solution. NH_4NO_3 is composed of the conjugates of the base NH_3 and the strong acid HNO_3 respectively. Thus, NH_4^+ is acidic and NO_3^- is neutral. As a salt, NH_4NO_3 is weakly acidic.

6-6
Salts

When considering salts, remember, all cations, except those of the alkali metals and the heavier alkaline earth metals (Ca^{2+}, Sr^{2+}, and Ba^{2+}), act as weak Lewis acids in aqueous solutions.

Copyright © 2005 Examkrackers, Inc.

Questions 129 through 136 are **NOT** based on a descriptive passage.

129. Which of the following is the K_b for the conjugate base of carbonic acid?

A. $\frac{[H_2CO_3]}{[H][HCO_3^-]}$

B. $\frac{[OH^-][HCO_3^-]}{[H_2CO_3]}$

C. $\frac{[H^+][H_2CO_3]}{[HCO_3^-]}$

D. $\frac{[OH^-][H_2CO_3]}{[HCO_3^-]}$

130. An aqueous solution of 0.1 M HBr has a pH of:

A. 0
B. 1
C. 2
D. 14

131. Carbonic acid has a K_a of 4.3×10^{-7}. What is the pH when 1 mole of $NaHCO_3$ is dissolved in 1 liter of water?

A. 3.2
B. 3.8
C. 10.2
D. 12.5

132. Stomach acid has a pH of approximately 2. Sour milk has a pH of 6. Stomach acid is:

A. 3 times as acidic as sour milk.
B. 4 times as acidic as sour milk.
C. 100 times as acidic as sour milk.
D. 10,000 times as acidic as sour milk.

133. Which of the following salts is the most basic?

A. NaI
B. $NaNO_3$
C. NH_4Cl
D. KF

134. The acid dissociation constant for HBrO is 2×10^{-9}. What is the base dissociation constant for BrO^-?

A. 5×10^{-5}
B. 5×10^{-6}
C. 5×10^{-7}
D. 5×10^{-8}

135. A solution of soapy water has a pH of 10. What is the hydroxide ion concentration?

A. 10^{-10} M
B. 10^{-7} M
C. 10^{-4} M
D. 10^{-1} M

136. When solid sodium acetate, $NaC_2H_3O_2$ is added to pure water, the pH of the solution will:

A. decrease because Na^+ acts as an acid.
B. increase because Na^+ acts as a base.
C. decrease because $C_2H_3O_2^-$ acts as an acid.
D. increase because $C_2H_3O_2^-$ acts as a base.

Copyright © 2005Examkrackers, Inc.

STOP.

A **titration** is the drop-by-drop mixing of an acid and a base. Titrations are performed in order to find the concentration of some unknown by comparing it with the concentration of the **titrant**. The changing pH of the unknown as the acidic or basic titrant is added is represented graphically as a sigmoidal curve. To the right is the **titration curve** of a strong acid titrated by a strong base.

Notice the portion of the graph that most nearly approximates a vertical line. The midpoint of this line is called the **equivalence point** or the **stoichiometric point**. The equivalence point for a monoprotic acid is the point in the titration when there are equal equivalents of acid and base in solution. (An *equivalent* is the mass of acid or base necessary to produce or consume one mole of protons.) For instance, since there is a one to one correspondence between HCl with NaOH, the equivalence point for a titration of HCl with NaOH will be reached when the same number of moles of HCl and NaOH exist in solution. This is not necessarily when they are at equal volumes. If the concentrations differ (and they probably will) the equivalence point will not be where the volumes are equal.

For equally strong acid-base titrations, the equivalence point will usually be at pH 7. (**Warning!** For a diprotic acid whose conjugate base is a strong acid, like H_2SO_4, this is not the case.)

The graph to the right is for the titration of a strong acid with a strong base. In other words, we are slowly adding base to an acid. This is clear because we start with a very low pH and finish with a very high pH. For a titration of a strong base with a strong acid, we would simply invert the graph.

6-7
Titrations

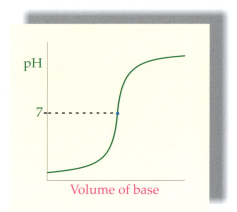

The titration of a weak acid with a strong base looks slightly different than the curve above, and is shown below. The equivalence point is also not as predictable. Of course, if the base is stronger than the acid, the equivalence point will be above 7, and if the acid is stronger than the base, the equivalence point will be below 7.

6-8
More Titrations and Buffered Solutions

Copyright © 2005 Examkrackers, Inc.

Notice the half equivalence point. This is probably more likely be tested by the MCAT than the equivalence point. The **half equivalence point** is the point where exactly one half of the acid has been neutralized by the base. In other words, the concentration of the acid is equal to the concentration of its conjugate base. Notice that the half equivalence point occurs at the midpoint of the section of the graph that most represents a horizontal line. This is the spot where we could add the largest amount of base or acid with the least amount of change in pH. Such a solution is considered to be **buffered**. The half equivalence point shows the point in the titration where the solution is the most well buffered.

Notice also that, at the half equivalence point, the pH of the solution is equal to the pK_a of the acid. This is predicted by the **Henderson-Hasselbalch equation**:

The Henderson-Hasselbalch equation is simply a form of the equilibrium expression for K_a:

$$K_a = \frac{[H^+][A^-]}{[HA]}$$

$$K_a = [H^+]\frac{[A^-]}{[HA]}$$

using the log rule: $-\log(K_a) = -\log[H^+] -\log\frac{[A^-]}{[HA]}$

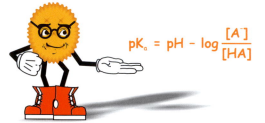

$$pK_a = pH - \log\frac{[A^-]}{[HA]}$$

There is no need to memorize it, since it is so easy and so quick to derive it.

$$pH = pK_a + \log\frac{[A^-]}{[HA]}$$

Recall that $\log(1) = 0$; thus when $[A^-] = [HA]$, $pH = pK_a$.

If we were to make a buffer solution, we would start with an acid whose pK_a is closest to the pH at which we want to buffer our solution. Next we would mix equal amounts of that acid with its conjugate base. We would want the concentration of our buffer solution to greatly exceed the concentration of outside acid or base affecting our solution. So, a buffer solution is made from equal and copious amounts of a weak acid and its conjugate base.

It appears from the Henderson-Hasselbalch equation that we could add an infinite amount of water to a buffered solution with no change in pH. Of course, this is ridiculous. Will adding Lake Tahoe to a beaker of buffered solution change the pH of that solution? The Henderson-Hasselbalch equation in the form above does not allow for *ion pairing*. (Ion pairing is when oppositely charged ions in solution bond momentarily to form a single particle.) Water will generally act like a base in acidic solution and an acid in basic solution. If you add a base or water to an acidic, buffered solution, it is clear from the titration curve that the pH will increase. It just won't increase as rapidly as other solutions less well buffered. However, a question on the MCAT is more likely to consider the ideal circumstance where adding a *small* amount of water to an ideally dilute, buffered solution will have no effect on the pH.

Warning! You cannot typically use the Henderson-Hasselbalch equation to find the pH at the equivalence point. Instead, you must use the K_b of the conjugate base. You can find the K_b from the K_a and the K_w. The concentration of the conjugate base at the equivalence point is equal to the number of moles of acid divided by the volume of acid plus the volume of base used to titrate. Don't forget to consider the volume of base used to titrate. Unless the base has no volume, the concentration of the conjugate at the equivalence point will not be equal to the original concentration of the acid. The pH at the equivalence point involves much more calculation than the pH at the half equivalence point. For this reason, it is more likely that the MCAT will ask about the pH at the half equivalence point.

Copyright © 2005 Examkrackers, Inc.

Finding the pH at the equivalence point is a good exercise, but you won't have to do it on the MCAT. Here are the steps:

Use K_a and K_w to find the K_b

$$K_b = \frac{K_w}{K_a}$$

Set up the K_b equilibrium expression.

$$K_b = \frac{[OH^-][HA]}{[A^-]}$$

Solve for the OH⁻ concentration, and find the pOH.

Subtract the pOH from 14 to find the pH.

$$14 - pOH = pH$$

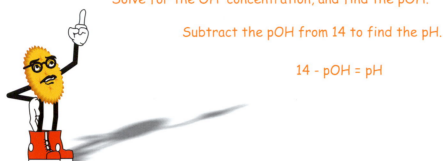

6-9
Indicators and the End Point

To find the equivalence point, a chemical called an **indicator** is used. (A pH meter can also be used.) The indicator is usually a weak acid whose conjugate base is a different color. We can designate an indicator as HIn, where In– represents the conjugate base. In order for the human eye to detect a color change, the new form of the indicator must reach 1/10 the concentration of the original form. For example, if we titrate an acid with a base, we add a small amount of indicator to our acid. (We add only a small amount because we don't want the indicator to affect the pH.) At the initial low pH, the HIn form of the indicator predominates. As we titrate, and the pH increases, the In– form of the indicator also increases. When the In– concentration reaches 1/10 of the HIn concentration, a color change can be detected by the human eye. If we titrate a base with an acid, the process works in reverse. Thus, the pH of the color change depends upon the direction of the titration. The pH values of the two points of color change give the **range** of an indicator. An indicator's range can be predicted by using the Henderson-Hasselbalch equation as follows:

You don't need to memorize this stuff about indicators, but it's useful to understand.

$$pH = pK_a + \log\frac{[In^-]}{[HIn]}$$

lower range of color change ==> $pH = pK_a + \log\frac{1}{10}$ ==> $pH = pK_a - 1$

upper range of color change ==> $pH = pK_a + \log\frac{10}{1}$ ==> $pH = pK_a + 1$

The point where the indicator changes color is called the **endpoint**. Do not confuse the equivalence point with the end point. We usually choose an indicator whose range will cover the equivalence point.

You can also monitor the pH with a pH meter. A pH meter is a concentration cell comparing the voltage difference between different concentrations of H⁺. (See Chemistry Lecture 7 for concentration cells.)

By the way, you can remember that the end point is where the indicator changes color by spelling indicator as:

Endicator

Copyright © 2005 Examkrackers, Inc.

Since we established that the Henderson-Hasselbalch equation is not useful to find the pH of the equivalence point, how can it be useful to find an indicator range that will include the equivalence point?

The answer is that we are using the indicator concentrations in the Henderson-Hasselbalch equation, and the indicator never reaches its equivalence point in the titration. The indicator ions do not approach zero concentration near the color change range.

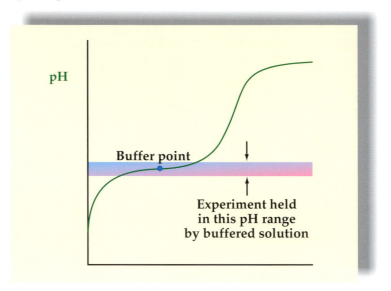

6-10
Polyprotic Titrations

Titrations of polyprotic acids will have more than one equivalence point and more than one half equivalence point. For the MCAT, assume that the first proton completely dissociates before the second proton begins to dissociate. (This assumption is only acceptable if the second proton is a much weaker acid than the first, which is usually the case.) Thus we have a titration curve like the one shown below.

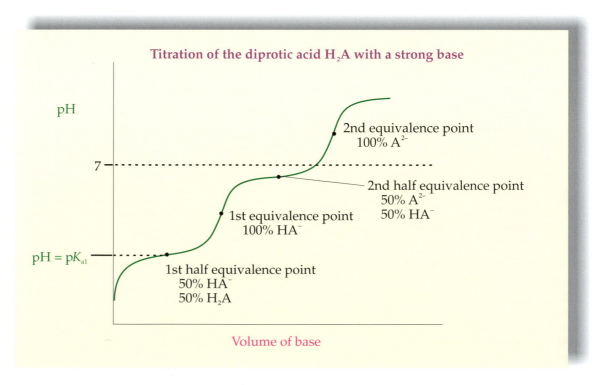

Copyright © 2005 Examkrackers, Inc.

Questions 137 through 144 are **NOT** based on a descriptive passage.

137. The titration curve below represents the titration of:

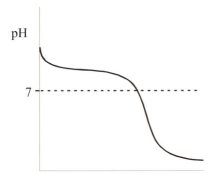

A. a strong acid with a weak base.
B. a strong base with a weak acid.
C. a weak acid with a strong base.
D. a weak base with a strong acid.

138. The following is a list of acid dissociation constants for 4 acids.

	K_a
Acid 1	1.2×10^{-7}
Acid 2	8.3×10^{-7}
Acid 3	3.3×10^{-6}
Acid 4	6.1×10^{-5}

Which acid should be used to manufacture a buffer at a pH of 6.1?

A. Acid 1
B. Acid 2
C. Acid 3
D. Acid 4

139. If the expected equivalence point for a titration is at a pH of 8.2, which of the following would be the best indicator for the titration?

Indicator	K_a
phenolphthalein	1.0×10^{-8}
bromthymol blue	7.9×10^{-8}
methyl orange	3.2×10^{-4}
methyl violet	1.4×10^{-3}

A. phenolphthalein
B. bromthymol blue
C. methyl orange
D. methyl violet

140. On the titration curve of the H_2CO_3 pictured below, at which of the following points is the concentration of HCO_3^- the greatest?

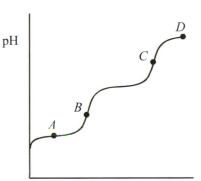

A. point *A*
B. point *B*
C. point *C*
D. point *D*

141. Which of the following is the equivalence point when the weak acid, acetic acid, is titrated with NaOH?

A. 4.3
B. 7
C. 8.7
D. 14

142. A buffered solution has a pH that cannot readily be changed. A buffered solution will be produced by mixing equal volumes of:

    A.   1 M HCl and 1 M $NaC_2H_3O_2$
    B.   1 M HCl and 1 M NaOH
    C.   1 M $HC_2H_3O_2$ and 1 M $NaC_2H_3O_2$
    D.   1 M $HC_2H_3O_2$ and 1 M NaOH

143. All of the following statements regarding HCO_3^- are true EXCEPT:

    A. HCO_3^- can act as a Bronsted Lowry acid.
    B. HCO_3^- can act as a Lewis base.
    C. HCO_3^- is amphoteric.
    D. HCO_3^- is a polyprotic acid.

144. The acid dissociation constant for $HC_6H_7O_6$ is 8.0×10^{-5}. If a solution contains equal concentrations of $HC_6H_7O_6$ and $C_6H_7O_6^-$, what will be the pH of the solution?

    A.   3.0
    B.   4.1
    C.   5.3
    D.   9.0

Lecture 7

Electrochemistry

7-1
Oxidation-Reduction

In an oxidation-reduction reaction (called a **redox reaction** for short), electrons are transferred from one atom to another. The atom that loses electrons is **oxidized**; the atom that gains electrons is **reduced**.

7-2
Oxidation States

In order to keep track of the electrons in a redox reaction, you must memorize the **oxidation states** of certain atoms. Oxidation states are the possible charge values that an atom may hold within a molecule. In many cases, these charges don't truly exist; it is simply a system to follow the electrons of a redox reaction. Even though they do not represent actual charges, the oxidation states must add up to the charge on the molecule or ion. For instance, the sum of the oxidation states of the atoms in a neutral molecule must equal zero. The oxidation states that you must memorize for the MCAT are given in Table 7-1. When a conflict arises, the rule occupying the higher position on the table is given priority.

Oxidation State	Atom
0	Atoms in their elemental form
–1	Fluorine
+1	Hydrogen (except when bonded to a metal: then –1.)
–2	Oxygen (except when it is in a peroxide like H_2O_2)

Table 7-1

For the MCAT, you *probably* won't need to memorize any other oxidation states than those in Table 7-1.

In general, when in a compound, elements in the following groups have the oxidation states listed in the table below. It is helpful to know Table 7-2 but not crucial for the MCAT.

Oxidation State	Group on Periodic Table
+1	Group 1 elements (alkali metals)
+2	Group 2 elements (alkaline earth metals)
–3	Group 15 elements (nitrogen family)
–2	Group 16 elements (oxygen family)
–1	Group 17 elements (halogens)

Table 7-2

To help keep oxidation and reduction straight, just remember:

GERrrrrr ...

This is definitely not in my contract.

Lose **E**lectrons **O**xidation — **the Lion says** — **G**ain **E**lectrons **R**eduction

The idea is simple; a general guideline for oxidation states is the atom's variance from a noble gas configuration. However, if all atoms had permanent oxidation states, no redox reactions could take place. The oxidation states in table 7-2 are to be used only as a general guideline. When the two tables conflict, the first table is given priority. For example, the oxidation state of nitrogen in NO_3^- is +5 because the –2 on the oxygens have priority and dictate the oxidation state on nitrogen. (Don't forget that the oxidation states for NO_3^- must add up to the 1– charge on the molecule.) The transition metals change oxidation states according to the atoms with which they are bonded. Although each transition metal has only certain oxidation states that it can attain, the MCAT will not require that you memorize these.

The following is an example of a redox reaction:

$$2H_2 + O_2 \rightarrow 2H_2O$$

Here oxygen and hydrogen begin in their elemental form, and thus have an oxidation state of zero. Once the water molecule is formed, hydrogen's oxidation state is +1, and oxygen's is –2. In this case, we say that hydrogen has been **oxidized**; hydrogen has lost electrons; its oxidation state has increased from 0 to +1. Oxygen, on the other hand, has been **reduced**; it has gained electrons; its oxidation state has been reduced from 0 to –2. Whenever there is oxidation, there must also be reduction.

Copyright © 2005 Examkrackers, Inc.

Since in any redox reaction one atom is oxidized and another atom is reduced, there is a **reducing agent** (also called the **reductant**) and an **oxidizing agent** (also called the **oxidant**). Because the reducing agent is giving electrons to an atom, an atom in the reducing agent must be giving up some of its own electrons. Since an atom in the reducing agent gives up electrons, an atom in the reducing agent is oxidized. The reverse is true for the oxidizing agent. Thus, the reducing agent is the compound containing the atom being oxidized, and the oxidizing agent is the compound containing the atom being reduced. For example, in the following reaction, methane is the reducing agent and dioxygen is the oxidizing agent.

Reducing Agent Salty

Carbon goes from –4 to +4.

$$CH_4 + 2O_2 \longrightarrow CO_2 + 2H_2O$$

Oxygen goes from 0 to –2.

Notice that the reducing agents and oxidizing agents are compounds, not atoms. In a redox reaction, the atom is oxidized or reduced; the compound is the oxidant or reductant. In the reaction:

$$Cd(s) + NiO_2(s) + 2H_2O(l) \rightarrow Cd(OH)_2(s) + Ni(OH)_2(s)$$

Ni is reduced. NiO_2 is the oxidizing agent.

7-3 Oxidation-Reduction Titrations

In order to find the molarity of a reducing agent, a sample can be titrated with a strong oxidizing agent. For instance, if we want to know the molarity of Sn^{2+} ions in a solution, we can titrate it with a known concentration of the strong oxidizing agent Ce^{4+}. Sn^{2+} ions oxidize to Sn^{4+}, while Ce^{4+} reduces to Ce^{3+}. Since only one electron is required to reduce Ce^{4+}, and two electrons are given up to oxidize Sn^{2+}, two Ce^{4+} ions are reduced for every Sn^{2+} ion oxidized. Thus, we know that the number of moles of Ce^{4+} required to reach the equivalence point is twice the number of moles of Sn^{2+} in solution. Instead of measuring the pH, we measure the voltage compared to a standard solution.

Knowledge of oxidation-reduction titrations is not required for the MCAT. However, it is possible that there will be a passage which explains them. They are included here just so you won't be shocked if you see one in a passage.

Copyright © 2005 Examkrackers, Inc.

145. What is the oxidation state of sulfur in HSO_4^-?

    A.   −2
    B.   +3
    C.   +6
    D.   +7

146. Which of the following statements is true concerning the reaction:

$$2Al_2O_3 + 3C \rightarrow 4Al + 3CO_2$$

    A.   Both aluminum and carbon are reduced.
    B.   Both aluminum and carbon are oxidized.
    C.   Aluminum is reduced and carbon is oxidized.
    D.   Carbon is reduced and aluminum is oxidized.

147. What is the reducing agent in the following reaction:

$$2HCl + Zn \rightarrow ZnCl_2 + H_2$$

    A.   Zn
    B. Zn^{2+}
    C. H^+
    D. Cl^-

148. The first step in producing pure lead from galena (PbS) is as follows:

$$2PbS(s) + 3O_2(g) \rightarrow 2PbO(s) + 2SO_2(g)$$

All of the following are true concerning this reaction EXCEPT:

    A.   Both lead and sulfur are oxidized.
    B.   Oxygen is the oxidizing agent.
    C.   Lead sulfide is the reducing agent.
    D.   Lead is neither oxidized nor reduced.

149. All of the following are always true concerning oxidation-reduction reactions EXCEPT:

    A.   An atom in the reducing agent is always oxidized.
    B.   If reduction takes place, so must oxidation.
    C.   An atom in the oxidizing agent gains electrons.
    D.   If an atom of the reductant loses two electrons, an atom of the oxidant gains two electrons.

150. The process below takes place in acidic solution.

$$NO_2^-(aq) \rightarrow NO_3^-(aq)$$

In this process, the oxidation state of nitrogen is:

    A.   reduced from +2 to +3.
    B.   oxidized from +2 to +3.
    C.   reduced from +3 to +5.
    D.   oxidized from +3 to +5.

151. Which of the following statements is true about the reaction below?

$$HNO_3 + NaHCO_3 \rightarrow NaNO_3 + H_2CO_3$$

    A.   Nitrogen is reduced and oxygen is oxidized.
    B.   Oxygen is reduced and carbon is oxidized.
    C.   Hydrogen is reduced and sodium is oxidized.
    D.   No oxidation or reduction takes place.

152. $Cl_2 + 2Br^- \rightarrow Br_2 + 2Cl^-$

In the reaction shown above,

    A. Cl_2 is the oxidizing agent and Br^- is oxidized.
    B. Cl_2 is the oxidizing agent and Br^- is reduced.
    C. Cl_2 is the reducing agent and Br^- is oxidized.
    D. Cl_2 is the reducing agent and Br^- is reduced.

Copyright © 2005 Examkrackers, Inc.

STOP.

Since in a redox reaction electrons are transferred, and since electrons have charge, there is an **electric potential** E associated with any redox reaction. The potentials for the oxidation component and reduction component of a reaction can be approximated separately based upon a *standard hydrogen electrode* (SHE) discussed later in this lecture. Each component is called a **half reaction**. Of course, no half reaction will occur by itself; any reduction half reaction must be accompanied by an oxidation half reaction. There is only one possible potential for any given half reaction. Since the reverse of a reduction half reaction is an oxidation half reaction, it would be redundant to list potentials for both the oxidation and reduction half reactions. Therefore, half reaction potentials are usually listed as **reduction potentials**. To find the oxidation potential for the reverse half reaction, the sign of the reduction potential is reversed. Below is a list of some common reduction potentials.

Standard Reduction Potentials at 25°C	
Half reaction	**Potential $E°$**
$Au^{3+}(aq) + 3e^- \rightarrow Au(s)$	1.50
$O_2(g) + 4H^+(aq) + 4e^- \rightarrow H_2O(l)$	1.23
$Pt^{2+}(aq) + 2e^- \rightarrow Pt(s)$	1.2
$Ag^{2+}(aq) + 2e^- \rightarrow Ag(s)$	0.80
$Hg^{2+}(aq) + 2e^- \rightarrow Hg(l)$	0.80
$Cu^+(aq) + e^- \rightarrow Cu(s)$	0.52
$Cu^{2+}(aq) + 2e^- \rightarrow Cu(s)$	0.34
$2H^+(aq) + 2e^- \rightarrow H_2(g)$	0.00
$Fe^{3+}(aq) + 3e^- \rightarrow Fe(s)$	−0.036
$Ni^{2+}(aq) + 2e^- \rightarrow Ni(s)$	−0.23
$Fe^{2+}(aq) + 2e^- \rightarrow Fe(s)$	−0.44
$Zn^{2+}(aq) + 2e^- \rightarrow Zn(s)$	−0.76
$H_2O(l) + 2e^- \rightarrow H_2(g) + 2OH^-(aq)$	−0.83

Table 7-3

Recall from physics that electric potential has no absolute value. Thus the values in the table above are assigned based upon the arbitrary assignment of a zero value to the half reaction that occurs at a standard hydrogen electrode:

$$\mathbf{2H^+ + 2e^- \rightarrow H_2} \qquad \mathbf{E° = 0.00\ V}$$

This is the only reduction potential that you need to memorize.

An example of an oxidation potential taken from the table above would be:

$$Ag(s) \rightarrow Ag^{2+}(aq) + 2e^- \quad E° = -0.80\ V$$

If we wish to find the potential of the following ionic reaction:

$$2Au^{3+} + 3Cu \rightarrow 3Cu^{2+} + 2Au$$

7-4
Potentials

Notice that, except for nickel, the metals used to make coins have negative oxidation potentials. In other words, unlike most metals, platinum, gold, silver, mercury, and copper do not oxidize (or dissolve) spontaneously under standard conditions in the presence of aqueous H^+.

Also notice that Table 7-3 gives us the reduction potential for $Ag^{2+}(aq)$ and the oxidation potential for $Ag(s)$. (**Warning**: The table does not give us the oxidation potential for Ag^{2+}.) The strongest oxidizing agent is shown on the upper left hand side of a reduction table. The strongest reducing agent is shown on the lower right hand side of a reduction table. Notice that water is both a poor oxidizing agent and a poor reducing agent.

Finally, notice that the second half reaction in Table 7-3 is part of the final reaction in aerobic respiration where oxygen accepts electrons to form water. Predictably, this reaction has a high positive potential.

Copyright © 2005 Examkrackers, Inc.

we can separate the reaction into its two half reactions and add the half reaction potentials:

$$2(Au^{3+} + 3e^- \rightarrow Au) \qquad E° = 1.50 \text{ V}$$
$$\underline{3(Cu \rightarrow Cu^{2+} + 2e^-) \qquad E° = -0.34 \text{ V}}$$
$$\phantom{3(Cu \rightarrow Cu^{2+} + 2e^-) \qquad E°} = 1.16 \text{ V}$$

Warning: Since reduction potentials are intensive properties, we do not multiply the half reaction potential by the number of times it occurs.

7-5
Balancing Redox Reactions

Balancing redox reactions can be tricky. When you have trouble, follow the steps below to balance a redox reaction that occurs in acidic solution.

1. Divide the reaction into its corresponding half reactions.

2. Balance the elements other than H and O.

3. Add H_2O to one side until the O atoms are balanced.

4. Add H^+ to one side until the H atoms are balanced.

5. Add e^- to one side until the charge is balanced.

All this effort to balance a redox reaction will get you, at most, one point on the MCAT. MCAT just doesn't require the balancing of redox reactions very often, so spend your time accordingly.

6. Multiply each half reaction by an integer so that an equal number of electrons are transferred in each reaction.

7. Add the two half reactions and simplify.

For redox reactions occurring in basic solution, follow the same steps, then neutralize the H^+ ions by adding the same number of OH^- ions to both sides of the reaction.

7-6
The Galvanic Cell

If two distinct electrically conducting chemical phases are placed in contact, and one charged species from one phase cannot freely flow to the other phase, a tiny amount of charge difference may result. This tiny charge difference creates an electric potential between the phases (typically one or two volts). By offering an alternative path for electron flow, a **galvanic cell** (also called a **voltaic cell**) uses the electric potential between such phases to generate a current of electrons from one phase to another in a conversion of chemical energy to electrical energy.

More simply put, a galvanic cell turns chemical energy into electrical energy.

A galvanic cell is made of a multiphase series of components with no component occurring in more than one phase. All phases must conduct electricity, but at least one phase must be impermeable to electrons. Otherwise, electrons would move freely throughout the circuit and come to a quick equilibrium. The phase that is impermeable to electrons is an ionic conductor carrying the current in the form of ions. The ionic conducting phase is usually an electrolyte solution in the form of a **salt bridge**. The components of a simple galvanic cell can be symbolized by the letter T-E-I-E'-T', where T represents the **terminals** (electronic conductors such as metal wires), E represents the electrodes (also electronic conductors), and I the ionic conductor (often the salt bridge). When the cell is formed, the emf is the electric potential difference between T and T'.

A simple galvanic cell has two **electrodes**: the **anode** and the **cathode**. The anode is marked with a negative sign and the cathode is marked with a positive sign. The oxidation half reaction takes place at the anode, and the reduction half reaction takes place at the cathode. Depending upon the text, electrodes may refer to only a

Copyright © 2005 Examkrackers, Inc.

strip of metal or both a strip of metal and the electrolyte solution in which it is submerged. The strip of metal and solution together may also be called a *half cell*.

Remember: RED CAT; AN OX: reduction cathode; anode oxidation.

Only potential differences between chemically identical forms of matter are easily measurable, so the two terminals of a galvanic cell must be made of the same material. The **cell potential E**, also called the **electromotive force (emf)**, is the potential difference between the terminals when they are not connected. Connecting the terminals reduces the potential difference due to internal resistance within the galvanic cell. The drop in the emf increases as the current increases. The current from one terminal to the other through the *load* (or resistance) flows in the direction opposite the electron flow. Since electrons in the anode have higher potential energy than those in the cathode, electrons flow through the load from the anode to the cathode.

The standard state cell potential is simply the sum of the standard state potentials of the corresponding half reactions. The cell potential for a galvanic cell is always positive; a galvanic cell always has chemical energy that can be converted to work. The real cell potential depends upon the half reactions, the concentrations of the reactants and products, and the temperature.

Electrons are negatively charged, so they are attracted to the positive cathode and repelled by the negative anode in a galvanic cell.

Below is an example of a simple galvanic cell with the standard hydrogen electrode. Hydrogen gas is bubbled over the platinum plate. The platinum acts as a catalyst in the production of H^+ ions. The half reaction is shown. The platinum plate carries an electron through the wire to the silver strip. Ag^+ accepts the electron converting it to solid silver and allowing a chloride ion to solvate into the aqueous solution.

$$H_2(g) \rightarrow 2H^+(aq) + 2e^- \qquad AgCl(s) + e^- \rightarrow Ag(s) + Cl^-(aq)$$

Galvanic Cell
with standard hydrogen electrode (SHE)

Since, by convention, the oxidation potential of hydrogen is zero, the cell potential of any electrode used in conjunction with the SHE will be exactly equal to the reduction potential of the half reaction occurring at the other electrode. Thus, some half reaction reduction potentials can be measured using the SHE.

Copyright © 2005 Examkrackers, Inc.

Notice that there is no salt bridge in the SHE Galvanic Cell. Both electrodes are in contact with the same solution so no salt bridge is necessary. When a cell contains two different solutions, a *liquid junction* is required to separate the solutions. Because ions can move across a liquid junction, any liquid junction creates an additional small potential difference that affects the potential of the galvanic cell. A **salt bridge** is a type of liquid junction that minimizes this potential difference. Typically a salt bridge is made from an aqueous solution of KCl. The salt bridge allows ionic conduction between solutions without creating a strong extra potential within the galvanic cell. It is able to minimize the potential because the K^+ ions move toward the cathode at about the same rate that the Cl^- move toward the anode. Below is an example of a simple galvanic cell that requires a salt bridge. Without the salt bridge, the solutions in the cell below would mix providing a low resistance path for electrons to move from $Zn(s)$ to $Cu^{2+}(aq)$ effectively short circuiting the cell, and leaving it with a cell potential of zero.

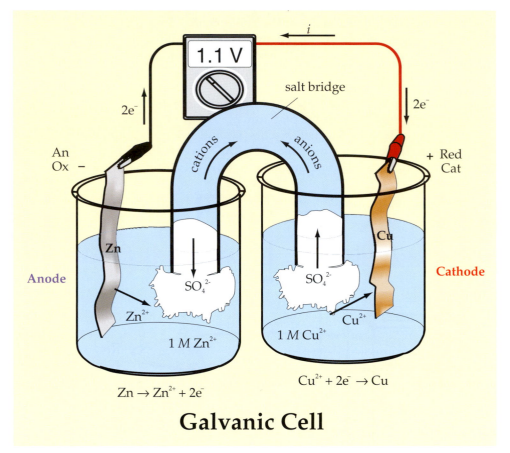

You should sketch a couple of your own galvanic cells so that you know how they are made. Notice that the concentrations are 1 M. This represents standard conditions and allows the use of the values from the reduction half reaction table to calculate the cell potential.

Galvanic Cell

Even in a galvanic cell with a salt bridge, there is some leakage of ions across the liquid junction, which causes the battery to lose its chemical potential over time. Commercial cells use an insoluble salt to prevent this from happening.

7-7
IUPAC Conventions

Galvanic cells can be represented by a *cell diagram*. Each phase is listed from left to right beginning with the terminal attached to the anode and ending with the terminal attached to the cathode. The terminals are often omitted because they are always the same material and do not take part in the reaction. A vertical line is placed between phases. A double vertical line is used to indicate a salt bridge. A dotted vertical line indicates a boundary between two miscible liquids, and species in the same phase are separated by a comma.

Copyright © 2005 Examkrackers, Inc.

$$Pt'(s)|Zn(s)|Zn^{2+}(aq)\|Cu^{2+}(aq)|Cu(s)|Pt(s)$$

Cell Diagram

The standard state emf can be found from the cell diagram by subtracting the potential of the reduction half reaction on the left (the reaction at the anode) from the potential of the reduction half reaction on the right (the reaction at the cathode).

It is unlikely that MCAT will require that you know the IUPAC conventions for a galvanic cell diagram. You can remember that the cathode is on the right because reduction and right both begin with an 'r'. Don't spend too much time here.

A positive cell potential indicates a spontaneous reaction as shown by the following equation:

$$\Delta G = -nFE_{max}$$

where n is the number of moles of electrons that are transferred in the balanced redox reaction, and F is Faraday's constant, which is the charge on one mole of electrons (96,486 C mol^{-1}). This equation says that the free energy represents the product of the total charge nF times the voltage E. Recall from Physics Lecture 7 that the product of charge and voltage equals work ($w = qV$). Since this is electrical work, it is not the result of a change in pressure or volume, so it represents nonPV work. Recall from Chemistry Lecture 3 that the change in Gibbs free energy represents the maximum amount of nonPV work available from a reaction at constant temperature and pressure. A negative ΔG indicates that the work is being done <u>by</u> the system and not <u>on</u> the system.

A positive cell potential indicates a negative ΔG and a spontaneous reaction.

When all the conditions are standard, we can write the equation above using the '$\circ$' symbol as follows (the 'max' is part of the definition of ΔG and is assumed):

$$\Delta G^{\circ} = -nFE^{\circ}$$

ΔG° can be found in books, but what about ΔG for non-standard state conditions? There are an infinite number of possible combinations of concentrations of reactants and products and temperatures with which we could start a reaction. How can we predict the maximum available work from these combinations? In order to make predictions about reactions that do not occur at standard state, we must use the following equation, which relates ΔG with ΔG°:

$$\Delta G = \Delta G^{\circ} + RT \ln(Q)$$

where Q is the reaction quotient discussed in Chemistry Lecture 2, and 'ln( )' is the natural logarithm. You may see this equation written using a base 10 logarithm as:

$$\Delta G = \Delta G^{\circ} + 2.3RT \log(Q)$$

This is based upon the crude approximation: $2.3\log(x) \approx \ln(x)$.

There is no need to confuse ΔG and ΔG°. ΔG° is a specific ΔG with specifically described parameters called standard conditions. Notice that if we use only one molar concentrations for Q, then $Q = 1$, and $RT\ln(Q) = 0$, leaving us with $\Delta G = \Delta G^{\circ}$. This is what we would expect for a reaction at standard conditions. (Remember, standard conditions don't actually indicate a particular temperature; you can have standard conditions at any temperature. Standard conditions are usually assumed to be 298 K.)

7-8

Free Energy and Chemical Energy

Memorizing this equation isn't nearly as important as understanding what it says about the relationship between ΔG, ΔG°, Q and K.

Copyright © 2005 Examkrackers, Inc.

Recall from Chemistry Lecture 3 that at equilibrium, there is no available free energy with which to do work; $\Delta G = 0$ by definition. Thus, if we have equilibrium conditions, we can plug in a value of 0 for ΔG, and rewrite "$\Delta G = \Delta G° + RT \ln(Q)$" as:

$$\Delta G° = -RT \ln(K)$$

In this equation, both K and $\Delta G°$ vary with temperature. Whenever you specify a new temperature, you must look up a new $\Delta G°$ for that temperature. Notice that since this equation uses the natural log of the equilibrium constant, a value of 1 for K will result in a value of 0 for $\Delta G°$. For the MCAT you should understand the relationship between K and $\Delta G°$.

$$\text{if} \quad K = 1 \quad \text{then} \quad \Delta G° = 0$$
$$\text{if} \quad K > 1 \quad \text{then} \quad \Delta G° < 0$$
$$\text{if} \quad K < 1 \quad \text{then} \quad \Delta G° > 0$$

Warning: This relationship does NOT say that if a reaction has an equilibrium constant that is greater than one, then the reaction is always spontaneous. That doesn't make any sense, since the spontaneity of a reaction depends upon starting concentrations of products and reactants. It does say that if a reaction has an equilibrium constant that is greater than one, the reaction is spontaneous at standard state (starting molar concentrations of exactly 1 M) and the prescribed temperature.

The galvanic cell pictured on page 116 was drawn with standard conditions of 1 M concentrations. That's great for the instant that the concentrations are all one molar, but what about for the rest of the time? How can we find the potential when the concentrations aren't one molar? If we take the equation:

$$\Delta G = \Delta G° + RT \ln(Q)$$

and substitute $-nFE$ for ΔG, and $-nFE°$ for $\Delta G°$, and then divide by $-nF$, we get:

$$E = E° - \frac{RT}{nF} \ln(Q)$$

This is the *Nernst equation*. At 298 K, and in base 10 logarithm form, the Nernst equation is:

$$E = E° - \frac{0.06}{n} \log(Q)$$

The Nernst equation allows us to plug in nonstandard concentrations to create Q and find the cell potential.

> This is pretty tricky stuff, but it's worth wracking your brains and killing some time on it now, rather than on the MCAT. Reread this section and make sure that you understand the relationship between K, Q, $\Delta G°$, ΔG, and T.

> You do not have to know the Nernst equation for the MCAT. However, you should understand how the Nernst equation expresses the relationship between chemical concentrations and potential difference. For instance, the Nernst equation could be used to express the resting potential across the membrane of a neuron. Such a situation would be similar to a concentration cell as discussed in the next section.

Copyright © 2005 Examkrackers, Inc.

153. Which of the following statements about a galvanic cell is false?

- **A.** If $E° = 0$, a reaction may still be spontaneous depending upon the chemical concentrations.
- **B.** A galvanic cell with a positive potential can perform work.
- **C.** Reduction takes place at the cathode.
- **D.** A salt bridge balances the charge by allowing positive ions to move to the anode.

154. The values of all of the following are reversed when a reaction is reversed EXCEPT:

- **A.** enthalpy
- **B.** Gibbs energy
- **C.** the rate constant
- **D.** reaction potential

155. Which of the following is true for a reaction, if $\Delta G°_{298} = 0$? (The 298 subscript indicates a temperature of 298 K.)

- **A.** The reaction is at equilibrium.
- **B.** At 298 K and 1 M concentrations of products and reactants the equilibrium constant equals one.
- **C.** ΔG is also zero.
- **D.** The reaction is spontaneous at temperatures greater than 298 K.

156. The following is a table of half reactions:

Half Reaction	$E°$ (V)
$Ag^{2+} + e^- \rightarrow Ag^+$	1.99
$Fe^{3+} + e^- \rightarrow Fe^{2+}$	0.77
$Cu^{2+} + 2e^- \rightarrow Cu$	0.34
$2H^+ + 2e^- \rightarrow H_2$	0.00
$Fe^{2+} + 2e^- \rightarrow Fe$	−0.44
$Zn^{2+} + 2e^- \rightarrow Zn$	−0.76

The strongest reducing agent shown in the table is:

- **A.** Zn
- **B.** Zn^{2+}
- **C.** Ag^+
- **D.** Ag^{2+}

157. A negative cell potential indicates which of the following:

- **A.** Both half reactions are nonspontaneous.
- **B.** The reduction half reaction potential is greater than the oxidation half reaction potential.
- **C.** The oxidation half reaction potential is greater than the reduction half reaction potential.
- **D.** The cell is electrolytic.

Questions 158 through 160 are based on the information below.

A galvanic cell uses the reaction between solid tin and aqueous copper ions to produce electrical power.

$$Sn(s) + 2Cu^{2+}(aq) \rightarrow Sn^{2+}(aq) + 2Cu(s)$$

$$Sn^{2+}(aq) + 2e^- \rightarrow Sn(s) \qquad E° = -0.14 \text{ V}$$
$$Cu^{2+}(aq) + 2e^- \rightarrow Cu(s) \qquad E° = 0.15 \text{ V}$$

158. The standard state cell potential for this reaction is:

- **A.** 0.01 V
- **B.** 0.16 V
- **C.** 0.29 V
- **D.** 0.44 V

159. The reaction in the cell is allowed to proceed. As the reaction in the cell progresses, the cell potential will:

- **A.** decrease as the concentration of Sn^{2+} increases.
- **B.** decrease as the concentration of Sn^{2+} decreases.
- **C.** increase as the concentration of Sn^{2+} increases.
- **D.** increase as the concentration of Sn^{2+} decreases.

160. Which of the following is true of the tin/copper cell reaction?

- **A.** $K > 1$ and $\Delta G° > 0$
- **B.** $K > 1$ and $\Delta G° < 0$
- **C.** $K < 1$ and $\Delta G° > 0$
- **D.** $K < 1$ and $\Delta G° < 0$

Copyright © 2005 Examkrackers, Inc.

STOP.

7-9
More Cells

The concentration cell is just a type of galvanic cell. It is never at standard conditions, so the Nernst equation is required to solve for the cell potential.

A **concentration cell** is a limited form of a galvanic cell with a reduction half reaction taking place in one half cell and the exact reverse of that half reaction taking place in the other half cell.

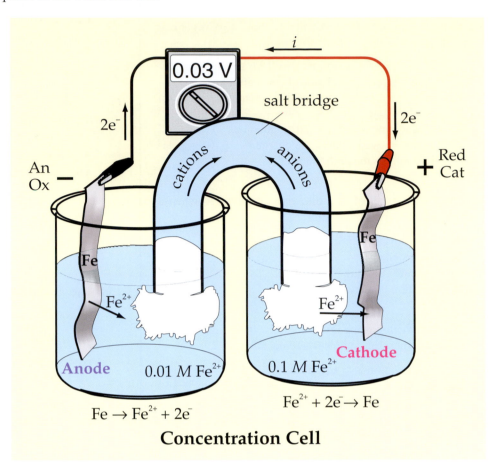

Concentration Cell

For cells, you should learn to diagram a galvanic cell by yourself. Once you can do that, the other cells can be created from the galvanic cell. Remember that galvanic cells have a positive cell potential; electrolytic cells have a negative potential. Galvanic cells are spontaneous; electrolytic are forced by an outside power source.

'Electrochemical' cell can mean either 'galvanic' or 'electrolytic' cell.

For any and all cells, remember 'Red Cat, An Ox'. This translates to Reduction at the Cathode, and Oxidation at the Anode.

Of course, when we add the two half reactions we get: $E° = 0$. If the concentrations were equal on both sides, the concentration cell potential would be zero. You can use the Nernst equation to find the potential for a concentration cell. (If you need the Nernst equation, the MCAT will give it to you.) It is much more likely that the MCAT will ask you a qualitative question like "In which direction will current flow in the concentration cell?" In this case, we must think about nature's tendency for balance; nature wants to create the greatest entropy. The more concentrated side will try to become less concentrated, and electrons will flow accordingly.

To use the Nernst equation to find the potential of a concentration cell at 25°C, we must realize that Fe^{2+} is both a product and a reactant. Thus, we simply substitute for Q the ratio of the Fe^{2+} concentrations on either side. For the case above we have:

$$E = E° - \frac{0.06}{2} \log\left(\frac{0.01}{0.1}\right)$$

$n = 2$ because 2 electrons are used each time the reaction occurs, and $E°$ equals zero. Concentration cells tend to have small potentials.

If we hook up a power source across the resistance of a galvanic cell, and force the cell to run backwards, we have created another type of cell, the **electrolytic cell**. Any electrolytic cell on the MCAT will have a negative emf. In the electrolytic cell, the cathode is marked negative and the anode is marked positive. Reduction still takes place at the cathode and oxidation at the anode.

Copyright © 2005 Examkrackers, Inc.

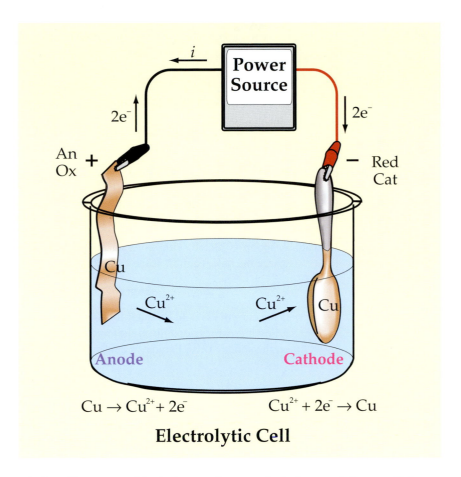

Electrolytic Cell

Electrolytic cells are used in industry for metal plating, and for purifying metals. For instance, pure sodium can be collected through electrolysis of sodium chloride solution in a *Downs cell*. The half reactions are as follows:

$$Na^+ + e^- \rightarrow Na \quad E° = -2.71 \text{ V}$$

$$2Cl^- \rightarrow 2e^- + Cl_2 \quad E° = -1.36 \text{ V}$$

Notice that this reaction will not run in aqueous solution because, from Table 7-3, we see that water has a less negative reduction potential than sodium. In fact, this indicates that solid sodium will oxidize spontaneously in water.

The assignment of positive and negative to electrodes in galvanic and electrolytic cells is based upon perspective. Galvanic cells are used to provide energy to an external load, so the electrodes are labeled so that negative electrons will flow toward the positive electrode. Electrons flow from the load to the cathode, so the cathode is labeled positive in the galvanic cell. The focus of electrolytic cells is within the cell itself. For instance, electrophoresis uses an electrolytic cell. It is important that negatively charged amino acids within the electrolytic cell flow toward the positive electrode, so the anode is labeled positive in the electrolytic cell.

Copyright © 2005 Examkrackers, Inc.

161. A galvanic cell is prepared with solutions of Mg^{2+} and Al^{3+} ions separated by a salt bridge. A potentiometer reads the difference across the electrodes to be 1.05 Volts. The following standard reduction potentials at 25°C apply:

Half Reaction $E°$ (V)	
$Al^{3+} + 3e^- \rightarrow Al$	-1.66
$Mg^{2+} + 2e^- \rightarrow Mg$	-2.37

Which of the following statements is true concerning the galvanic cell at 25°C?

A. Magnesium is reduced at the cathode.
B. The concentrations of ions are 1 M.
C. The reaction is spontaneous.
D. For every aluminum atom reduced, an equal number of magnesium atoms are oxidized.

162. Which of the following is true for an electrolytic cell?

A. Reduction takes place at the anode.
B. The reaction is spontaneous.
C. electrons flow to the cathode.
D. An electrolytic cell requires a salt bridge.

163. A concentration cell contains 0.5 M aqueous Ag^+ on one side and 0.1 M aqueous Ag^+ on the other. All of the following are true EXCEPT:

A. Electrons will move from the less concentrated side to the more concentrated side.
B. Electrons will move from the anode to the cathode.
C. As the cell potential moves toward zero, the concentrations of both sides will tend to even out.
D. $\Delta G > 0$

164. According to the Nernst equation:

$$E = E° - \frac{0.06}{n} \log\left(\frac{x}{y}\right)$$

if a concentration cell has a potential of 0.12 V, and a concentration of 0.1 M Ag^+ at the anode, what is the concentration of Ag^+ at the cathode?

A. 10^{-3} M
B. 10^{-1} M
C. 1 M
D. 10 M

165. A spoon is plated with silver in an electrolytic process where the half reaction at the cathode is:

$$Ag^+(aq) + e^- \rightarrow Ag(s) \quad E° = 0.8 \text{ V}$$

If the current i is held constant for t seconds, which of the following expressions gives the mass of silver deposited on the spoon? (F is Faraday's constant.)

A. $107.8 \, itF$

B. $107.8 \dfrac{it}{F}$

C. $107.8 \dfrac{i}{tF}$

D. $107.8 \dfrac{iF}{t}$

166. The charge on 1 mole of electrons is given by Faraday's constant, 96,500 C/mole. A galvanic cell was operated continuously for 5 minutes and 0.01 moles of electrons were passed through the wire. If the voltage remained constant for the entire time, what is the current generated by the cell?

A. 3 A
B. 5 A
C. 6 A
D. 9 A

167. The reduction potential for two half reactions are given below.

$$2H_2O(l) + 2e^- \rightarrow H_2(g) + 2OH^-(aq) \quad E° = -0.8 \text{ V}$$

$$Na^+(aq) + e^- \rightarrow Na(s) \quad E° = -2.7 \text{ V}$$

Aqueous sodium cannot be reduced to solid sodium in an electrolytic cell because:

A. aqueous sodium will combine with aqueous hydroxide to form solid sodium hydroxide.
B. liquid water is more easily reduced than aqueous sodium.
C. aqueous sodium must be oxidized to form solid sodium.
D. hydrogen gas is more easily oxidized than solid sodium.

168. The reaction above takes place in a galvanic cell. Which of the following is true?

$$2Ag^{2+} + Fe \rightarrow 2Ag^+ + Fe^{2+} \quad E° = 2.4 \text{ V}$$

A. Ag^{2+} is reduced at the anode.
B. Ag^{2+} is oxidized at the anode.
C. Ag^{2+} is reduced at the cathode.
D. Ag^{2+} is oxidized at the cathode.

STOP!

DO NOT LOOK AT THESE EXAMS UNTIL CLASS.

30-MINUTE
IN-CLASS EXAM
FOR LECTURE 1

There are five types of interactions within and between molecules. Intramolecular interactions include covalent and ionic bonds. Intermolecular interactions include van der Waals's forces, dipole-dipole, and hydrogen bonds. Table 1 lists the typical energies for these interactions.

Interaction	Typical Energy kJ mol^{-1}
Van der Waals's	0.1 – 5
Dipole-dipole	5 – 20
Hydrogen bond	5 – 50
Ionic bond	400 – 500
Covalent bond	150 – 900

Table 1 Energies of interactions

The boiling point of a substance increases with the strength of its intermolecular bonds. Figure 1 shows the boiling points of hydrides for some main-group elements and of the noble gases.

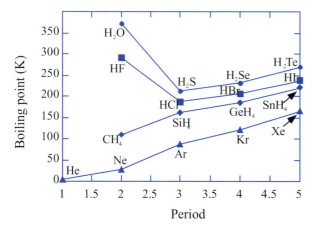

Figure 1 Boiling points of some main-group hydrides and the noble gases.

1. Why does the boiling point of H_2O and HF deviate from the trend in Figure 1?

   A. F and O both occur in the second period.
   B. The size of H_2O and HF are small relative to the other molecules
   C. H_2O and HF are less polarizable.
   D. H_2O and HF can hydrogen bond.

2. What type of bonding holds together the compound $MgCl_2$?

   A. covalent
   B. ionic
   C. hydrogen
   D. van der Waals's

3. Why do the boiling points of the noble gases increase as the period increases?

   A. The bonds are stronger because larger atoms are more polarizable as period increases.
   B. The bonds are weaker because larger atoms are more polarizable as period increases.
   C. The bonds are stronger because larger atoms are less polarizable as period increases.
   D. The bonds are weaker because larger atoms are less polarizable as period increases.

4. The atomic radius of Ne is:

   A. greater than Ar
   B. less than Ar
   C. the same as Ar
   D. cannot be determined

5. Why are boiling points a better indication of intermolecular bonding than melting points?

   A. Vaporization requires more energy than melting.
   B. Vaporization requires less energy than melting.
   C. Transition from solid to liquid involves other factors such as crystalline lattice structures.
   D. Vaporization is easier to measure.

6. What type of intermolecular bonding occurs in gaseous CH_4?

   A. covalent
   B. ionic
   C. hydrogen
   D. van der Waals's

7. Why is a dipole-dipole interaction stronger than a van der Waals's interaction?

   A. Dipole-dipole is an electrostatic interaction.
   B. Van der Waals's interactions rely on temporarily induced dipoles.
   C. Van der Waals's interactions require a large surface area.
   D. Dipole-dipole interactions only occur with ionically bonded compounds.

Copyright © 2005 Examkrackers, Inc.

GO ON TO THE NEXT PAGE.

Passage II (Questions 8-15)

Figure 1 shows atomic radius as a function of atomic number for the first three periods of the periodic table. Within a period the atomic radius decreases as the atomic number increases, but the atomic radius increases as the period increases.

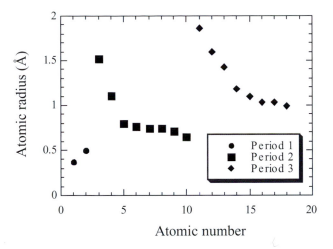

Figure 1 Atomic radius as a function of atomic number

Electronegativity of an atom also follows a trend in the periodic table. Electronegativity for any element (X) is based upon the difference (Δ) between the actual bond energy of a bond between element X and hydrogen and the expected bond energy of the same bond:

$$\Delta = (H\text{---}X)_{\text{actual bond energy}} - (H\text{---}X)_{\text{expected bond energy}}$$

where the expected bond energy is given by:

$$H\text{---}X_{\text{exp bond energy}} = \frac{H\text{---}H_{\text{bond energy}} + X\text{---}X_{\text{bond energy}}}{2}$$

Pauling electronegativity values are assigned to each element based upon its Δ value with respect to fluorine. Flourine is arbitrarily given a value of 4.0. The electronegativity of elements may be used to predict the type of bonding found in a molecule. Large differences in electronegativities of atoms in a bond result in an ionic bond.

8. If Se has an atomic radius of 1.16 Å, what is the predicted atomic radius of As?

- **A.** 1.05 Å
- **B.** 1.15 Å
- **C.** 1.25 Å
- **D.** 1.97 Å

9. Which of the following elements is the most chemically similar to Na?

- **A.** H
- **B.** Mg
- **C.** C
- **D.** Cs

10. Which element has the largest atomic radius?

- **A.** Li
- **B.** Ne
- **C.** Rb
- **D.** Br

11. Why is the electronegativity scale adjusted to fluorine?

- **A.** The researcher who discovered electronegativity was working with fluorine.
- **B.** Fluorine has the smallest atomic radius.
- **C.** Fluorine has the smallest electronegativity.
- **D.** Fluorine has the greatest electronegativity.

12. How does electron affinity change with atomic number?

- **A.** Electron affinity becomes more exothermic as atomic number increases in a period and a group.
- **B.** Electron affinity becomes less exothermic as atomic number increases in a period and a group.
- **C.** Electron affinity becomes more exothermic as atomic number increases in a period and less exothermic as atomic number increases in a group.
- **D.** Electron affinity becomes less exothermic as atomic number increases in a period and more exothermic as atomic number increases in a group.

13. Why does the atomic radius follow the trends observed in Figure 1?

- **A.** As the atomic number increases, the nuclear charge increases.
- **B.** As the atomic number increases, the nuclear charge decreases.
- **C.** As the atomic number increases, the nuclear charge increases and as the period increases the number of electron shells increases.
- **D.** As the atomic number increases, the nuclear charge increases and as the period increases the number of electron shells decreases.

Copyright © 2005 Examkrackers, Inc.

GO ON TO THE NEXT PAGE.

14. Hydrogen has a Pauling electronegativity of 2.1. What is the value of Δ for hydrogen?

    A.   0
    B.   1.0
    C.   2.1
    D.   4.0

15. What type of intramolecular bonding is found in a CO molecule?

    A.   covalent
    B.   ionic
    C.   hydrogen
    D.   van der Waals's

Passage III (Questions 16-21)

The empirical formula of a hydrocarbon can be determined using an instrument similar to the one shown in Figure 1. A sample hydrocarbon is combusted. The absorption chambers absorb all the water and carbon dioxide from the reaction. $CaCl_2$ can absorb both water and CO_2. The masses of the chambers before and after the reaction are compared to find the moles of carbon and hydrogen in the sample.

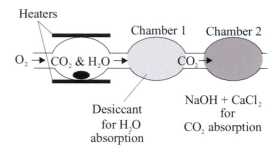

Figure 1 A combustion train

For example: propane can be combusted in the apparatus as follows:

$$C_3H_8 + 5O_2 \rightarrow 4H_2O + 3CO_2$$

In an experiment using the combustion train, a gaseous fuel used in welding (containing only C and H) is reacted with O_2. The mass of the absorbers in Chamber 1 increases by 0.9 grams and the mass of the absorbers in chamber 2 increases by 4.4 grams.

The density of the welding gas is 1.1 g L^{-1} at 25°C and atmospheric pressure. At the same conditions, O_2 has a density of 1.3 g L^{-1}.

16. What is the empirical formula of the welding gas?

    A.   CHO
    B.   CH
    C. C_2H_2
    D. C_3H_8

17. What is the molecular weight of the gas?

    A.   13 g/mol
    B.   26 g/mol
    C.   32 g/mol
    D.   60 g/mol

Copyright © 2005 Examkrackers, Inc.

GO ON TO THE NEXT PAGE.

18. A compound has an empirical formula of CH_2O. Using osmotic pressure, the molecular weight is determined to be 120 g/mol. What is the molecular formula for this compound?

    A. CH_2O
    B. $C_4H_4O_3$
    C. $C_3H_6O_3$
    D. $C_4H_8O_4$

19. If 1 mole of C_3H_8 is reacted with 2.5 moles of O_2, how many moles of H_2O will be produced?

    A.   1 mole of H_2O
    B.   2 moles of H_2O
    C.   3 moles of H_2O
    D.   4 moles of H_2O

20. What would happen if the order of the chambers in the combustion train were reversed?

    A.   The amount of CO_2 calculated would be higher than the actual amount produced.
    B.   The amount of CO_2 calculated would be lower than the actual amount produced.
    C.   The amount of H_2O calculated would be higher than the actual amount produced.
    D.   Nothing, the experiment would still give the same results.

21. Why is it necessary to react the O_2 in excess when using a combustion train?

    A.   In addition to the combustion reaction, the O_2 is used as a carrier gas.
    B.   In addition to the combustion reaction, the O_2 is used as a source of energy to propel the non-spontaneous reaction.
    C. O_2 needs to be the limiting reagent in order for the calculations to be correct.
    D.   The sample needs to be the limiting reagent in order for the calculations to be correct.

Questions 22 through 23 are **NOT** based on a descriptive passage.

22. What is the electron configuration of a chloride ion?

    A.   [Ne] $3s^2\ 3p^5$
    B.   [Ne] $3s^2\ 3p^6$
    C.   [Ne] $3s^2\ 3d^{10}\ 3p^5$
    D.   [Ar] $3s^2\ 3p^6$

23. According to the Heisenberg uncertainty principle, which of the following pairs of properties of an electron cannot be known with certainty at the same time?

    A.   charge and velocity
    B.   spin and subshell
    C.   average radius and energy level
    D.   momentum and position

STOP. IF YOU FINISH BEFORE TIME IS CALLED, CHECK YOUR WORK. YOU MAY GO BACK TO ANY QUESTION IN THIS TEST BOOKLET.

30-MINUTE
IN-CLASS EXAM
FOR LECTURE 2

Passage I (Questions 24-29)

Over the years, many attempts have been made to find an equation which represents the behavior of non-ideal gases. Although none of the equations are completely accurate, they do allow an investigation of some of the macroscopic properties of real gases. The most commonly used of these is the *van der Waals equation:*

$$\left(P + a\frac{n^2}{v^2}\right)(V - nb) = nRT$$

where P is the absolute pressure, n is the number of moles, V is the volume, T is the absolute temperature, R is the gas constant (0.08206 L atm/mol K), and a and b are constants determined experimentally for each gas studied. Table 1 gives the values of a and b for some common gases:

Gas	a (atm L^2/mol)	b (L/mol)
Ar	1.4	0.032
HCl	3.7	0.041
Cl$_2$	6.4	0.054
H$_2$	0.25	0.027
NH$_3$	4.3	0.037
O$_2$	1.4	0.032

Table 1 van der Waals Constants for Various gases

To help quantify the deviation of a real gas from ideality, a *compression factor Z* has been defined by $Z = PV/nRT$. Figure 1 shows how the compression factor for ammonia depends on pressure at several different temperatures.

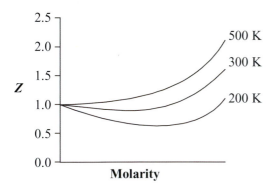

Figure 1 Compression factors for ammonia

24. For an ideal gas, which of the following is most likely the correct graph?

A.

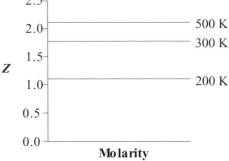

B.

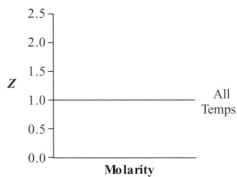

C.

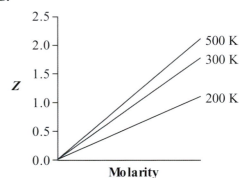

D.

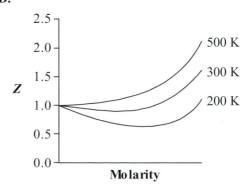

Copyright © 2005 Examkrackers, Inc.

GO ON TO THE NEXT PAGE.

25. For an ideal gas, what can be said about the constants a and b?

   A. They are both zero.
   B. They are both positive and equal to each other.
   C. They depend on the temperature of the gas.
   D. They must be determined experimentally.

26. Based on the information in the passage, under which of the following conditions does ammonia behave most ideally?

   A. Low temperatures and low pressures
   B. Low temperatures and high pressures
   C. High temperatures and low pressures
   D. High temperatures and high pressures

27. Which of the following statements is NOT true for an ideal gas?

   A. The average kinetic energy of the molecules depends only on the temperature of the gas.
   B. At constant volume in a sealed container, the pressure of the gas is directly proportional to its temperature.
   C. At constant temperature in a sealed container, the volume of the gas is directly proportional to its pressure.
   D. The intermolecular attractions between the gas molecules are negligible.

28. Which of the following demonstrates nonideal behavior of a gas?

   A. Some of the molecules move more rapidly than others.
   B. Condensation occurs at low temperatures.
   C. The gas exerts a force on the walls of its container.
   D. The average speed of the molecules in the gas is proportional to the square root of the absolute temperature.

29. Why must absolute temperature be used in the van der Waals equation?

   A. Because the van der Waals equation is a nonrelativistic equation.
   B. Because it is impossible to have a negative absolute temperature.
   C. Because ratios of temperatures on other scales, such as the Celsius scale, are meaningless.
   D. Because international convention requires it.

Passage II (Questions 30-37)

In 1889, Svante Arrhenius proposed that the rate constant for a given reaction is given by the formula:

$$k = Ae^{-\frac{E_a}{RT}}$$

where E_a is the *activation energy* for the reaction, R is the gas constant (8.314 J/mol K), T is the absolute temperature, and A is a factor, which depends on factors such as molecular size. *Catalysts* change the reaction pathway, which may result in a change in E_a, A, or both.

In *heterogeneous catalysis,* the catalyst is in a different phase from the reactants and products. For example, a solid may catalyze a fluid-phase reaction. Such a catalysis involves the following steps:

1. A reactant molecule diffuses through the liquid to the surface of the catalyst.

2. The reactant molecule bonds to the catalyst (*adsorption*).

3. Adsorbed molecules bond with each other or with a molecule which collides with the adsorbed molecules.

4. The product leaves the catalyst.

In *homogeneous catalysis,* the catalyst is in the same phase as the reactants and products. Acids often act by this mechanism.

30. Which of the following is true of a catalyzed reaction?

   A. A catalyst may be the limiting reagent.
   B. At equilibrium, more products are produced when a catalyst is present.
   C. The catalyzed reaction pathway has a lower energy of activation than the uncatalyzed reacton pathway.
   D. The rate of the reverse reacton will be slower for the catalyzed reaction.

31. Consider the following mechanism:

$$Cl + O_3 \rightarrow ClO + O_2$$
$$ClO + O \rightarrow Cl + O_2$$

   In this mechanism, what is the catalyst?

   A. Cl
   B. O_3
   C. ClO
   D. O_2

Copyright © 2005 Examkrackers, Inc.

GO ON TO THE NEXT PAGE.

32. As the temperature of a reaction increases, which of the following always occurs?

- **A.** The rate constant increases.
- **B.** The rate constant decreases.
- **C.** The activation energy increases.
- **D.** The activation energy decreases.

33. Consider a reversible reaction. If the activation energy for the forward reaction is lowered by a catalyst, what can be said about the activation energy for the reverse reaction?

- **A.** It is also lowered.
- **B.** It is raised.
- **C.** It is unaffected by the catalyst.
- **D.** The effect of the catalyst on the reverse reaction cannot be predicted without more information.

34. Suppose a reaction is acid-catalyzed by a solution of pH 3.0. What can be said about the pH of the resulting solution?

- **A.** It will be greater than 3.0 because the acid is consumed.
- **B.** It will be equal to 3.0 because the acid is regenerated.
- **C.** It will be equal to 3.0 because catalysts have no effect on equilibrium.
- **D.** It cannot be predicted without information on the acidity of the reactants and products.

35. The rate of a reaction may depend on which of the following?

- **I.** Concentrations of the reactants
- **II.** Concentration of a catalyst
- **III.** Surface area of a heterogeneous catalyst
- **IV.** Temperature

- **A.** I only
- **B.** IV only
- **C.** I and IV only
- **D.** I, II, III, and IV

36. H_2 can be added to ethylene in the presence of a heterogeneous catalyst such as solid platinum. What might account for the initial attraction between the hydrogen molecules and the solid platinum?

- **A.** hydrogen bonding
- **B.** metallic bonding
- **C.** van der Waals attraction
- **D.** the plasma continuum effect

37. If the solid line in the graph below represents the reaction profile for an uncatalyzed reaction, which line might represent the reaction profile for the catalyzed reaction?

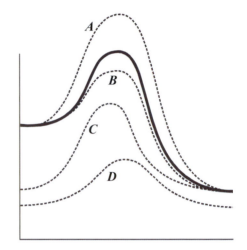

- **A.** *A*
- **B.** *B*
- **C.** *C*
- **D.** *D*

Copyright © 2005 Examkrackers, Inc.

GO ON TO THE NEXT PAGE.

Peroxydisulfate (persulfate) ion reacts with the iodide anion according to Reaction 1.

$$S_2O_8^{2-} (aq) + 3I^- (aq) \rightleftharpoons 2SO_4^{2-} (aq) + I_3^- (aq)$$

Reaction 1

The amount of I_3^- formed can be determined by adding a known amount of $S_2O_3^{2-}$ and allowing it to react according to Reaction 2.

$$2S_2O_3^{2-} (aq) + I_3^- (aq) \rightleftharpoons S_4O_6^{2-} (aq) + 3I^- (aq)$$

Reaction 2

If starch is also added, any excess I_3^- will react to form a blue-black I_2 complex. The formation of this complex indicates the completion of Reaction 2. The rate of Reaction 1 can be determined by the following equation where t is the elapsed time from the addition of the last component to the formation of the blue-black starch, I_2 complex.

$$rate = \frac{\frac{1}{2}\left[S_2O_3^{2-}\right]}{t}$$

Equation 1

38. Why can Equation 1 be used to measure the rate of Reaction 1?

 A. Reaction 2 must be much faster than Reaction 1, thus the rate in Equation 1 is the rate of formation of I_3^-.
 B. Reaction 2 must be much slower than Reaction 1, thus the rate in Equation 1 is the rate of formation of I_3^-.
 C. Reactions 1 and 2 must occur at the same rate, thus the rate in Equation 1 is the rate of formation of I_3^-.
 D. Equation 1 can be derived directly from the rate laws of Reactions 1 and 2.

39. What would happen to the time and the rate in Equation 1, if the temperature were reduced?

 A. Time would increase and rate would decrease.
 B. Time would decrease and rate would increase.
 C. Time would increase and rate would remain unchanged.
 D. Time would remain the same and rate would increase.

40. The following table gives the relative concentrations and rates found using the method described in the passage. What is the rate law for Reaction 1?

	1	2	3
$[I^-]$, (M)	0.060	0.030	0.030
$[S_2O_8^{2-}]$, (M)	0.030	0.030	0.015
Rate, $(M$/sec$)$	6.0×10^{-6}	3.0×10^{-6}	1.5×10^{-6}

 A. $k[I^-]^2[S_2O_8^{2-}]^2$
 B. $k[I^-]^{1/2}[S_2O_8^{2-}]^2$
 C. $k[I^-]^3[S_2O_8^{2-}]$
 D. $k[I^-][S_2O_8^{2-}]$

41. The rate expression for the reaction of H_2 with Br_2 is:

$$rate = k[H_2][Br_2].$$

 A. The rate is first order with respect to H_2, and first order overall.
 B. The rate is first order with respect to H_2, and second order overall.
 C. The rate is second order with respect to H_2, and first order overall.
 D. The rate is second order with respect to H_2, and second order overall.

42. A student is performing the kinetic study described in the passage and forgets to add starch. What will be the result of the experiment?

 A. The rates of both reactions as measured by the student will increase because the starch slows the reactions.
 B. The rate of Reaction 1 as measured by the student will decrease because starch speeds up the reaction.
 C. The rate of Reaction 1 as measured by the student will stay the same because starch has no effect on the rate.
 D. The rate of Reaction 1 as measured by the student will not be able to be determined by the method described in the passage.

Copyright © 2005 Examkrackers, Inc.

43. What would happen to the time and the rate in Equation 1, if more $S_2O_3^{2-}$ were added, and all other conditions remained the same?

   A.   Time would increase and rate would decrease.
   B.   Time would decrease and rate would increase.
   C.   Time would increase and rate would remain unchanged.
   D.   Time would remain the same and rate would increase.

44. What would happen to the time and the rate in Equation 1, if a catalyst is added to Reaction 1, and all other conditions remain the same?

   A.   Time would increase and rate would decrease.
   B.   Time would decrease and rate would increase.
   C.   Time would increase and rate would remain unchanged.
   D.   Time would remain the same and rate would increase.

Questions 45 through 46 are **NOT** based on a descriptive passage.

45. Which of the following are true concerning any reaction at equilibrium?

   I.   The concentration of products is equal to the concentration of reactants.
   II.   The rate of change in the concentration of the products is equal to the rate of change in the concentration of reactants.
   III.   The rate constant of the forward reaction is equal to the rate constant of the reverse reaction.

   A.   II only
   B.   I and II only
   C.   II and III only
   D.   I, II, and III

46. Equal concentrations of hydrogen and oxygen gas are placed on side 1 of the container shown below. Side 2 contains a vacuum. A small pin hole exists in the barrier separating side 1 and side 2. Which of the following statements is true?

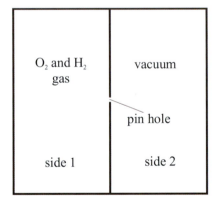

   A.   The partial pressure of oxygen on side 1 will increase.
   B.   The partial pressure of hydrogen on side 1 will increase.
   C.   The mole fraction of oxygen on side 1 will increase.
   D.   The mole fraction of hydrogen on side 1 will increase.

STOP. IF YOU FINISH BEFORE TIME IS CALLED, CHECK YOUR WORK. YOU MAY GO BACK TO ANY QUESTION IN THIS TEST BOOKLET.

30-MINUTE
IN-CLASS EXAM
FOR LECTURE 3

Nickel is purified by the Mond process, which relies on the equilibrium:

$$Ni(s) + 4CO(g) \rightleftharpoons Ni(CO)_4(g)$$

$$\Delta H° = -160.8 \text{ kJ}, \Delta S° = -409.5 \text{ JK}^{-1} \text{ at } 25°C$$

Reaction 1 The Mond process

Two chemists analyze the equilibrium.

Chemist A

Chemist A argues that Reaction 1 will be spontaneous in the forward direction because the product is more stable than the reactants. Furthermore, if the temperature is raised, the reaction will run in reverse because it is an exothermic reaction.

Chemist B

Chemist B argues that Reaction 1 will be spontaneous in the reverse direction because the entropy is higher for the reactants than for the products. Furthermore, if the temperature is raised, the spontaneity of the reverse reaction will increase.

47. The $\Delta H°_f$ for Ni(s) is:

- **A.** 0 kJ/mol
- **B.** −160.8 kJ/mol
- **C.** 160.8 kJ/mol
- **D.** 409.5 kJ/mol

48. Which of the following is a logical conclusion of Chemist A's argument?

- **A.** The enthalpy change of a reaction is an indicator of the relative stability of the reactants and products.
- **B.** The entropy change of a reaction is an indicator of the relative stability of the reactants and products.
- **C.** At higher temperatures, the reactants of Reaction 1 will be more stable than the products.
- **D.** Reactions do not necessarily need to increase the entropy of the universe in order to be spontaneous.

49. What are the most efficient conditions for purifying nickel when using the Mond process?

- **A.** low pressure and low temperature
- **B.** low pressure and high temperature
- **C.** high pressure and low temperature
- **D.** high pressure and high temperature

50. Which of the following explains the error in Chemist B's argument?

- **A.** Higher temperatures favor a reaction that decreases entropy.
- **B.** The entropy change of a reaction is the entropy change of the universe.
- **C.** A positive entropy of reaction does not necessarily indicate an entropy increase for the universe.
- **D.** The reaction will only run in the reverse direction until entropy is maximized for the reaction system.

51. What is the change in Gibbs free energy for Reaction 1 at standard state and 25°C?

- **A.** −38 kJ
- **B.** 38 kJ
- **C.** −150.5 kJ
- **D.** 150.5 kJ

52. Consider the reaction below:

$$C(s) + O_2 (g) \rightarrow CO_2 (g)$$

$\Delta H°$ is −393.51 kJ and $\Delta S°$ is 2.86 JK^{-1} at 25°C

If solid carbon is exposed to 1atm of oxygen and 1 atm of carbon dioxide gas at room temperature, will carbon dioxide gas form spontaneously?

- **A.** No, because the enthalpy of formation for CO_2 is negative.
- **B.** No, because the change in Gibbs energy is negative.
- **C.** Yes, because the enthalpy of formation for CO_2 is negative.
- **D.** Yes, because the change in Gibbs energy is negative.

A heat engine converts heat energy to work via a cyclical process which necessarily results in some of the heat energy being transferred from a higher temperature heat reservoir to a lower temperature heat reservoir. A heat engine obeys the *First Law of Thermodynamics*. The efficiency e of a heat engine is the fraction of heat energy input converted to useful work and is given by:

$$e = \frac{W}{Q_h}$$

where W is the work done by the heat engine on the surroundings and Q_h is the heat removed from the higher temperature reservoir. Work on the surroundings can also be represented by:

$$W = Q_h - Q_c$$

where Q_c is the heat energy expelled into the cold reservoir.

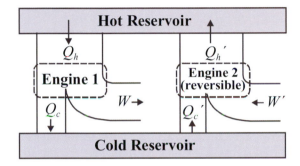

Figure 1 A schematic diaram of two heat engines operating between the same two heat reservoirs. (Not drawn to scale.)

The *Carnot theorem* states: No engine working between two heat reservoirs can be more efficient than a reversible engine working between those same reservoirs. Such a reversible engine is called a Carnot engine. This theorem can be proven with the *Second Law of Thermodynamics,* which states that for any process other than a reversible process the entropy change of the universe is greater than zero, and for a reversible process the entropy change of the universe is zero. Thus a Carnot engine obeys the following equation:

$$\Delta S = \frac{Q_c}{T_c} - \frac{Q_h}{T_h} = 0$$

Figure 1 shows a schematic representation of two heat engines working between the same two reservoirs. Engine 1 is absorbing heat energy from the hot reservoir and doing work while emitting heat energy into the cold reservoir. Engine 2 is a Carnot engine and is being run backwards removing heat energy from the cold reservoir and rejecting heat energy into the hot reservoir.

53. If both Engines 1 and 2 are operating at the same time as shown in Figure 1, and the rate of heat energy being removed from each reservoir is equal to the rate of heat energy being added then:

A. $W' > W$.
B. $W' < W$.
C. Engine 1 is a Carnot engine.
D. The efficiency of Engine 2 is greater than the efficiency of Engine 1.

54. Which of the following is true of the engines in Figure 1 if Engine 1 is not a Carnot engine and the work from Engine 1 is used to run Engine 2?

A. $Q_c < Q_c{}'$ and $Q_h < Q_h{}'$.
B. $Q_c > Q_c{}'$ and $Q_h < Q_h{}'$.
C. $Q_c > Q_c{}'$ and $Q_h > Q_h{}'$.
D. The work from Engine 1 cannot be used to run Engine 2.

55. Assume Engine 2 is running in the opposite direction as shown in Figure 1. Which of the following changes to Engine 2 will increase its efficiency as a heat engine?

A. increasing $Q_h{}'$
B. decreasing $Q_c{}'$
C. decreasing the temperature difference between the reservoirs
D. increasing the temperature difference between the reservoirs

56. Which of the following would allow a Carnot engine to operate at 100% efficiency where $e = 1$.

A. The work on the surroundings must be very large.
B. The engine must be reversible.
C. The hot reservoir must be at the same temperature as the cold reservoir.
D. The cold reservoir must be at a temperature of absolute zero.

57. What is the minimum power required for a heat engine to lift a 80 kg mass 5 m in 20 s if it releases 1000 J of heat energy from its exhaust each second?

A. 200 W
B. 500 W
C. 1200 W
D. 3000 W

Copyright © 2005 Examkrackers, Inc.

GO ON TO THE NEXT PAGE.

58. A certain Carnot engine requires 18 kg of water in the form of steam as its working substance. When 5×10^5 J of heat energy are added at a constant temperature of 400 K the gas expands to 4 m³. What is the approximate pressure of the gas after the initial expansion? (The ideal gas constant is $R = 8.314$ J/K mol)

A. 8.3×10^5 Pa
B. 8.3×10^7 Pa
C. 1.3×10^6 Pa
D. 1.3×10^8 Pa

Passage III (Questions 59-65)

As shown in Figure 1, Reaction 1 is thermodynamically favored because the products are at a lower energy state than the reactants. However, at low temperatures this reaction will be too slow to be observed because the reactant molecules do not have enough energy to form the activated complex.

$$NO_2 + CO \rightleftharpoons NO + CO_2$$
Reaction 1

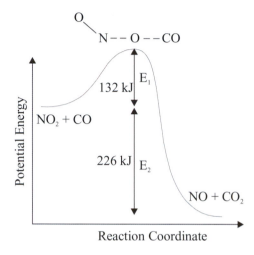

Figure 1 Energy diagram for Reaction 1.

As shown in Figure 2, Reaction 2 is not thermo-dynamically favored, but it has a smaller reaction barrier. The reactants require less energy to form the activated complex.

$$H_2 + Br \rightleftharpoons H + HBr$$
Reaction 2

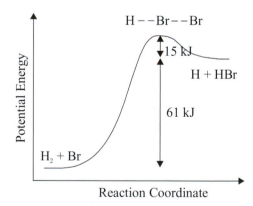

Figure 2 Energy diagram for Reaction 2

Copyright © 2005 Examkrackers, Inc.
GO ON TO THE NEXT PAGE.

59. What does the symbol H--Br--Br represent in Figure 2?

    A.   an intermediate
    B.   a transition state
    C.   a reactant of the second step of the reaction
    D.   a product of the first step of the reaction

60. What is E_a for Reaction 2 as written?

    A.   15 kJ/mole
    B.   61 kJ/mole
    C.   76 kJ/mole
    D.   132 kJ/mole

61. Which reaction is most kinetically favored?

    A. $NO_2 + CO \rightarrow NO + CO_2$
    B. $NO + CO_2 \rightarrow NO_2 + CO$
    C. $H_2 + Br \rightarrow H + HBr$
    D. $H + HBr \rightarrow H_2 + Br$

62. Which reaction is most thermodynamically favored?

    A. $NO_2 + CO \rightarrow NO + CO_2$
    B. $NO + CO_2 \rightarrow NO_2 + CO$
    C. $H_2 + Br \rightarrow H + HBr$
    D. $H + HBr \rightarrow H_2 + Br$

63. If a catalyst were added to Reaction 1, what would happen?

    A. E_1 would be less than 132 kJ but E_2 would remain unchanged.
    B. E_1 would be less than 132 kJ and E_2 would be less than 226 kJ.
    C. E_2 would be less than 226 but E_1 would remain unchanged.
    D.   A catalyst doesn't affect the thermodynamic properties of the reactants and products. E_1 and E_2 would remain unchanged but the reaction rate would increase.

64. What is ΔE for Reaction 2 as written?

    A.   15 kJ/mole
    B.   61 kJ/mole
    C.   76 kJ/mole
    D.   −76 kJ/mole

65. For the reaction,

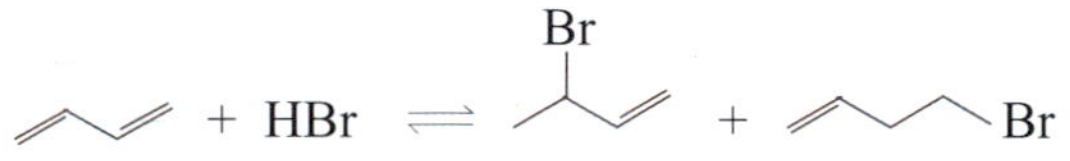

the ratio of products changes with temperature. At −80°C, 80% of 1 and 20% of 2 form. At 40°C, 15% of 1 and 85% of 2 form. Assuming the relative stability of products vs. reactants does not change significantly with the change in temperature, which product is the kinetically favored one?

    A.   1
    B.   2
    C.   both 1 and 2
    D.   neither 1 nor 2

Questions 66 through 69 are **NOT** based on a descriptive passage.

66. An iron skillet is laid on a hot stove. After a few minutes the handle gets hot. The method of heat transfer described is:

   A. convection.
   B. conduction.
   C. radiation.
   D. translation.

67. A man straightens up his room. His action does not violate the second law of thermodynamics because:

   A. the entropy of his room increased.
   B. energy of the universe was conserved.
   C. the entropy increase by the breakdown of nutrients in his body is greater than the entropy decrease by the straightening of his room.
   D. his action does violate the second law of thermodynamics.

68. A metal rod is in thermal contact with two heat reservoirs both at constant temperature, one at 100 K and the other at 200 K. The rod conducts 1000 J of heat from the warmer to the colder reservoir. If no energy is exchanged with the surroundings, what is the total change of entropy?

   A. −5 J/K
   B. 0 J/K
   C. 5 J/K
   D. 10 J/K

69. Two ideal gases, A and B, are at the same temperature, volume and pressure. Gas A is reversibly expanded at constant temperature to a volume V. Gas B is allowed to expand into an evacuated chamber until it also has a total volume V, but without exchanging heat with its surroundings. Which of the following most accurately describes the two gases?

   A. Gas A has a higher temperature and enthalpy than gas B.
   B. Gas A has a higher temperature but a lower enthalpy than gas B.
   C. Gas B has a higher temperature and enthalpy than gas A.
   D. Gas A and B have equal temperatures and enthalpies.

STOP. IF YOU FINISH BEFORE TIME IS CALLED, CHECK YOUR WORK. YOU MAY GO BACK TO ANY QUESTION IN THIS TEST BOOKLET.

30-MINUTE
IN-CLASS EXAM
FOR LECTURE 4

The following tests were carried out on samples of an unknown solution in order to identify any presence of nitrate and nitrite ions.

Experiment 1

In acidic solution nitrites react with sulfamic acid (HNH_2SO_3) according to the following reaction:

$$NO_2^- + NH_2SO_3^- \rightarrow N_2(g) + SO_4^{2-} + H_2O$$

Barium sulfate is insoluble while barium sulfamate is soluble.

In a test tube, $BaCl_2$ is added to a few drops of a sample of the unknown solution. No precipitate is formed. A few crystals of sulfamic acid are then mixed into the sample.

No visible reaction occurs.

Experiment 2

Active metals such as aluminum and zinc in alkaline solution reduce nitrate to ammonia. Nitrite ion will also form ammonia under these conditions. Devarda's alloy (50% Cu, 45% Al, 5% Zn) gives the following reaction with nitrate ion:

$$Al + NO_3^- \rightarrow Al(OH)_4^- + NH_3(g)$$

Several drops of the unknown solution are mixed with an equal amount of 6 *M* NaOH and placed into a dry test tube. Care is taken not to wet the walls of the tube. Devarda's alloy is then added and a loose cotton plug pushed one third of the way down the tube. The tube is warmed briefly in a water bath and removed. A bent strip of red litmus with a moistened fold is then placed at the top of the tube as shone in Figure 1.

The moistened section of the litmus turns blue.

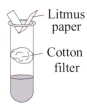

— Litmus paper

— Cotton filter

Figure 1

70. The unknown solution contains which of the following ions:

    A.   nitrite but not nitrate
    B.   both nitrite and nitrate
    C.   nitrate but not nitrite
    D.   neither nitrite nor nitrate

71. In Experiment 1, why is $BaCl_2$ added before the sulfamic acid crystals?

    A.   to acidify the solution
    B.   to remove any sulfate ions existing prior to the reaction with nitrite
    C.   to prevent sulfamic acid from reacting with $BaCl_2$
    D. $BaCl_2$ is needed to react with nitrite and form the precipitate.

72. If the unknown solution contained nitrite what would be the expected result of Experiment 1?

    A.   A precipitate would be formed before the addition of sulfamic acid.
    B.   Bubbles and precipitate would be observed after the addition of sulfamic acid.
    C.   Bubbles but no precipitate would be observed after the addition of sulfamic acid.
    D.   No visible reaction would be observed after the addition of sulfamic acid.

73. If carbonate ion is present in the unknown, which of the following reactions might interfere with Experiment 1?

    A. $2H^+ + CO_3^{2-} \rightarrow CO_2(g) + H_2O$
    B. $Ba^{2+} + 2OH^- + CO_2 \rightarrow BaCO(s) + H_2O$
    C. $NH_4^+ + CO_3^{2-} \rightarrow NH_3 + HCO_3^-$
    D. $H_2CO_3 \rightarrow CO(g) + O_2(g) + H_2(g)$

74. When the solution in Experiment 2 is warmed in the water bath, all of the following may be true EXCEPT:

    A.   The equilibrium constant *K* of the reaction changes.
    B.   The rate constant *k* of the reaction changes.
    C.   The rate of the reaction decreases.
    D.   The rate of the reaction increases.

75. Which of the following represents the reaction taking place in the litmus paper in Experiment 2?

    A. $NO_3^- + H_2O \rightarrow OH^- + HNO_3$
    B. $HNO_3 + H_2O \rightarrow H_3O^+ + NO_3^-$
    C. $NH_4^+ + H_2O \rightarrow H_3O^+ + NH_3$
    D. $NH_3 + H_2O \rightarrow NH_4^+ + OH^-$

Passage II (Questions 76-82)

When $Ca(IO_3)_2$ dissolves in a solution containing H^+ the following two reactions occur.

$$Ca(IO_3)_2 \rightleftharpoons Ca^{2+} + 2IO_3^-$$

Reaction 1

$$H^+ + IO_3^- \rightleftharpoons HIO_3$$

Reaction 2

HIO_3 is a weak acid. The K_{sp} for $Ca(IO_3)_2$ and the K_a for HIO_3 can be determined from the solubility (S) of $Ca(IO_3)_2$ for solutions of varying $[H^+]$. The solubility is related to the initial hydrogen ion concentration $[H^+]$ by the following equation:

$$2(S)^{\frac{3}{2}} = K_{sp}^{\frac{1}{2}} + \left[\frac{K_{sp}^{\frac{1}{2}}}{K_a} \right] [H^+]$$

A student prepared four saturated solutions by mixing $Ca(IO_3)_2$ with a strong acid. Excess solid was filtered off. The student found the S for each solution with constant ionic strength, using iodometric titrations. The resulting data are shown in Table 1.

Solution	$[H^+]$ (mol/l)	S (mol/l)
1	1.0×10^{-7}	5.4×10^{-3}
2	2.5×10^{-1}	9.9×10^{-3}
3	5.0×10^{-1}	1.4×10^{-2}
4	1	2.0×10^{-2}

Table 1 Solubility data for $Ca(IO_3)_2$

76. The K_{sp} for $Ca(IO_3)_2$ and the K_a for HIO_3, respectively are:

A. $[Ca^{2+}][IO_3^-]^2$ and $\dfrac{[H^+][IO_3^-]}{[HIO_3]}$

B. $\dfrac{[Ca^{2+}][IO_3^-]^2}{[Ca(IO_3)_2]}$ and $\dfrac{[H^+][IO_3^-]}{[HIO_3]}$

C. $[Ca^{2+}][IO_3^-]^2$ and $[H^+][IO_3^-]$

D. $[Ca^{2+}][IO_3^-]^2$ and $\dfrac{[HIO_3]}{[H^+][IO_3^-]}$

77. As $[H^+]$ increases, the solubility of $Ca(IO_3)_2$:

A.   increases and K_{sp} increases.
B.   decreases and K_{sp} decreases.
C.   increases and K_{sp} does not change.
D.   does not change and K_{sp} increases.

78. The graph of $2(S)^{3/2}$ versus $[H^+]$ for the data shown in Table 1 would most closely resemble which of the following?

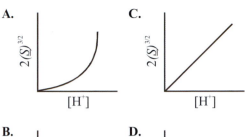

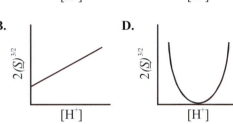

79. After filtering out excess solid, a student adds HCl to Solution 1 in Table 1. He then adds a small amount of $CaSO_4$, which dissolves completely. Which of the following also occurs in the new solution?

A.   Some $Ca(IO_3)_2$ precipitates when the $CaSO_4$ is added.
B.   Undissociated HIO_3 increases when the HCl is added.
C.   Aqueous IO_3^- decreases when $CaSO_4$ is added.
D.   Aqueous Ca^{2+} decreases when $CaSO_4$ is added.

80. According to Table 1, what is the value of K_{sp} for $Ca(IO_3)_2$?

A. 1.0×10^{-14}
B. 6.4×10^{-7}
C. 5.4×10^{-3}
D. 1.1×10^{-1}

81. If $Ca(OH)_2$ is added to the Solution 3 in Table 1:

A.   the concentration of H^+ will increase.
B.   the concentration of HIO_3 will increase.
C.   the concentration of IO_3^- will increase
D. $Ca(IO_3)_2$ will precipitate.

82. How will the addition of HIO_3 affect Solution 2 from Table 1?

A.   The lower pH will shift Reaction 2 to the right.
B.   The increased hydrogen ion concentration will dissolve more $Ca(IO_3)_2$.
C.   The common ion effect will shift Reaction 1 to the left.
D.   The lower pH will balance out the common ion effect and the equilibrium will not change.

Copyright © 2005 Examkrackers, Inc.

GO ON TO THE NEXT PAGE.

Passage III (Questions 83-89)

Many carbonate minerals are found in the earth's crust. As a result, the waters of several lakes, rivers, and even oceans are in contact with these minerals. $CaCO_3$ is the primary component of limestone and marble, while dolomite ($CaMg(CO_3)_2$) and magnesite ($MgCO_3$) are minerals found in other rock formations.

Limestone lines many of the river and lake beds resulting in contamination of the fresh water supply with Ca^{2+} and Mg^{2+}. The amount of these minerals present in water can be measured in parts per million (ppm). The "hardness" of water is determined by the ppm of Ca^{2+} and Mg^{2+} present. Hard water is the cause of many problems in the home. Scale buildup in pipes, on pots and pans, and in washing machines are just a few of the problems.

The hardness of water can be measured by titrating a sample of water with the ligand ethylenediamine tetraacetic acid (EDTA) and the indicator eriochrome black T. This ligand forms a coordination complex with metal cations (M) in a one-to-one stochiometry in the following association reaction:

$$EDTA + M \rightarrow EDTA–M$$

The structure of EDTA is shown in Figure 1. It has six binding sites to form a very stable complex ion with most metal ions.

Figure 1 The structure of EDTA

The association constants for EDTA with several metal ions are listed in Table 1.

Metal	K_{assoc}
Hg^{2+}	6×10^{21}
Mg^{2+}	5×10^{8}
Ca^{2+}	5×10^{10}
Al^{3+}	1×10^{16}
Fe^{2+}	2×10^{14}
Fe^{3+}	1×10^{25}
Cu^{2+}	6×10^{18}

Table 1 Association constants for EDTA with metal ions

Many households soften hard water using ion exchange resins. These resins replace the Ca^{2+} and Mg^{2+} ions with smaller cations such as Na^+ and H^+.

83. A scientist determines how hard the tap water is in the laboratory, using an EDTA titration. If the pipes in the building are old and some rust dissolves into the tap water, how will the results of the test change?

   A. The results will not change because the EDTA titration only works with Ca^{2+} and Mg^{2+}.
   B. The titration will not be able to be carried out because the tap water will be colored.
   C. The tap water will appear to have less Ca^{2+} and Mg^{2+} present.
   D. The tap water will appear to have more Ca^{2+} and Mg^{2+} present.

84. When EDTA reacts with a metal ion to form a complex ion, EDTA is acting as a(n):

   A. oxidizing agent.
   B. reducing agent.
   C. Lewis base.
   D. Lewis acid.

85. Salt water contains a high concentration of Cl^- ions. These ions form complexes ($CaCl^+$) with Ca^{2+}. How will the solubility of limestone change in ocean water compared to fresh water?

   A. It will increase.
   B. It will decrease.
   C. It will remain the same.
   D. The change in solubility cannot be determined.

86. A 25 mL sample of hard water is titrated with a 0.001 M solution of EDTA, and the endpoint of the titration is reached at 50 mL of EDTA added. What is the concentration of Ca^{2+} and Mg^{2+} ions in solution?

   A. 0.0005 M
   B. 0.001 M
   C. 0.002 M
   D. 0.006 M

87. The EDTA titrations are carried out at a pH of 10. Why is it necessary to buffer the pH at 10?

    A. A low pH will cause metal hydroxides to form.
    B. $CaCO_3$ requires a high pH in order to dissolve.
    C. The indicator requires pH 10 to change color.
    D. The coordinating atoms must be deprotonated in order to bond with the metal ion.

88. Why does replacing the cations found in hard water with Na^+ or H^+ soften the water (i.e., reduce the unwanted residue produced by hard water)?

    A. The smaller cations do not form insoluble mineral deposits.
    B. Twice as many smaller ions are necessary to react with soaps and other ligands.
    C. No minerals contain Na and H.
    D. H is found in water so there is no addition of new atoms.

89. 9 ppm is equivalent to an aqueous concentration of approximately 5×10^{-4} mol/L. If a water sample were reduced from 18 ppm Mg^{2+} to 9 ppm Mg^{2+} by the addition of EDTA, according to Table 1 what would be the concentration of the remaining unbound EDTA?

    A. 2×10^{-9} mol/L
    B. 5×10^{-4} mol/L
    C. 1×10^{-3} mol/L
    D. 5×10^{-3} mol/L

Questions 90 through 92 are **NOT** based on a descriptive passage.

90. The vapor pressure of pure water at 25°C is approximately 23.8 torr. Which of the following is the vapor pressure of pure water at 95°C?

    A. 10 torr
    B. 23.8 torr
    C. 633.9 torr
    D. 800 torr

91. Benzene and toluene form a nearly ideal solution. If the vapor pressure for benzene and toluene at 25°C is 94 mm Hg and 29 mm Hg respectively, what is the approximate vapor pressure of a solution made from 25% benzene and 75% toluene at the same temperature?

    A. 29 mm Hg
    B. 45 mm Hg
    C. 94 mm Hg
    D. 123 mm Hg

92. When volatile solvents A and B are mixed in equal proportions heat is given off to the surroundings. If pure A has a higher boiling point than pure B, which of the following could NOT be true?

    A. The boiling point of the mixture is less than pure A.
    B. The boiling point of the mixture is less than pure B.
    C. The vapor pressure of the mixture is less than pure A.
    D. The vapor pressure of the mixture is less than pure B.

STOP. IF YOU FINISH BEFORE TIME IS CALLED, CHECK YOUR WORK. YOU MAY GO BACK TO ANY QUESTION IN THIS TEST BOOKLET.

30-MINUTE
IN-CLASS EXAM
FOR LECTURE 5

Two students performed the following experiment to calculate the molecular weight of an unknown substance. The apparatus shown in Figure 1 was used.

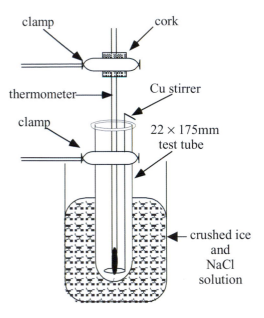

Figure 1 Freezing Point Apparatus

Both students placed 10.00 mL of cyclohexane into the test tube at room temperature. Next 0.500 gram of an unknown solid was dissolved in the cyclohexane. The test tube and contents were lowered into the ice bath, which was maintained at a temperature of –5.0°C by adjusting the relative amounts of NaCl, ice, and water. The students monitored the temperature of the cyclohexane mixtures by taking readings from the thermometer at 30 seconds intervals. The freezing point of the solution for a given trial is the temperature maintained for four consecutive readings. The experiment was repeated two more times by warming the cyclohexane to room temperature then freezing it again.

The results obtained by the students are recorded in Table 1.

Time, seconds	30	60	90	120	150	180	210	240
Student 1	22.0	6.0	4.0	–3.5	–3.5	–3.5	–3.5	–3.5
Student 2	22.0	12.0	6.0	0.6	0.6	0.6	0.6	0.4

Table 1 Solution temperature (°C) with time

(The K_f for cyclohexane is 20.2°C kg/mol, the freezing point is 6.6°C, and the density is 0.78 g/mL. The K_f for water is 1.86°C kg/mol.)

93. Why was NaCl added to the ice bath?

A. To lower the freezing point of the water and cool the cyclohexane solution more quickly.
B. To lower the freezing point of the cyclohexane solution below the freezing point of the water.
C. To lower the freezing point of the water below the freezing point of the cyclohexane solution.
D. To raise the freezing point of the water.

94. Which salt is the most efficient per gram at lowering the freezing point of water?

A. $Ba(OH)_2$
B. $MgSO_4$
C. NaCl
D. $CaCl_2$

95. The purpose of the copper stirrer is:

A. to ensure that the solid stays in solution.
B. to create heat to offset the chilling effect of the ice bath.
C. to ensure that the solution temperature remains homogenous.
D. to allow the student to see when crystals begin to form.

96. According to the results in Table 1, which student had the unknown with the greatest molecular weight? (Assume no dissociation of the unknown solids occurs.)

A. Student 1
B. Student 2
C. The molecular weights were the same.
D. It cannot be determined based on the given information.

97. Student 1 recorded a lower freezing point for the experiment because:

A. the concentration of particles in Student 1's crushed ice solution was lower than in Student 2's crushed ice solution.
B. the concentration of particles in Student 1's crushed ice solution was greater than in Student 2's crushed ice solution.
C. the concentration of particles in Student 1's cyclohexane solution was lower than in Student 2's cyclohexane solution.
D. the concentration of particles in Student 1's cyclohexane solution was greater than in Student 2's cyclohexane solution.

98. In order to calculate the molecular weight of their unknown solid the students probably used all of the following data EXCEPT:

    A. the mass of the unknown solid added to the solution.

    B. the time required for the cyclhexane solution to freeze.

    C. the temperature at the freezing point of the cycloexane solution.

    D. the volume of the cyclohexane solution.

99. A professor must choose the unknown from the following solutes. Which of the following would be the most appropriate for the experiment in the passage?

    A. NaCl

    B. $Mg(OH)_2$

    C. CH_3OH

    D. $C_{10}H_8$

100. Why does the temperature in Student 2's experiment begin to drop after 210 seconds?

    A. Student 2 used too much ice in the ice bath.

    B. Student 2's cyclohexane solution was completely frozen at 210 seconds.

    C. Student 2 stopped stirring the solution at 180 seconds.

    D. Student 2 stopped dissolving the unknown solid.

Passage II (Questions 101-106)

A series of experiments are performed using the calorimeter shown in Figure 1.

Figure 1 Coffee Cup Calorimeter

A volume of 0.5 *M* NaOH is placed near the calorimeter, which contains an equal volume of 0.5 *M* HCl. The temperatures of both solutions are monitored until they equilibrate to room temperature.

The NaOH solution is added to the HCl solution through the funnel. The temperature is recorded every 30 seconds for 5 minutes. The experiment is repeated three times with three different volumes of HCl and NaOH. The results of one of these experiments are shown in the graph in Figure 2. The data for all experiments are recorded in Table 1.

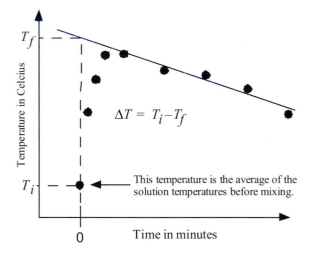

Figure 2 Temperature change of solution over time

Copyright © 2005 Examkrackers, Inc.

GO ON TO THE NEXT PAGE.

In-Class Exams

Trial	Volume of HCL and NaOH (ml)	Initial Temperature °C	Final Temperature °C
1	30	22.0	25.3
2	40	20.0	23.3
3	50	21.0	24.3

Table 1

101. What reaction is taking place in the calorimeter to cause the temperature change?

A. $H^+ + OH^- \rightarrow H_2O$
B. $Na^+ + Cl^- \rightarrow NaCl$
C. $NaCl \rightarrow Na^+ + Cl^-$
D. $Na^+ + 1e^- \rightarrow Na$

102. The reaction in the calorimeter is an:

A. endothermic reaction.
B. exothermic reaction.
C. oxidation reaction.
D. isothermic reaction.

103. Assuming that the heat capacity of the solution is the same as the heat capacity of water, what is the enthalpy change for the reaction in Trial 2 as recorded in Table 1? (The heat capacity for water is 1.0 cal °C^{-1} mL^{-1})

A. −132 cal
B. 132 cal
C. −330 cal
D. 330 cal

104. If 0.5 M NH$_4$OH (a weaker base) were used instead of NaOH, how would this affect the results of the experiment?

A. The temperature change would be greater because more energy is required to dissociate NH$_4$OH.
B. The temperature change would be less because more energy is required to dissociate NH$_4$OH.
C. The temperature change would be greater because less energy is required to dissociate NH$_4$OH.
D. It would not change the results because both bases are ionic compounds and the energy required to separate equal charges is always the same.

105. Which trial would be expected to result in the greatest heat of solution per mole of reactants?

A. 1
B. 2
C. 3
D. They should all be the same.

106. If the solutions in the experiment began at room temperature, which of the following explains the heat transfer between the calorimeter and its surroundings for the experiment shown in Figure 2?

A. Initially heat is transferred from the surroundings to the calorimeter, and then heat is transferred from the calorimeter to the surroundings.
B. Initially heat is transferred from the calorimeter to the surroundings, and then heat is transferred from the surroundings to the calorimeter.
C. Heat is transferred from the surroundings to the calorimeter throughout the experiment.
D. Heat is transferred from the calorimeter to the surroundings throughout the experiment.

Copyright © 2005 Examkrackers, Inc.

GO ON TO THE NEXT PAGE.

Passage III (Questions 107-113)

Phase diagrams show the changes in phase of a material as a function of temperature and pressure. Student A prepared a phase diagram for CO_2. After observing the phase diagram, he concluded that raising the pressure isothermally promotes a substance to change from a gas to a liquid to a solid as demonstrated by the dashed line in Figure 1.

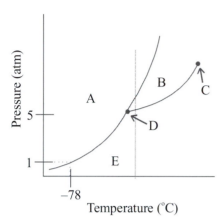

Figure 1 Phase diagram of CO_2

Student B chose to make a phase diagram of H_2O. She observed that raising the pressure isothermally promotes a substance to convert from vapor to solid then to liquid as indicated by the dashed line in Figure 2.

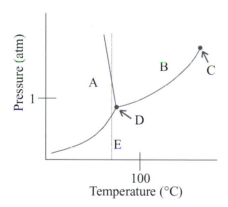

Figure 2 Phase diagram of H_2O

107. Which of the following explains the discrepancy between the observations of the two students?

   A. Water expands when going from liquid to solid, where as CO_2 contracts.
   B. CO_2 expands when going from liquid to solid, where as water contracts.
   C. The two chemists observed the phase changes at different temperatures.
   D. CO_2 is a gas at room temperature, while H_2O is a liquid.

108. According to Figure 1, at –78°C and 1 atm CO_2 will:

   A. exist as a liquid.
   B. exist in equilibrium as a gas and liquid.
   C. exist in equilibrium as a gas and solid.
   D. exist in equilibrium as a liquid and solid.

109. The temperature and pressure above which the gas and liquid phases of a substance can not be distinguished is called the:

   A. critical point
   B. triple point
   C. boiling point
   D. super point

110. At temperatures and pressures greater than point C in Figure 1:

   A. CO_2 is a vapor.
   B. CO_2 is a liquid.
   C. CO_2 is in both liquid and vapor phase.
   D. the vapor and liquid phases of CO_2 cannot be distinguished.

111. According to Figure 2, as the pressure increases the melting point of H_2O?

   A. increases
   B. decreases
   C. does not change
   D. increases than decreases

112. The normal boiling point for O_2 is 90.2 K. Which of the following could be the triple point for O_2?

   A. 1.14 mmHg and 54.4 K
   B. 1.14 mmHg and 154.6 K
   C. 800 mmHg and 54.4 K
   D. 37,800 mmHg and 154.6 K

113. Describe the phase change for H_2O as the pressure is raised at 100°C.

   A. sublimation
   B. vaporization
   C. condensation
   D. melting

Copyright © 2005 Examkrackers, Inc.

GO ON TO THE NEXT PAGE.

Questions 114 through 115 are **NOT** based on a descriptive passage.

114. During a solid to liquid phase change, energy is:

    A.   absorbed by bond breakage.
    B.   released by bond breakage.
    C.   absorbed by increased kinetic energy of the liquid molecules.
    D.   released by increased kinetic energy of the liquid molecules.

115. On his honeymoon the chemist, Joule, took with him a long thermometer with which to measure the temperature difference between the waters at the top and the bottom of Niagra Falls. If the height of the falls is 60 meters and the specific heat of water is approximately 4200 J kg^{-1} K^{-1}, what is the expected temperature difference?

    A.   1/7 K
    B.   7 K
    C.   70 K
    D.   700 K

STOP. IF YOU FINISH BEFORE TIME IS CALLED, CHECK YOUR WORK. YOU MAY GO BACK TO ANY QUESTION IN THIS TEST BOOKLET.

30-MINUTE
IN-CLASS EXAM
FOR LECTURE 6

Passage I (Questions 116-121)

The solubility of $Ca(OH)_2$ (Reaction 1) can be determined by titrating the saturated solution containing no precipitate against a standardized HCl solution and determining $[OH^-]$.

$$Ca(OH)_2 \rightleftharpoons Ca^{2+} + 2OH^-$$

Reaction 1

Once $[OH^-]$ is determined, the solubility *(S)* of $Ca(OH)_2$ is calculated using the following equation:

$$S = \frac{1}{2}\left[OH^-\right]_{Ca(OH)_2}$$

Equation 1

where $[OH^-]_{Ca(OH)_2}$ is the concentration of hydroxide ion due only to $Ca(OH)_2$. The solubilities of $Ca(OH)_2$ in a variety of solutions of varying $[OH^-]$ concentrations were determined by the above method, but the calculation of *S* had to be altered slightly due to the presence of additional hydroxide ions.

$$S = \frac{1}{2}\left\{\left[OH^-\right]_{total} - \left[OH^-\right]_{solvent}\right\}$$

Equation 2

The results of the experiment are summarized in Table 1.

Trial	Solution	Solubility
1	H_2O	0.0199 *M*
2	0.01793 *M* NaOH	0.0100 *M*
3	0.03614 *M* NaOH	0.0047 *M*
4	0.07119 *M* NaOH	0.0015 *M*

Table 1 Solubility data for $Ca(OH)_2$

116. How does the solubility of $Ca(OH)_2$ change as the $[OH^-]$ in the solvent increases?

- **A.** It decreases because the increase in OH^- shifts Reaction 1 toward the left.
- **B.** It decreases because the increase in OH^- interferes with the acid titration.
- **C.** It increases because the increase in OH^- shifts Reaction 1 toward the left.
- **D.** It increases because the increase in OH^- interferes with the acid titration.

117. How do the titrations in Trials 1 and 3 compare?

- **A.** The pH of the equivalence points are the same, but more HCl is required to reach the equivalence point in Trial 3.
- **B.** The pH of the equivalence point in Trial 1 is higher, and less HCl is required to reach it.
- **C.** The pH of the equivalence point in Trial 3 is higher, and less HCl is required to reach it.
- **D.** The pH of the equivalence point in Trial 3 is higher, and more HCl is required to reach it.

118. The K_{sp} for Reaction 1 in the presence of NaOH is:

- **A.** $[Ca^{2+}][OH^-]^2_{Ca(OH)_2}$
- **B.** $[Ca^{2+}][OH^-]^2_{Total}$
- **C.** $[Ca^{2+}][2OH^-]^2_{Ca(OH)_2}$
- **D.** $[Ca^{2+}][2OH^-]^2_{Total}$

119. What is the pH of the solution in Trial 3 before the titration?

- **A.** 1.1
- **B.** 7.0
- **C.** 9.3
- **D.** 12.7

120. Which indicator would be best for the titration in this experiment?

- **A.** Phenolphthalein: (acid color is colorless, base is red, and the transition pH is 8.0 – 9.6).
- **B.** Thymolphthalein: (acid color is colorless, base is blue, and the transition pH is 8.3 – 10.5).
- **C.** Bromocresol purple: (acid color is yellow, base is purple, and the transition pH is 5.2 – 6.8).
- **D.** Neutral red: (acid color is red, base color is yellow, and the transition pH is 6.8 – 8.0).

Copyright © 2005 Examkrackers, Inc.

GO ON TO THE NEXT PAGE.

121. If a pH meter were placed into the titration beaker, what would be the resulting curve for Trial 1?

A.

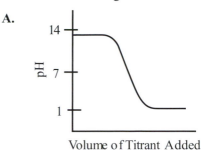

Volume of Titrant Added

B.

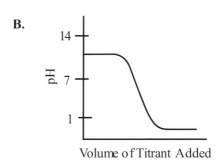

Volume of Titrant Added

C.

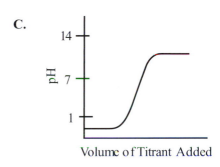

Volume of Titrant Added

D.

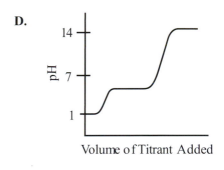

Volume of Titrant Added

Passage II (Questions 122-127)

The reaction for the autoionization of water is shown below:

$$2H_2O \rightarrow H_3O^+ + OH^-$$

The equilibrium constant (K_w) is temperature dependent. Table 1 lists the value of K_w at several temperatures.

Temperature (°C)	K_w
0	0.114×10^{-14}
10	0.292×10^{-14}
20	0.681×10^{-14}
25	1.01×10^{-14}
30	1.47×10^{-14}
40	2.92×10^{-14}
50	5.47×10^{-14}
60	9.61×10^{-14}

Table 1 Equilibrium constants for water at different temperatures

Water has a leveling effect on acids. Any acid stronger than H_3O^+ appears to have the same behavior in aqueous solution. For example, 1 M HCl and 1 M HClO$_4$ have the same concentration of H_3O^+ even though in anhydrous acetic acid, HClO$_4$ is a stronger acid.

122. What is the pH of H_2O at 40°C?

    A.   7.5
    B.   7.0
    C.   6.7
    D.   6.0

123. At 10°C, the concentration of OH^- in 1 M HCl is approximately:

    A. $1 \times 10^{-7} M$
    B. $1 \times 10^{-14} M$
    C. $3 \times 10^{-15} M$
    D. $1 \times 10^{-15} M$

124. As temperature increases, the pH of pure water:

    A.   increases.
    B.   decreases.
    C.   becomes less than the pOH.
    D.   becomes greater than the pOH.

Copyright © 2005 Examkrackers, Inc.

GO ON TO THE NEXT PAGE.

125. What is the conjugate base of H_2SO_4?

    A. H_2O
    B. OH^-
    C. HSO_4^-
    D. SO_4^{2-}

126. Why can the relative strength of HCl and $HClO_4$ be determined in acetic acid but not in water?

    A.   because acetic acid is a weaker acid than H_3O^+
    B.   because acetic acid is a stronger acid than H_3O^+
    C.   because acetic acid is a weaker Bronsted-Lowry base than H_2O
    D.   because acetic acid is a stronger Bronsted-Lowry base than H_2O

127. The equation for K_w at 50°C is:

    A. $[OH^-][H_3O^+]$

    B. $\dfrac{[OH^-][H_3O^+]}{[H_2O]^2}$

    C. $\dfrac{[OH^-][H_3O^+]}{[H_2O]}$

    D. $[H_3O^+]$

Passage III (Questions 128-134)

Acid rain results when $SO_3(g)$, produced by the industrial burning of fuel, dissolves in the moist atmosphere.

$$SO_3(g) + H_2O(l) \rightarrow H_2SO_4(aq)$$

The rain formed from the condensation of this acidic water is an environmental hazard destroying trees and killing the fish in some lakes. (The pH of the water varies depending upon the level of pollution in the area. The pK_a values are about −2 for H_2SO_4 and 1.92 for HSO_4^-.)

Another pollutant which dissolves in water vapor and reacts to form acid rain is $SO_2(g)$. This gas forms $H_2SO_3(aq)$ which can be oxidized to H_2SO_4. (The pK_a values are 1.81 for H_2SO_3 and 6.91 for HSO_3^-.)

The table below gives the color changes of many acid base indicators used to test the pH of water.

Indicator	Color Change	pH of color change
Malachite green	yellow to green	0.2 – 1.8
Thymol blue	red to yellow	1.2 – 2.8
Methyl orange	red to yellow	3.2 – 4.4
Methyl red	red to yellow	4.8 – 6.0
Phenolphthalein	clear to red	8.2 – 10.0
Alizarin yellow	yellow to red	10.1 – 12.0

Table 1

128. A sample of rainwater tested with methyl orange results in a yellow color, and the addition of methyl red to a fresh sample of the same water results in a red color. What is the pH of the sample?

    A.   between 1.2 and 1.8
    B.   between 3.2 and 4.4
    C.   between 4.4 and 4.8
    D.   between 4.8 and 6.0

Copyright © 2005 Examkrackers, Inc.

GO ON TO THE NEXT PAGE.

129. If there is no oxidant present in the air and the same number of moles of SO_2 and SO_3 are dissolved, which gas would produce acid rain with a lower pH?

A. SO_2 because H_2SO_3 has a higher pK_a than H_2SO_4.
B. SO_2 because HSO_3^- has a higher pK_a than HSO_4^-.
C. SO_3 because H_2SO_4 has a lower pK_a than H_2SO_3.
D. SO_3 because HSO_4^- has a lower pK_a than HSO_3^-.

130. What is the pK_b for HSO_3^-?

A. 0
B. 6.91
C. 7.09
D. 12.19

131. H_2SO_4 is a stronger acid than:

I. H_2O
II. H_3O^+
III. H_2SO_3

A. III only
B. I and II only
C. I and III only
D. I, II, and III

132. What is the oxidation state of sulfur in H_2SO_4 and H_2SO_3 respectively?

A. +6, +4
B. +4, +6
C. –6, –4
D. –4, –6

133. What is the pH of a 5.0×10^{-8} M aqueous solution of H_2SO_4 at room temperature?

A. 8.3
B. 7.3
C. 6.8
D. 6.0

134. A sample of rainwater polluted with SO_3 is titrated with NaOH. Which of the following most resembles the shape of titration curve.

A.

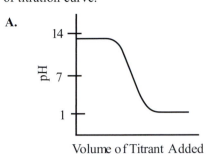

B.

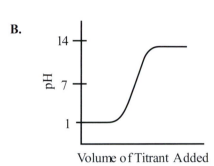

C.

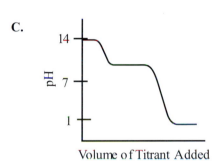

D.

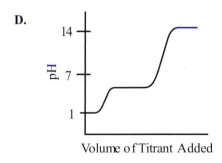

Questions 135 through 138 are **NOT** based on a descriptive passage.

135. Which of the following is the strongest base?

    A. ClO^-
    B. ClO_2^-
    C. ClO_3^-
    D. ClO_4^-

136. A weak acid is titrated with a strong base. When the concentration of the conjugate base is equal to the concentration of the acid, the titration is at the:

    A. stoichiometric point.
    B. equivalence point.
    C. half equivalence point.
    D. end point.

137. A buffer solution is created using acetic acid and its conjugate base. If the ratio of acetic acid to its conjugate base is 10 to 1, what is the approximate pH of the solution? (The K_a of acetic acid is 1.8×10^{-5})

    A. 3.7
    B. 4.7
    C. 5.7
    D. 7.0

138. NH_3 has a K_b of 1.8×10^{-5}. Which of the following has a K_a of 5.6×10^{-10}?

    A. NH_3
    B. NH_4^+
    C. NH_2^-
    D. H^+

STOP. IF YOU FINISH BEFORE TIME IS CALLED, CHECK YOUR WORK. YOU MAY GO BACK TO ANY QUESTION IN THIS TEST BOOKLET.

Copyright © 2005 Examkrackers, Inc.

STOP.

30-MINUTE
IN-CLASS EXAM
FOR LECTURE 7

When Fe^{2+} is titrated with dichromate $(Cr_2O_7^{2-})$ according to Reaction 1, the titration curve similar to the one shown in Figure 1 results. The curve was generated by measuring the potential difference between the reaction solution and a standard solution after each addition of a known volume and concentration of dichromate. The potential is measured using a voltmeter attached to an *orp* electrode.

$$6Fe^{2+} + Cr_2O_7^{2-} + 14H^+ \rightleftharpoons 2Cr^{3+} + 7H_2O + 6Fe^{3+}$$

$$E° = 1.33 \text{ V}$$

Reaction 1

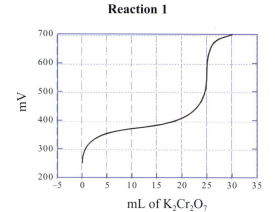

Figure 1. Titration Curve for Reaction 1

Chromium (III) is green in color, and dichromate solution is orange. The orange is not intense enough to be used as an indicator. Instead, the endpoint of the titration can be indicated by the redox indicator diphenylamine sulfonic acid (DAS), which changes from colorless to violet when oxidized. The color change observed during the titration is from green to violet. After all the Fe^{2+} ions have been oxidized, the dichromate ion oxidizes DAS. However, the formal potential of the Fe^{2+} solution must be lowered in order to match the endpoint with the equivalence point of the titration. This is accomplished by the addition of H_2SO_4 and H_3PO_4 immediately before titration.

139. Which of the following is true concerning Reaction 1?

    A. Cr is oxidized and $Cr_2O_7^{2-}$ is the oxidizing agent.

    B. Cr is reduced and $Cr_2O_7^{2-}$ is the reducing agent.

    C. Cr is reduced and $Cr_2O_7^{2-}$ is the oxidizing agent.

    D. Cr is oxidized and $Cr_2O_7^{2-}$ is the reducing agent.

140. What is the oxidation state of Cr in $Cr_2O_7^{2-}$?

    A. +12

    B. +7

    C. +6

    D. +3

141. What is the volume of dichromate added to the titration at the equivalence point?

    A. 13 mL

    B. 15 mL

    C. 25 mL

    D. 30 mL

142. Which of the following expressions gives the concentration of Fe^{2+} in the unknown solution in terms of the volume of dichromate added $V_{Cr_2O_7^{2-}}$, the molarity of dichromate $M_{Cr_2O_7^{2-}}$, and the original volume of Fe^{2+} solution V_{Fe}?

    A. $\dfrac{\left(V_{Cr_2O_7^{2-}}\right)\left(M_{Cr_2O_7^{2-}}\right)}{V_{Fe}}$

    B. $\dfrac{\left(6V_{Cr_2O_7^{2-}}\right)\left(M_{Cr_2O_7^{2-}}\right)}{V_{Fe}}$

    C. $\dfrac{\left(V_{Cr_2O_7^{2-}}\right)\left(M_{Cr_2O_7^{2-}}\right)}{6V_{Fe}}$

    D. $\dfrac{\left(2V_{Cr_2O_7^{2-}}\right)\left(M_{Cr_2O_7^{2-}}\right)}{V_{Fe}}$

143. If the formal potential of the solution is not lowered, which of the following will be the result of the titration when DAS is used as the indicator?

    A. The solution will turn violet before the equivalence point is reached.

    B. The solution will turn violet after the equivalence point is reached.

    C. Dichromate ion will not be able to oxidize DAS.

    D. Dichromate ion will reduce DAS to its colorless form.

144. Which of the following statements is true at the equivalence point of the titration in the passage?

    A. Each iron ion has lost one electron and each chromium ion has gained three electrons.

    B. Each iron ion has lost one electron and each chromium ion has gained six electrons.

    C. Each iron ion has gained one electron and each chromium ion has lost three electrons.

    D. Each iron ion has gained one electron and each chromium ion has lost six electrons.

Copyright © 2005 Examkrackers, Inc.

GO ON TO THE NEXT PAGE.

Passage II (Questions 145-151)

Rechargeable batteries have become an essential part of our environmentally conscientious society. The nickel-cadmium cell battery is a rechargeable battery used in small electronic devices. The half reactions that take place in the nickel-cadmium battery during discharge are:

$$Cd(OH)_2(s) + 2e^- \rightarrow Cd(s) + 2OH^-$$
$$E° = -0.4 \text{ V}$$

Half Reaction 1

$$2NiO_2(s) + H_2O + 2e^- \rightarrow 2Ni(OH)_2(s) + 2OH^-$$
$$E° = 0.5 \text{ V}$$

Half Reaction 2

Other types of rechargeable batteries currently being developed are those using sodium or lithium metal as the anode and sulfur as the cathode. These batteries must operate at high temperatures because the metals must be in the liquid state, but they provide a high energy density, which means the batteries will be very light weight.

145. The reaction taking place at the anode when the nickel-cadmium batteries are discharging is:

   A. $Cd(s) + 2OH^- \rightarrow Cd(OH)_2(s) + 2e^-$
   B. $2NiO_2(s) + H_2O + 2e^- \rightarrow 2Ni(OH)_2(s) + 2OH^-$
   C. $Cd(OH)_2(s) + 2e^- \rightarrow Cd(s) + 2OH^-$
   D. $2Ni(OH)_2(s) + 2OH^- \rightarrow 2NiO_2(s) + H_2O + 2e^-$

146. When the nickel-cadmium battery is recharging, what is the reaction at the anode?

   A. $Cd(s) + 2OH^- \rightarrow Cd(OH)_2(s) + 2e^-$
   B. $2NiO_2(s) + H_2O + 2e^- \rightarrow 2Ni(OH)_2(s) + 2OH^-$
   C. $Cd(OH)_2(s) + 2e^- \rightarrow Cd(s) + 2OH^-$
   D. $2Ni(OH)_2(s) + 2OH^- \rightarrow 2NiO_2(s) + H_2O + 2e^-$

147. What is the oxidizing agent in the nickel cadmium battery during discharge?

   A.   Cd
   B. $Cd(OH)_2$
   C. NiO_2
   D. $2Ni(OH)_2$

148. Which of the following is true concerning the nickel-cadmium battery when it is recharging?

   A.   The cell is a nonspontaneous electrolytic cell.
   B.   The cell is a nonspontaneous galvanic cell.
   C.   The cell is a spontaneous electrolytic cell.
   D.   The cell is a spontaneous galvanic cell.

149. In order to recharge the nickel-cadmium battery back to standard conditions, what is the minimum voltage that must be applied across its electrodes?

   A.   0.1 V
   B.   0.2 V
   C.   0.9 V
   D.   1.8 V

150. In a sodium-sulfur battery, what is the half reaction for sodium in the spontaneous direction?

   A. $Na^+ + e^- \rightarrow Na$
   B. $Na \rightarrow Na^+ + e^-$
   C. $Na \rightarrow Na^{2+} + 2e^-$
   D. $Na^+ + OH^- \rightarrow NaOH$

151. The nickel-cadmium battery is used to power a light bulb. The current in the light bulb flows:

   A.   in the same direction as the flow of electrons, from the side with Half Reaction 1 to the side with Half Reaction 2.
   B.   in the same direction as the flow of electrons, from the side with Half Reaction 2 to the side with Half Reaction 1.
   C.   in the opposite direction to the flow of electrons, from the side with Half Reaction 1 to the side with Half Reaction 2.
   D.   in the opposite direction to the flow of electrons, from the side with Half Reaction 2 to the side with Half Reaction 1.

Copyright © 2005 Examkrackers, Inc.

GO ON TO THE NEXT PAGE.

A pH meter is a concentration cell which measures the potential difference between a reference solution and a test solution and reports the difference in terms of pH. In a simplified version of a pH meter the half reactions are:

$$H_2 + 2H_2O \rightarrow 2H_3O^+ + 2e^-$$
$$2H_3O^+ + 2e^- \rightarrow H_2 + 2H_2O$$

The potential difference between the two solutions is derived from the Nernst equation as follows:

$$E = -\frac{0.0592}{2} \log \left(\frac{[H_3O^+]_{\text{test solution}}}{[H_3O^+]_{\text{reference solution}}} \right)^2$$

where E is given in volts. This equation can be rewritten in terms of the pH of the solutions as follows:

$$E = 0.059(pH_{\text{test}} - pH_{\text{reference}})$$

Because it is inconvenient to bubble H_2 gas through a solution, a more sophisticated pH meter is used in standard laboratory practice. Dilute hydrochloric acid is used as the reference solution. The test solution is in contact with a thin glass membrane in which a silver wire coated with silver chloride is imbedded. This glass membrane is dipped into the test solution and the potential difference between the solutions is measured and interpreted by a computer, which displays the pH of the test solution. The same equation holds for both pH meters.

152. What is the reaction quotient (*Q*) in the Nernst equation for the simple pH meter?

A. $\dfrac{[H_3O^+]^2_{\text{test solution}}}{[H_2]}$

B. $\dfrac{[H_2]}{[H_3O^+]^2_{\text{test solution}}}$

C. $\dfrac{[H_3O^+]^2_{\text{test solution}}[H_2]_{\text{reference solution}}}{[H_3O^+]^2_{\text{reference solution}}[H_2]_{\text{test solution}}}$

D. $\dfrac{[H_3O^+]^2_{\text{test solution}}}{[H_3O^+]^2_{\text{reference solution}}}$

153. What would be the approximate potential difference measured by a pH meter if the test solution had a pH of 2 and the reference solution had a pH of 4?

A. −118 mV
B. −59 mV
C. 59 mV
D. 118 mV

154. The potential difference measured by a pH meter is directly proportional to:

A. the difference in the hydrogen ion concentrations of the test and reference solution.
B. the difference in the pH of the test and reference solution.
C. the pH of the test solution.
D. the hydrogen ion concentration of the test solution.

155. If the reference solution of a pH meter were 1 *M* HCl, and the potential difference measured by the meter were 59 mV, what would be the pH of the test solution?

A. 0
B. 1
C. 2
D. 8

156. How would the potential difference registered by a pH meter change for a given test solution if the hydrogen ion concentration of the reference solution were increased by a factor of 10?

A. The potential difference would increase by 59 mV.
B. The potential difference would decrease by 59 mV.
C. The potential difference would increase by a factor of 10.
D. The potential difference would decrease by a factor of 10.

Copyright © 2005 Examkrackers, Inc.

GO ON TO THE NEXT PAGE.

157. A galvanic cell is prepared by connecting two half cells with a salt bridge and a wire. One cell has a Cu electrode and 1 M $CuSO_4$, and the other has a Cu electrode and 2 M $CuSO_4$. Which direction will the current flow through the wire?

   A.   toward the 1M $CuSO_4$ solution.
   B.   toward the 2M $CuSO_4$ solution.
   C.   current will not flow because the half reactions are the same for both sides.
   D.   current will not flow because both half cells have Cu electrodes.

158. Which of the following is true for an acid-base concentration cell such as the one used by the pH meter?

   A.   Current always flows toward the more acidic solution.
   B.   Current always flows toward the more basic solution.
   C.   Current always flows toward the more neutral solution.
   D.   Current always flows away from the more neutral solution.

Questions 159 through 161 are **NOT** based on a descriptive passage.

---

159. Consider the reduction potential:

$$Zn^{2+} + 2e^- \rightarrow Zn(s) \qquad E° = -0.76 \text{ V}.$$

When solid Zinc is added to aqueous HCl, under standard conditions, does a reaction take place?

   A.   No, because the oxidation potential for Cl^- is positive.
   B.   No, because the reduction potential for Cl^- is negative.
   C.   Yes, because the reduction potential for H^+ is positive.
   D.   Yes, because the reduction potential for H^+ is zero.

160. Chemicals are mixed in a redox reaction and allowed to come to equilibrium. Which of the following must be true concerning the solution at equilibrium?

   A. $K = 1$
   B. $\Delta G° = 0$
   C. $E = 0$
   D. $\Delta G° = \Delta G$

161. At 298 K all reactants and products in a certain oxidation-reduction reaction are in aqueous phase at initial concentrations of 1 M. If the total potential for the reaction is $E = 20$ mV, which of the following must be true?

   A. $K = 1$
   B. $E°_{298} = 20$ mV
   C. ΔG is positive
   D. $K < 1$

STOP. IF YOU FINISH BEFORE TIME IS CALLED, CHECK YOUR WORK. YOU MAY GO BACK TO ANY QUESTION IN THIS TEST BOOKLET.

Copyright © 2005 Examkrackers, Inc.

STOP.

ANSWERS & EXPLANATIONS

FOR

30-MINUTE

IN-CLASS EXAMS

ANSWERS FOR THE 30-MINUTE IN-CLASS EXAMS

Lecture 1	Lecture 2	Lecture 3	Lecture 4	Lecture 5	Lecture 6	Lecture 7
1. D	24. B	47. A	70. C	93. C	116. A	139. C
2. B	25. A	48. C	71. B	94. C	117. A	140. C
3. A	26. C	49. B	72. B	95. C	118. B	141. C
4. B	27. C	50. C	73. A	96. B	119. D	142. B
5. C	28. B	51. A	74. C	97. D	120. D	143. A
6. D	29. C	52. D	75. D	98. B	121. A	144. A
7. B	30. C	53. C	76. A	99. D	122. C	145. A
8. C	31. A	54. C	77. C	100. B	123. C	146. D
9. D	32. A	55. D	78. B	101. A	124. B	147. C
10. C	33. A	56. D	79. B	102. B	125. C	148. A
11. D	34. D	57. C	80. B	103. A	126. C	149. C
12. C	35. D	58. A	81. D	104. B	127. A	150. B
13. C	36. C	59. B	82. C	105. D	128. C	151. D
14. A	37. B	60. C	83. D	106. D	129. C	152. D
15. A	38. A	61. D	84. C	107. A	130. D	153. A
16. B	39. A	62. A	85. A	108. C	131. D	154. B
17. B	40. D	63. A	86. C	109. A	132. A	155. B
18. D	41. B	64. B	87. D	110. D	133. C	156. A
19. B	42. D	65. A	88. A	111. B	134. D	157. A
20. A	43. C	66. B	89. A	112. A	135. A	158. B
21. D	44. B	67. C	90. C	113. C	136. C	159. D
22. B	45. A	68. C	91. B	114. A	137. A	160. C
23. D	46. C	69. D	92. B	115. A	138. B	161. B

PHYSICAL SCIENCES

Raw Score	Estimated Scaled Score
23	15
22	14
21	13
19–20	12
18	11
16–17	10
15	9
13–14	8
12	7
10–11	6
9	5
7–8	4

Copyright © 2005 Examkrackers, Inc.

EXPLANATIONS TO IN-CLASS EXAM FOR LECTURE 1

Passage I

1. **D is correct.** If you get a boiling point question on the MCAT, look for hydrogen bonding. It increases the strength of intermolecular attractions. Stronger intermolecular attractions leads to higher boiling point.

2. **B is correct.** You should recognize this compound as ionic because alkaline earth metals like to form ionic compounds with halogens.

3. **A is correct.** In order to explain an increase in boiling point, we have to look for a reason that intermolecular bond strength would increase. The intermolecular bonds in noble gases are totally due to van der Waals forces. If the atoms are more polarizable, instantaneous dipoles can have greater strength. Larger atoms are more polarizable because the electrons can get farther from the nucleus and create a larger dipole moment.

4. **B is correct.** This is a periodic trend. Radius increases going down and to the left on the periodic table.

5. **C is correct.** Crystallization depends upon molecular symmetry as well as intermolecular bonding. Boiling point is strongly dependent upon intermolecular bond strength.

6. **D is correct.** Methane is nonpolar, so its only intermolecular bonding is through van der Waals forces.

7. **B is correct.** All intermolecular bonding is via electrostatic forces. The dipoles in van der Waals forces are temporal whereas dipole-dipole interactions may be due to permanent dipoles.

Passage II

8. **C is correct.** 'As' is just to the left of 'Se' on the periodic table. Therefore, its radius should be slightly larger than Se.

9. **D is correct.** Elements in the same family tend to be chemically similar. Hydrogen is an exception.

10. **C is correct.** Atomic radius is a periodic trend increasing down and to the left.

11. **D is correct.** Only D is a true statement. A is knowledge that would not be required by the MCAT.

12. **C is correct.** Electron affinity is a periodic trend increasing (becoming more exothermic) to the right and up.

13. **C is correct.** The answer we are looking for must explain shielding. With each new period, a new shell is added which shields the new electrons from the greater nuclear charge.

14. **A is correct.** If you substitute H for X in the equation for Δ in the passage, you can only arrive at zero.

15. **A is correct.** C and O are close together in electronegativity and will form a covalent bond.

Passage III

16. **B is correct.** Only water is caught in chamber 1. The change in mass of chamber 1, 0.9 grams, is all water. 0.9 grams of water divided by 18 g/mol gives 0.05 mole of water. All the hydrogen came from the sample, and all the oxygen came from the excess oxygen. For every mole of water, there are 2 moles of hydrogens, so there is $0.05 \times 2 = 0.1$ mole of hydrogen in the sample. Doing the same with the carbon dioxide caught in chamber 2 we have: $4.4/44.2 = 0.1$ of CO_2, or 0.1 mole of carbon from the sample. This is a 1:1 ratio. The empirical formula is CH.

17. **B is correct.** The molarity of O_2 is equal to the molarity of the welding gas or any other ideal gas at the same temperature and pressure. Density divided by molecular weight is molarity. Therefore, we can set the ratios of density to molecular weight for oxygen and the welding gas equal to each other. We get: $1.3/32 = 1.1/M.W$.

18. **D is correct.** CH_2O has a molecular weight of 30 g/mol. Thus, we must multiply this by 4 to get 120. So, for the molecular formula we need four times as many atoms of each element from the empirical formula.

19. **B is correct.** O_2 is the limiting reagent. Only 0.5 mole of propane can react, producing 2 moles of water.

20. **A is correct.** The passage says that $CaCl_2$ absorbs water. Thus if chamber 2 were in front of chamber 1, it would weigh more because it would absorb both water and carbon dioxide. The amount of carbon dioxide is calculated from the weight of chamber 2, so the calculated value would be too high.

Copyright © 2005 Examkrackers, Inc.

21. **D is correct.** All of the welding gas must be reacted because the mass of the original sample is divided by the moles of carbon and hydrogen to find the molecular weight. If all the gas were not reacted, the calculated molecular weight would be too large. Adding excess oxygen ensures that all of the welding gas reacts.

Stand Alones

22. **B is correct.** Chlorine takes on an additional electron to become an ion.

23. **D is correct.** This is the Heisenberg uncertainty principle.

EXPLANATIONS TO IN-CLASS EXAM FOR LECTURE 2

Passage I

24. **B is correct.** The definition of $Z = PV/(nRT)$ is always 1 for an ideal gas.

25. **A is correct.** If a and b are both zero, the van der Waals equation becomes $PV = nRT$, the ideal gas law.

26. **C is correct.** You can figure this out from the passage, but it's a lot easier to fall back on your previous knowledge: gases behave most ideally at high temperature and low pressures.

27. **C is correct.** Volume is inversely proportional to pressure. A: $K.E. = 3/2 \, kT$. B: $PV = nRT$, D: This is one of the assumptions underlying the derivation of the ideal gas law.

28. **B is correct.** Condensation is due to intermolecular attractions, which are neglected for ideal gases. For D, start with $K.E. = 3/2 \, kT$. Then $1/2 \, mv^2 = 3/2 \, kT$, so v is proportional to the square root of T.

29. **C is correct.** Equations involving products or ratios of temperature are meaningless if the zero of the temperature scale is not absolute zero. A and B are true statements, but they don't explain why absolute temperature must be used.

Passage II

30. **C is correct.** A catalyst acts to lower the activation energy of a reaction, so the catalyzed reactioin will have a lower activation energy than the uncatalyzed reaction.

31. **A is correct.** A catalyst is neither produced nor consumed in a reaction and does not appear in the net reaction. The net rection for the mechanism shown is:

$$O_3 + O \rightarrow 2O_2$$

The catalyst, Cl, does not appear. ClO aslo does not appear, but it is produced and consume in the recaction making it an intermediate.

32. **A is correct.** See the Arrhenius equation:

$$k = zpe^{-Ea/RT}$$

You should also memorize the fact that temperature always increases the rate of a reaction. Even in the case of biologically catalyzed reactions, heat increases the reaction rate until the enzyme is denatured. Once the enzyme is denatured, although the reaction rate slows, the reaction takes a new pathway, and is no longer the same reaction.

33. **A is correct.** If a catalyst only affected the rate in one direction, the equilibrium would be affected. A catalyst doesn't change the equilibrium. This can also be seen from a reaction profile diagram as shown in question 37.

34. **D is correct.** The catalyst is not necessarily the only factor influencing pH.

Copyright © 2005 Examkrackers, Inc.

35.   **D is correct.** Choice I is seen from the standard form of the rate law: rate = k[A][B]. For choice II, imagine the saturation kinetics exhibited by enzyme catalysts:

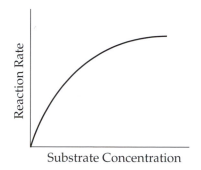

This should make it clear that the ratio of concentrations of the catalyst and the substrates affect the rate of a reaction. This ratio can be changed by changing the concentration of the catalyst. Thus the concentration of a catalyst can affect the rate of a reaction. For choice III, a heterogeneous catalyst is one that is not in the same phase as the reactants. Increasing the surface area of a heterogeneous catalyst is like increasing the concentration. The reaction is affected for the same reasons as in choice II. The reason that a heterogeneous catalyst is typically in the form of metal shavings as opposed to a solid metal bar is to increase surface area. Choice IV you should know from the Arrhenius equation: $k = zpe^{-Ea/RT}$.

36.   **C is correct.** The MCAT sometimes uses the phrase "van der Waals" forces as a synonym for London Dispersion Forces. A more modern meaning is as a synonym for intermolecular forces. In either case, this is a correct answer. Hydrogen bonding requires a hydrogen atom bonded to a nitrogen, fluorine, or oxygen. D is from an episode of Star Trek.

37.   **B is correct.** Only the activation energy is changed by a catalyst. The initial and final states are not affected!

Passage III

In this experiment, Reaction 2 uses up I_3^- as it is formed. When all the $S_2O_3^{2-}$ is used up in Reaction 2, the I_3^- reacts with the starch to turn black. The black color signals the experimenter that all the $S_2O_3^{2-}$ is used up. The experimenter now knows that half as much I_3^- was used up in the same time, and can calculate the rate for Reaction 1. This depends upon Reaction 2 being the fastest reaction.

38.   **A is correct.** If we look at Reactions 1 and 2 as two steps of a single reaction, we know that the rate of the slow step is equal to the rate of the overall reaction. Equation 1 measures the time necessary for a specific number of moles of I_3^- to be used by Reaction 2. (Notice that the rate of change of $\frac{1}{2}[S_2O_3^{2-}]$ will be equal to the rate of change of $[I_3^-]$) If Reaction 2 were not the fast step, then Equation 1 would not measure the rate of Reaction 1 accurately. Since Reaction 2 is the fast step, the time t required to use up $\frac{1}{2}[S_2O_3^{2-}]$ is equal to the time needed to produce $[I_3^-]$. The $[I_3^-]$ concentration produced divided by the time necessary to produce it is the rate of Reaction 1. Equation 1 is not derivable from the rate laws of Reactions 1 and 2.

39.   **A is correct.** A temperature decrease reduces rate and makes the reaction take longer.

40.   **D is correct.** The rate law is found by comparing the rate change from one trial to the next when the concentration of only one reaction is changed. Comparing trials 1 and 2, when the concentration of I⁻ is reduced by a factor of two, the rate is also reduced by a factor of two. This indicates a first order reaction with respect to I⁻. D is the only possible answer.

41.   **B is correct.** The exponents in the rate law indicate the order of the reaction with respect to each concentration.

42.   **D is correct.** The starch is used to measure the rate of Reaction 1, and does not affect the rate. Although C is true, it does not answer the question as well as D.

43.   **C is correct.** Equation 1 gives the rate of Reaction 1. $S_2O_3^{2-}$ is not part of Reaction 1 and its concentration does not change the rate. If rate doesn't change, then, according to Equation 1, t must increase with $S_2O_3^{2-}$.

44.   **B is correct.** A catalyst increases the rate of a reaction.

Copyright © 2005 Examkrackers, Inc.

Stand Alones

45. **A is correct.** In a reaction at equilibrium, the rate of change in the concentrations of both products and reactants is zero. This does not mean that the concentrations of reactants and products are equal, nor that the rate constants are equal.

46. **C is correct.** Some of both gases will effuse from side 1 to side 2. This means that the partial pressures of both gases will decrease. (Remember, partial pressure is the pressure of the gas as if it were alone in the container. Thus if we reduce the number of moles of a gas at constant volume and temperature, we reduce its partial pressure.) Since hydrogen will diffuse more rapidly than oxygen, the mole fraction of oxygen will increase.

EXPLANATIONS TO IN-CLASS EXAM FOR LECTURE 3

Passage I

47. **A is correct.** Nickel is an element and is a solid in its natural state at 298 K. Thus, the enthalpy of formation of solid nickel at 298 K is zero.

48. **C is correct.** Chemist A chooses the direction of the reaction based upon chemical stability, and then says that the direction will change at higher temperatures. This is tantamount to saying that the stability will switch at higher temperatures, which, by the way, is also correct. D is, of course, a false statement. The entropy shown for Reaction 1 is the entropy of the reaction. In other words, it is the entropy of the system, and not the entropy of the universe. Chemist A's statement is correct, and does not contradict the second law of thermodynamics. A and B are contradicted because Chemist A says the direction is temperature dependent.

49. **B is correct.** Use Le Chatelier's principle. Read the first sentence of the passage carefully, and notice that to purify nickel, the reaction must move to the left. There are four gas molecules on the left side of the reaction and only one on the right. Pressure pushes the reaction to the right. The reaction is exothermic when moving to the right, so high temperature pushes the reaction to the left.

50. **C is correct.** The reaction is the system, and everything outside the reaction makes up the surroundings. The entropy change given in the passage refers to the system not the universe. The second law of thermodynamics says that a reaction is spontaneous when the entropy of the universe is positive. The entropy of the system may be positive or negative. A and B are false statements. D is a false statement as well. The reaction runs until the entropy of the universe is maximized.

51. **A is correct.** Use $\Delta G = \Delta H - T\Delta S$. Don't forget to convert J/K to kJ/K.

52. **D is correct.** Spontaneity is dictated by Gibbs energy. 1 atmos. is standard state for a gas, so $\Delta G = \Delta G°$. When Gibbs energy is negative, a reaction is spontaneous. If enthalpy change is negative and entropy change is positive, then Gibbs energy change must be negative. You can use $\Delta G° = \Delta H° - T\Delta S°$. Check this as follows: If the partial pressures are 1, then the reaction quotient Q is 1, and the log of the reaction quotient is zero. From the equation $\Delta G = \Delta G° + RT\ln Q$ we see that $\Delta G = \Delta G°$. The reaction is spontaneous.

Passage II

Note: A heat engine obeys the first law of thermodynamics. It must expel the same amount of energy as it takes in.

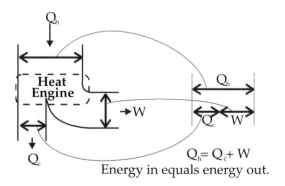

Energy in equals energy out.

Copyright © 2005 Examkrackers, Inc.

Lecture Question Expls.

53. **C is correct.** If $Q_h' = Q_h$ and $Q_c' = Q_c$ then $W' = W$. Thus the efficiencies of the engines must be equal. Since only a Carnot engine can be as efficient as another Carnot engine, Engine 1 must be a Carnot engine.

54. **C is correct.** If the all the work done by Engine 1 is done on Engine 2, the net work is zero. Since Engine 1 is not a Carnot engine, the entire process is not reversible. The result of any nonreversible process where no work is done must be that heat energy is transferred from the hot reservoir to the cold reservoir. Engine 1 has a lower e than Engine 2 and thus requires more heat energy to create as much work. According to conservation of energy, this extra heat energy input must be matched by extra heat energy output.

55. **D is correct.** Engine 2 is a Carnot engine, and, as the passage states, it has the highest possible efficiency of any engine working between the existing heat reservoirs. Thus only a change in the heat reservoirs will increase its efficiency. **The answer must therefore be C or D.** For greatest efficiency we want to remove the most heat energy possible from the hot reservoir and expel the least amount possible to the cold reservoir thus getting the most work with the least amount of wasted energy. Removing heat energy from the hot reservoir decreases its entropy, while adding heat energy to the cold reservoir increases its entropy. As the temperature of the hot reservoir increases, removing heat energy has less effect on the change in entropy, so more heat energy can be removed. The reverse is true for the cold reservoir. Since, in a Carnot engine, the change in entropy must be zero, the extra heat energy removed from the hot reservoir must be added to work. The engine becomes more efficient. Thus maximizing the temperature difference increases efficiency. This can be derived from the equation in the passage (the long method) as follows. Considering magnitudes only we have:

$$\frac{Q_h}{T_h} = \frac{Q_c}{T_c} \qquad \frac{Q_c}{Q_h} = \frac{T_c}{T_h}$$

$$e = \frac{W}{Q_h} \qquad e = \frac{(Q_h - Q_c)}{Q_h} \qquad e = 1 - \frac{Q_c}{Q_h}$$

substituting $\dfrac{T_c}{T_h}$ for $\dfrac{Q_c}{Q_h}$ we have:

$$e = 1 - \frac{T_c}{T_h}.$$

56. **D is correct.** From the derivation for efficiency in the previous explanation, if T_c is zero, $e = 1$. However, it is probably easier to eliminate the other answer choices instead. Choice A is wrong because by the equation for efficiency given in the passage, $e = W/Q_h$, a large W by itself won't give $e = 1$. Choice B is wrong because as per the passage all Carnot engines are reversible, but all Carnot engines are not 100% efficient. Choice C is wrong because from the entropy formula, if T_c and T_h were at the same temperature, Q_h and Q_c would also have to be at the same temperature, which gives $W = Q_h - Q_c = 0$, and an efficiency of zero. 100% efficiency is an impossibility.

57. **C is correct.** The exhaust is wasted energy. $Q_h = W + Q_c$. $P = Q_h/t = W/t + Q_c/t = (mgh)/20\,s + 1000\,J/s = 4000/20 + 1000 = 1200\,J$.

58. **A is correct.** $PV = nRT = (m/M.W.)RT$. $P = 1000 \times 8.314 \times 400/4 = 8.314 \times 10^5$ Pa. By the way, if the gas did not behave ideally, the real pressure would be lower. There is no answer lower than A, and the gas does behave very nearly ideally because it is at high temperature.

Passage III

59. **B is correct.** The transition state corresponds to the top of the energy curve.

60. **C is correct.** The energy of activation is given by the vertical displacement from the reactants to the top of the energy curve.

61. **D is correct.** The smallest energy of activation is the most kinetically favored.

62. **A is correct.** The largest drop in energy is the most thermodynamically favored.

63. **A is correct.** A catalyst lowers the energy of activation but does not change the energy difference between the reactants and products.

Copyright © 2005 Examkrackers, Inc.

64.   **B is correct.** The change in energy is energy of products minus reactants.

65.   **A is correct.** The kinetically favored product is the one with a lower energy of activation. The difference in their equilibrium is due to conflicting thermodynamics and kinetics. At a low temperature (T_2), the thermodynamically favored product does not have enough energy to reach the activated complex, so no reaction occurs. The kinetically favored reaction does reach the activated state and a reaction can occur. At the high temperature (T_1) both reactions occur but the reverse of the thermodynamically favored occurs only with a relatively lower probability. Thus the thermodynamically favored reaction predominates. This is not always true but is a concept of which you must be aware.

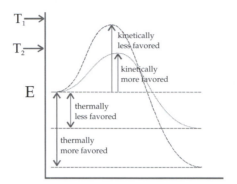

Stand Alones

66.   **B is correct.** Transfer by contact is conduction.

67.   **C is correct.** The second law of thermodynamics says that entropy of the universe increases for any process. By straightening up his room, the man increased the order in his room, and thus decreased its entropy. In order for the entropy of the universe to have increased, there must be a larger increase in entropy of the surroundings. Only C provides an explanation for this.

68.   **C is correct.** The entropy of the system is equal to change in entropy of the two reservoirs. $\Delta S = Q/T$ for each reservoir. The change in entropy of the first reservoir is negative because heat energy is leaving the system ($-1000/200 = -5$), and the change in entropy of the second reservoir is positive because heat energy is entering the system ($1000/100 = 10$). The sum of the two entropy changes is $+5$. You should have at least narrowed down the possibilities to C and D because the change in entropy for any isolated system must be positive for any process.

69.   **D is correct.** The temperature of Gas A remains constant because the question says so. Temperature is kinetic energy (due to random motion) per mole. Gas B does no work and doesn't exchange heat so its energy doesn't change; it has the same kinetic energy (due to random motion) per mole as when it began. Thus, its temperature doesn't change either.

        Enthalpy is $PV + U$. P and V are the same for both gases because they are at the same temp, volume and therefore pressure ($PV = nRT$). U doesn't change for Gas A because any energy removed is replaced to keep the temperature the same. U doesn't change for Gas B because no energy is exchanged with the surroundings for Gas B.

EXPLANATIONS TO IN-CLASS EXAM FOR LECTURE 4

Passage I

70.   **C is correct.** The first experiment shows that no nitrite was in the solution. Had there been nitrite, nitrogen bubbles would have formed as per the reaction, and then barium sulfate would have precipitated upon the addition of barium chloride. The second experiment demonstrates that nitrates exist. The water in the moistened litmus paper reacted with ammonia gas to make OH^- ions turning the paper blue. Ammonia gas resulted from the reaction of nitrate with Devarda's alloy.

Copyright © 2005 Examkrackers, Inc.

71. **B is correct.** Any sulfate ions that exist in solutin before sulfamic acid is added must be removed. They are removed by the addition of $BaCl_2$. Choice A is incorrect because $BaCl_2$ does not acidify the solution. Choice C is incorrect because $BaCl_2$ doesn't react with sulfamic acid, it reacts with sulfate. Choice D is incorrect because nitrite doesn't form a precipitate with $BaCl_2$, sulfate does.

72. **B is correct.** The precipitate would result when the sulfate ion from the reaction reacts with the barium ion to form barium sulfate. The bubbles would be created by the formation of nitrogen gas.

73. **A is correct.** Choice A produces gas bubbles which could be confused with nitrogen gas bubbles. The $BaCl_2$ actually prevents this from happening by forming a precipitate with carbonate before the sulfamic acid-nitrite reaction. Choice B is incorrect because the solution in Experiment 1 is acidic not basic, and because the precipitate would come out before the sulfamic acid-nitrite reaction. Choice C is incorrect because there is no ammonium in solution. Choice D is not carbonate ion, and although carbonic acid is formed by carbonate ion in aqueous solution, you should know that it breaks down to water and carbon dioxide, not carbon monoxide, hydrogen, and oxygen. A reaction you should know: $H_2CO_3 \rightarrow CO_2(g) + H_2O$

74. **C is correct.** Change in temperature can change the rate constant and the equilibrium constant but it can only increase the rate of the reaction.

75. **D is correct.** The litmus paper is turned blue when the basic ammonia gas from the reaction in the experiment reacts with the water in the paper.

Passage II

76. **A is correct.** This is definitional: products over reactants excluding pure liquids and solids.

77. **C is correct.** K_{sp} is a constant; solubility of $Ca(IO_3)_2$ is not. By Reaction 2, as acidity increases, IO_3^- ions are used up, pulling Reaction 1 to the right. Or just look at Table 1. If you want to see why you can't just use Le Chatelier's principle on Reaction 2, simply add the two equations together to get:

$$Ca(IO_3)_2 + H^+ \rightarrow Ca^{2+} + IO_3^- + HIO_3$$

Now when you add H^+ to this equation, it moves to the right, dissolving $Ca(IO_3)_2$.

78. **B is correct.** You should recognize the $y = mx + b$ form of the equation. This is the equation of a line. The b in this case is not zero, but is (K_{sp}).

79. **B is correct.** You must realize that the new solution is no longer saturated. These means that Reaction 1 is not in equilibrium. No precipitate exists. New Ca^{2+} ions do not immediately create precipitate because the solution is not saturated. There is no leftward shift because there is no equilibrium. Thus A, C and D are wrong. Iodic acid is in equilibrium however. Increasing H^+ ions shifts Reaction 2 to the right, creating more HIO_3. This is, of course, why Solution 1 is no longer saturated after adding the acid.

80. **B is correct.** The easiest way to find the K_{sp} is to plug the value of S for Solution 1 into the equation. Notice that the $[H^+]$ value in Solution 1 is for neutral water. It is so small that the second term in the solubility equation becomes negligible. The equation becomes

$$2S^{3/2} = K_{sp}^{1/2}.$$

Squaring both sides gives: $4S^3 = K_{sp}$

$$\Rightarrow 4 \times (5.4 \times 10^{-3})^3 = K_{sp}.$$

The only answer that is even close is choice B at 10^{-7}.

81. **D is correct.** The net equation is $Ca(IO_3)_2(s) + H^+(aq) \rightarrow Ca^{2+}(aq) + IO_3^-(aq) + HIO_3(aq)$. $CaOH_2$ in aqueous solution will produce both OH^- and Ca^{2+}. The OH^- will reduce the H^+ in solution. Since the solution is saturated (in equilibrium), Le Chatelier's principle predicts that both of these changes will shift the reaction to the left producing $Ca(IO_3)_2(s)$.

Copyright © 2005 Examkrackers, Inc.

82. **C is correct.** Reaction 2 will shift left via Le Chatelier's principle. The resulting increase in IO_3^- will shift Reaction 1 to the left due to the common ion effect, creating precipitate in the already saturated solution. The H^+ ion concentration in the formula for solubility is from hydrogen ions in solution before iodic acid is added. If a different acid were added (like HCl), the H^+ ion concentration would move Reaction 2 to the right and thus Reaction 1 to the right.

Passage III

A ligand is an ion or neutral molecule that can donate a pair of electrons to form a coordinate covalent bond with a metal ion. EDTA is a chelating agent (a ligand that makes more than one bond to a <u>single</u> metal ion). It wraps around its metal ion like a claw. Chele (χηλη) means claw in Greek.

83. **D is correct.** The passage states that EDTA reacts with other metal ions. If more EDTA is used up, the scientist will assume that it is being used up by calcium and magnesium ions. This will result in an overestimation of these ions.

84. **C is correct.** EDTA is donating a pair of electrons in a coordinate covalent bond, so it is a Lewis Base.

85. **A is correct.** This is LeChatelier's Principle. The chlorine ion will remove some of the Ca^{2+} pulling the reaction to the right.

86. **C is correct.** The passage states that there is a one-to-one stoichiometry between EDTA and its metal ion. (50 mL)(0.001 mol/L) = (25 mL)x. x = 0.002 mol/L

87. **D is correct.** D is the best explanation. Under high pH conditions, protons are stripped from the carboxylic acids allowing the ligand to bond to the cation. Indicators change color over a range so C is wrong. Calcium carbonate dissolves in an acid solution so B is wrong. A is irrelevant.

88. **A is correct.** You should know that Na^+ is very soluble, and H^+ does not form mineral deposits.

89. **A is correct.** The association constant from Table 1 is 5×10^8. The association reaction is:

$$Mg^{2+} + EDTA \rightarrow EDTA - Mg.$$

$$\text{The } K_{assoc} = 5 \times 10^8 = [EDTA - Mg]/[EDTA][Mg^{2+}]$$

Since half the magnesium is bound, [EDTA-Mg] is 9 ppm, which is 5×10^{-4}. The remaining half of $[Mg^{2+}]$ is 9 ppm, which is also 5×10^{-4}. Plugging these into the equilibrium expression leaves the remaining concentration [EDTA] = $1/(5 \times 10^8)$ or 2×10^{-9}.

Stand Alones

90. **C is correct.** Water boils at 100°C and atmospheric pressure, 760 torr. Boiling point is where vapor pressure meets atmospheric pressure. Thus water vapor pressure must be below 760 at 95°C. But it must also rise with increasing temperature, so it must be above 23.8 torr.

91. **B is correct.** No calculations are required since the vapor pressure would be somewhere between the vapor pressures of the pure liquids. The solution follows Raoult's law.

Copyright © 2005 Examkrackers, Inc.

92. **B is correct.** Since the reaction was exothermic, the vapor pressure deviated negatively from Raoult's law. Depending upon the ratios of the liquids in solution, the vapor pressure could be lower than either or just lower than B. (A has a higher boiling point thus a lower vapor pressure.) The boiling point must have gone up from B because the vapor pressure went down from B.

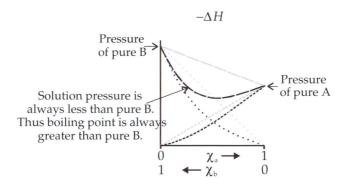

EXPLANATIONS TO IN-CLASS EXAM FOR LECTURE 5

Passage I

93. **C is correct.** The salt lowers the freezing point of water. This is necessary in order to insure that the water can bring the unknown solution to its freezing point.

94. **C is correct.** Even if the others completely dissociate, NaCl still releases more particles per gram than the others. (2 particles/58 grams) (A = 3/172, B = 2/120, and D = 3/115)

95. **C is correct.** The copper stirrer acts to evenly distribute the heat throughout the solution by convection.

96. **B is correct.** Since the freezing point depression was lower for Student 1, there must have been more particles for the same amount of mass. Thus Student 1 had an unknown with lower molecular weight.

97. **D is correct.** A greater concentration of particles lowers freezing point more. The freezing point data was collected and recorded for the cyclohexane solution, not the crushed ice solution.

98. **B is correct.** Time is not a factor in the calculation of the molecuar weight of the unknown solid. The molecular weight of the unknown solid can be calculated as follows:

$$\Delta T = K_f m:$$

$$m = (\text{grams}_{\text{solute}}/\text{M.W.})/(\text{volume}_{\text{solvent}} \times \text{density}_{\text{solvent}} \times \text{kg/gram})$$

plugging into $\Delta T = K_f m$ and rearranging we have:

$$\text{M.W.} = (K_f) (\text{grams}_{\text{solute}}) / \{(\Delta T) (\text{volume}_{\text{solvent}} \times \text{density}_{\text{solvent}} \times \text{kg/gram})\}$$

$$K_f = 20.2, (\text{grams}_{\text{solute}}) = 0.5, \ \Delta T = (6.6 - -3.5) = 10.1,$$
$$\text{volume}_{\text{solvent}} = 10.0, \text{density}_{\text{solvent}} = 0.78, \text{kg/gram} = 1/1000$$

Thus

$$\text{M.W.} = (K_f) (\text{grams}_{\text{solute}}) / \{(\Delta T) (\text{volume}_{\text{solvent}} \times \text{density}_{\text{solvent}} \times \text{kg/gram})\}$$

99. **D is correct.** D is the only nonvolatile, nonpolar solute that is soluble in cyclohexane.

100. **B is correct.** The only explanation is B. As long as some solution remains liquid, the energy removed by the ice bath creates bonds forming a solid. As soon as the entire solution is frozen, the energy removed from solution lowers the temperature.

Copyright © 2005 Examkrackers, Inc.

Passage II

101. **A is correct.** The acid and base are totally dissociated to begin with. This reaction takes high energy molecules and makes a low energy molecule, releasing heat.

102. **B is correct.** Heat is released.

103. **A is correct.** 40 mL × 1 cal/°C mL × –3.3°C = –132 cal. Since heat is released, we already know the answer is negative.

104. **B is correct.** The ammonium nitrate would require energy to dissociate before releasing energy to form water.

105. **D is correct.** Heat per mole is an intensive property.

106. **D is correct.** The temperature of the calorimeter is higher than the surroundings throughout the experiment. Heat always moves from hot to cold.

Passage III

107. **A is correct.** The negative slope on the phase diagram demonstrates that water expands when freezing.

108. **C is correct.** The line between A and E represents equilibrium of gas and solid.

109. **A is correct.** Point C in Figure 1 is the critical point, which is the temperature and pressure above which the gas and liquid phases cannot be distinguished.

110. **D is correct.** Point C in Figure 1 is the critical point, which is the temperature and pressure above which the gas and liquid phases cannot be distinguished.

111. **B is correct.** The negative slope between the solid and liquid phases of water in Figure 2 represents melting point at different temperatures and pressures. As pressure increases, the temperature decreases moving along the line.

112. **A is correct.** The normal boiling point is the boiling point at local atmospheric conditions (1 atm). To have a normal boiling point, the triple point must be at a pressure below 1 atm. In that case, the temperature of the triple point will be below the temperature of the normal boiling point.

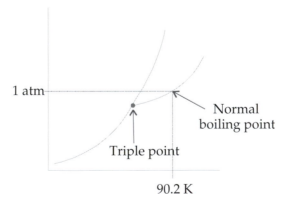

113. **C is correct.** See the graph.

Stand Alones

114. **A is correct.** During a phase change, temperature, and thus molecular kinetic energy, is constant. Breaking bonds always absorbs energy. Ice cools things when it melts.

115. **A is correct.** The potential energy of the water at the top of the falls becomes kinetic energy as it drops, and then thermal energy at the bottom of the falls. Thus $mgh = Q = mc\Delta T$, or $\Delta T = gh/c$.

Copyright © 2005 Examkrackers, Inc.

EXPLANATIONS TO IN-CLASS EXAM FOR LECTURE 6

Passage I

116. **A is correct.** This is the common ion effect in Reaction 1.

117. **A is correct.** For all trials, at the equivalence point there are Ca^{2+} ions, Na^+ and Cl^- ions. (Trial 1 has no Na^+ ions, but these don't affect pH anyway.) The Ca^{2+} started as a saturated solution. As OH^- ions are removed from solution by the acid, there is no precipitation of $Ca(OH)_2$. When all the OH^- ions are neutralized by the acid, the pH is 7 for all trials. The equivalence point is 7 for all trials. For trials with NaOH, the pH begins higher. More HCl is required to neutralize this extra base. The curves are exactly the same, but the trial one curve starts at a lower pH and requires less HCl.

118. **B is correct.** This is just the normal K_{sp}.

119. **D is correct.** $pOH = -\log[OH^-]$ In this case, the significant OH^- ion contribution comes completely from NaOH which dissociates completely. $1 > pOH > 2$ The pH is $14 - pOH =$ between 12 and 13.

120. **D is correct.** The $Ca(OH)_2$ solution begins as basic, and when the $Ca(OH)_2$ is totally dissolved, it should be neutral. See answer to question #117.

121. **A is correct.** This is the titration of a strong base with a strong acid. See question #117.

Passage II

122. **C is correct.** Since the K_w is higher, the hydrogen ion concentration will be higher also. But it would have to be 10 times higher in order for the pH to be higher.

123. **C is correct.** Set K_w equal to 1 mole of hydrogen ions times the OH concentration.

124. **B is correct.** As T increases, the hydrogen ion concentration increases.

125. **C is correct.** A proton is lost to form the conjugate base of a Bronsted acid.

126. **C is correct.** The leveling effect in water occurs because water readily accepts all protons from both acids. The equilibrium in water is so far to the right for both reactions that no comparison can be made. Although acetic acid accepts protons from both HCl and $HClO_4$, it does not do so as readily as water (it is a weaker proton acceptor or Bronsted-Lowry base). Thus, an equilibrium is established for both reactions, and the equilibriums can be compared.

127. **A is correct.** Definitional.

Passage III

128. **C is correct.** The pH must be where both indicators can have the proper color.

129. **C is correct.** The lower pK_a of sulfuric acid demonstrates that it is a stronger acid than sulfurous acid. The second proton is not the major contributor to the acid strength, so D is wrong.

130. **D is correct.** The K_b is found by adding the base to water. If the pK_a is known, the pK_b of the conjugate base can be found by subtracting the pK_a from 14. HSO_3^- is the conjugate base of H_2SO_3. The pK_a of H_2SO_3 is given as 1.81. $14 - 1.81 = 12.19$.

131. **D is correct.** The lowest pK_a is the strongest acid. You should know that sulfuric acid is stronger than the other acids.

132. **A is correct.** Minus eight for the oxygens, plus two for the hydrogens leaves minus six which must be counter balanced. Minus six for the oxygens, plus two for the hydrogens leaves minus four which must be counter balanced.

133. **C is correct.** We could never raise the pH by adding an acid. Water is the main contributor of H^+. To find the pH, we add the 5×10^{-8} ions contributed by H_2SO_4 to the 1×10^{-7} ions contributed by water. This leaves $1.5 \times 10^{-7} H^+$.

Copyright © 2005 Examkrackers, Inc.

134. **D is correct.** This is the titration of a diprotic acid with a strong base.

Stand Alones

135. **A is correct.** Perchloric acid is the strongest acid, thus it has the weakest conjugate base. In oxy acids, the more oxygens, the greater the acid strength.

136. **C is correct.** This is the definition of the half equivalence point.

137. **A is correct.** Use the Henderson-Hasselbalch equation. $pH = pK_a + \log(A^-/HA) \Rightarrow pH = -\log(1.8 \times 10^{-5}) + \log(1/10) \Rightarrow pH = 4.7 - 1 = 3.7$

138. **B is correct.** The conjugate acid has the K_a that equals K_w/K_b.

EXPLANATIONS TO IN-CLASS EXAM FOR LECTURE 7

Passage I

139. **C is correct.** $Cr_2O_7^{2-}$ is reduced to Cr^{3+}. Although this doesn't look like reduction from the charges, Cr in the dichromate has an original oxidation state of +6.

140. **C is correct.** Oxygen is –2. There are 7 oxygens which make –14. The 2– charge on the ion takes care of 2 of the 14 negatives. The 2 chromiums must take care of the other 12. That's +6 for each chromium.

141. **C is correct.** This is simply reading the graph.

142. **B is correct.** For each mole of dichromate that is reduced, 6 moles of Fe are oxidized. The top portion of B gives the number of moles of dichromate reduced times six, which is the number of moles of Fe oxidized. (The equivalence point is where all the iron has been oxidized.) We divide this by the original volume of Fe solution and get the molarity.

143. **A is correct.** The equivalence point is defined as the point when the Fe^{2+} is completely oxidized. Changing the formal potential won't change that definition. The Endpoint is when the indicator changes color. This should be at the equivalence point, but it doesn't have to be. The passage says that the formal potential is *lowered* so that the equivalence point and endpoint will coincide. This indicates that the indicator will change color at a low potential. If the formal potential isn't lowered, the indicator will change color early (still at the low potential) before the equivalence point is reached. The passage states that the indicator changes from colorless to violet; choice A. Dichromate ion will still oxidize DAS, but it will do so before oxidizing Fe^{2+}, so choice C is incorrect. Dichromate ion is an oxidizing agent and will not reduce anything, so choice D is incorrect.

144. **A is correct.** Each iron goes from a +2 to a +3 oxidation state by losing one electron. Each chromium goes from a +6 to a +3 oxidation state by gaining 3 electrons.

Passage II

145. **A is correct.** The half reactions must be rearranged in such a fashion so as the total voltage is positive (meaning the battery is discharging). This requires reversing the top half reaction. When reversed, this reaction becomes oxidation, which takes place at the anode.

146. **D is correct.** When we recharge the battery, the reactions are both reversed from the positions in question one.

147. **C is correct.** Ni is being reduced, so NiO_2 is the oxidizing agent. The compound with many oxygens is often the oxidizing agent.

148. **A is correct.** The cell has a negative potential and is forced to run in the nonspontaneous direction.

149. **C is correct.** The two half reaction potentials must be added after they have been rearranged to represent the galvanic cell. This means that the first half reaction is reversed. If this potential is applied, the cell can be recharged back to this potential which is the standard potential.

Copyright © 2005 Examkrackers, Inc.

150. **B is correct.** The passage tells us that sodium is at the anode so it is oxidized. Sodium is not normally oxidized to a +2.

151. **D is correct.** Current moves opposite to electrons. Since electrons flow from Half Reaction 1 to 2, current flows from Half Reaction 2 to 1.

Passage III

152. **D is correct.** The reaction quotient is in the same form as the equilibrium constant. Pure solids and liquids should not be used in the law of mass action to solve for the equilibrium constant.

153. **A is correct.** Plug the numbers into the Nernst equation. $(10^2)^2$ is 10^4. The log of 10^4 is 4. Thus the potential is negative and the voltage is twice 0.0592 V.

154. **B is correct.** See the last equation in the passage.

155. **B is correct.** See the last equation in the passage. A 1 M solution of HCl has a pH of 0.

156. **A is correct.** An increase of H^+ by a factor of 10 is a decrease in pH of 1. $E = 0.059$ (pH$_{test}$ – pH$_{reference}$) Each decrease in pH$_{reference}$ of 1 amounts to an increase in E of 0.059 V or 59 mV.

157. **A is correct.** The current will try to even the charges in the solutions. Since we have more positive charge on the concentrated side, the current moves to the less concentrated side.

158. **B is correct.** Again, current flows toward the less positive side, which is the basic side, which has less H^+ ions.

Stand Alones

159. **D is correct.** You should know this one reduction potential which is: $2H^+ + 2e^- \rightarrow H_2$ $E = 0$. When this is added to the oxidation of solid zinc, the potential is positive, which means spontaneous.

160. **C is correct.** At equilibrium, there can be no potential; neither direction of the reaction is favored.

161. **B is correct.** The products and reactants are at standard state, and therefore their potential defines the standard potential $E°$. A is wrong because they are not at equilibrium when $Q = 1$. C is wrong because the potential is positive. D is wrong because Q is at 1 and Q will move toward K. The reaction is spontaneous from here so products will increase, and Q will increase. Therefore, K must be greater than 1.

ANSWERS &
EXPLANATIONS
FOR
LECTURE QUESTIONS

ANSWERS FOR THE LECTURE QUESTIONS

Lecture 1	Lecture 2	Lecture 3	Lecture 4	Lecture 5	Lecture 6	Lecture 7
1. C	25. C	49. D	73. C	97. D	121. B	145. C
2. C	26. B	50. A	74. D	98. A	122. C	146. C
3. A	27. A	51. C	75. A	99. B	123. C	147. A
4. B	28. D	52. D	76. D	100. D	124. A	148. A
5. A	29. B	53. D	77. C	101. D	125. A	149. D
6. B	30. C	54. B	78. D	102. C	126. B	150. D
7. B	31. D	55. D	79. B	103. A	127. B	151. D
8. B	32. D	56. A	80. B	104. B	128. A	152. A
9. C	33. B	57. B	81. D	105. D	129. D	153. D
10. D	34. D	58. D	82. A	106. B	130. B	154. C
11. B	35. A	59. A	83. C	107. C	131. C	155. B
12. C	36. A	60. B	84. B	108. C	132. D	156. A
13. B	37. C	61. B	85. C	109. A	133. D	157. D
14. D	38. C	62. C	86. B	110. B	134. B	158. C
15. B	39. B	63. D	87. D	111. D	135. C	159. A
16. A	40. B	64. A	88. C	112. A	136. D	160. B
17. B	41. D	65. D	89. D	113. A	137. D	161. C
18. B	42. C	66. A	90. C	114. C	138. B	162. C
19. B	43. A	67. D	91. D	115. B	139. A	163. D
20. C	44. C	68. D	92. C	116. B	140. B	164. D
21. B	45. C	69. A	93. C	117. C	141. C	165. B
22. C	46. D	70. D	94. A	118. D	142. C	166. A
23. B	47. A	71. A	95. A	119. A	143. D	167. B
24. A	48. A	72. D	96. B	120. D	144. B	168. C

Copyright © 2005 Examkrackers, Inc.

ANSWERS & EXPLANATIONS FOR LECTURE QUESTIONS

1. **C is correct.** A family or group is the name for any vertical column on the periodic table. Of the choices given, only atomic radius increases going down a column. Although electron affinity is a possible choice depending upon the definition used, atomic radius is an unambiguous choice.

2. **C is correct.** The dipole moment will be greatest for the atoms with greatest difference in electronegativity. Based upon periodic trends, H and F will have the greatest dipole moment.

3. **A is correct.** By definition there are 12 amu in one atom of ^{12}C.

4. **B is correct.** Metals are lustrous, but they are also malleable and good conductors of electricity and heat. Silicon is positioned along the diagonal of elements in the periodic table sometimes referred to as metalloids.

5. **A is correct.** This is an isoelectronic series, which means that the number of electrons on each ion is the same. In an isoelectronic series of ions, the nuclear charge increases with increasing atomic number and draws the electrons inward with greater force. The ion with fewest protons produces the weakest attractive force on the electrons and thus has the largest size.

6. **B is correct.** Don't do any complicated calculations. This is the type of problem that everyone will get right, but many will spend too much time trying to be exact. First assume that 100% of the sample is ^{12}C. Now use the formula: moles = grams/molecular weight. This is very close to 4. The 1% that is not ^{12}C is insignificant.

7. **B is correct.** We are looking for an answer that would allow for the prediction of the order of atomic number. If atomic number increases with atomic weight, the scientists could have made accurate predictions.

8. **B is correct.** Sulfur can form four bonds. In choice A, Cl has the wrong number of electrons. In choice C, Se is too large to form stable pi bonds, so it can't double bond. In choice D, fluorine cannot make more than one bond. This question may require a little too much detailed knowledge to be on the MCAT.

---

9. **C is correct.** We start by assuming a 100 gram sample. By dividing grams by molecular weight, we obtain moles. $58.6/16 \approx 3.6$, $2.4/1 = 2.4$, $39/32 = 1.2$. Now we divide through by the lowest number of moles: $3.6/1.2 = 3$; $2.4/1.2 = 2$; $1.2/1.2 = 1$. This gives you the molar ratio of each element. Just to reduce the necessary calculations, the question tells you that it is a <u>neutral</u> compound. Nevertheless, MCAT questions with this much calculation occasionally come up, but they are few and far between. Maybe three on one entire exam.

10. **D is correct.** Silicon is too large to form pi bonds like carbon does. In order to complete its octet, it must make four bonds. It makes one bond with each of four oxygens. Each oxygen bonds with two silicon atoms.

11. **B is correct.** C has 12 g/mol and O has 16 g/mol. The total weight of CO_2 is 44 g/mol. Carbon's weight divided by the total weight is $12/44 = 0.27$. We multiply by 100 to get 27%.

12. **C is correct.** When one mole of sulfur dioxide is oxidized, one mole of sulfur trioxide is produced. One mole of sulfur trioxide has a mass of 80 g.

13. **B is correct.** Normally, 34 grams of ammonia (2 moles) could make 28 grams of nitrogen (1 mole), but here, only 26 grams were made. In a reaction that runs to completion, this must be due to lack of CuO.

14. **D is correct.** Each perchlorate ion has a 1– charge giving the copper ion a 2+ charge.

15. **B is correct.** This is an unusual looking reaction because it is a polymerization. Here it is drawn in a more representative form showing the repeated unit of the polymer as the product:

$$n CH_2 = CH_2 \longrightarrow \left(\begin{array}{cc} H & H \\ | & | \\ -C - C- \\ | & | \\ H & H \end{array} \right)_n$$

16. **A is correct.** This reaction has the form A + B → C. This is the form of a combination reaction.

Copyright © 2005 Examkrackers, Inc.

17. **B is correct.** The quickest way to see this is by realizing that atoms like to form ions with electron configurations similar to the nearest noble gas. Of course a noble gas does not have any unpaired electrons. You should recognize that Ca likes to form a 2+ ion not a 1+ ion.

18. **B is correct.** This question borders on requiring too much specific knowledge for the MCAT. The knowledge that the 4s and 3d orbitals are at the same energy level for the first row transition metals is probably beyond the MCAT. Rather than memorize specific exceptions to the Aufbau principle, answer this question by eliminating that A, C, and D must be wrong. A is wrong because there is no reason to skip the s subshell entirely. C is wrong because it contains the wrong number of electrons. D is wrong because we should be in the 3d subshell, not the 4d subshell. You may be able to see that, by Hund's rule, each electron would rather take its own orbital than share an orbital at the same energy level with another electron. Thus for Chromium, electrons fill the orbitals like this:

Chromium looks like this: [Ar] ↑/4s ↑/3d ↑/3d ↑/3d ↑/3d ↑/3d

not like this: [Ar] ↑↓/4s ↑/3d ↑/3d ↑/3d ↑/3d __/3d

Copper is the only other first row transition metal that breaks the Aufbau principle. Its electron configuration is [Ar] $4s^1 3d^{10}$.

19. **B is correct.** According to the Heisenberg uncertainty principle, both the position and the momentum mv of an electron cannot be known with absolute certainty at the same time. Since we know the mass of an electron, the uncertainty must lie in the velocity.

20. **C is correct.** The atom must absorb energy in order for one of its electrons to move to a higher energy level orbital.

21. **B is correct.** The principle quantum number (n) represents the energy level of the electron. The lowest energy shell is $n = 1$. As n increases, the shells move farther from the nucleus and energy increases.

22. **C is correct.** Because sulfur is larger than oxygen, sulfur has 3d subshells available that allow electrons to form bonds and break the octet rule of the Lewis structure.

23. **B is correct.** Hund's rule says that electrons added to the same subshell will occupy empty orbitals first and the unpaired electrons will have parallel spins.

24. **A is correct.** Since chromium forms more than one oxidation state and aluminum forms only one, chromium requires the variability in number of bonds formed. This means choices C and D are out. Chromium has electrons in the orbitals of the 2p subshell, but these are core electrons and not used for making bonds. Chromium has 6 valence electrons, 5 of which are in the orbitals of the 3d subshell.

Lecture 2

25. **C is correct.** You should recognize that 1 mole of gas occupies 22.4 liters at STP, so there is 0.5 moles of gas in the sample. 13 g/0.5 mol = 26 g/mol.

26. **B is correct.** Since density (ρ) is mass (m) divided by volume (V), and mass is moles (n) times molecular weight (MW), we have $(nMW)/V = \rho$. After some algebra we have: $MW = (\rho V)/n$. From the ideal gas law we know that $V/n = RT/P$. Substituting we have answer B.

27. **A is correct.** The number of moles of gas is extra information. If the container began at 11 atm then each gas is contributing a pressure in accordance with its stoichiometric coefficient. When the reaction runs to completion, the only gas in the container is nitrogen dioxide, so the partial pressure of nitrogen dioxide is the total pressure. The volume of the container remains constant, so the pressure is in accordance with the stoichiometric coefficient of nitrogen dioxide.

Copyright © 2005 Examkrackers, Inc.

28. **D is correct.** An ideal gas has a PV/RT equal to one. Real volume is greater than predicted by the ideal gas law, and real pressure is less than predicted by the ideal gas law. Volume deviations are due to the volume of the molecules, and pressure deviations are due to the intermolecular forces. Thus, a negative deviation in this ratio would indicate that the intermolecular forces are having a greater affect on the nonideal behavior than the volume of the molecules. (see the graph on page 27)

29. **B is correct.** The force does work on the gas, which means that the internal energy of the gas is increased. Since the internal energy of the gas is increased, and the number of moles remains the same, the temperature, which is average kinetic energy per mole, also increases.

30. **C is correct.** From Graham's law we know that the effusion rate for hydrogen is four times that of oxygen.

$$\frac{\text{H}_{2\text{ effusion rate}}}{\text{O}_{2\text{ effusion rate}}} = \sqrt{\frac{\text{M.W.}_{\text{oxygen}}}{\text{M.W.}_{\text{hydrogen}}}} = \sqrt{\frac{32}{2}} = 4$$

Since we don't know how many moles of gas were initially in container A, nor how many moles effused out, we don't know the ratio of hydrogen to oxygen. However, since we know that four times as many moles of hydrogen effused from container A into B, we know that container B contains four times as many moles of hydrogen. We can neglect any effusion in the reverse direction since the question says a "very short time".

31. **D is correct.** The diffusion rate for NH_3 is 1.5 times that of HCl. If HCl diffuses 4 cm, NH_3 will diffuse 6 cm. 4 cm + 6 cm = 10 cm.

$$\frac{\text{diffusion rate of NH}_3}{\text{diffusion rate of HCl}} = \frac{\sqrt{M_{\text{HCl}}}}{\sqrt{M_{\text{NH}_3}}} = \sqrt{\frac{36.5}{17}} = 1.5$$

32. **D is correct.** At STP, equal volumes of any gas behaving ideally contain the same number or moles.

33. **B is correct.** Changing the concentration of the reactants will not change the rate constant. Increasing the concentration of a catalyst will only increase the rate of the reaction if the supply of catalyst is so small that the reactants are waiting for a catalyst. Most of the time on the MCAT, you can assume that the supply of catalyst is large enough so that a change in concentration will not change the reaction rate. (See Biology Lecture 2 for the graph relating reaction rate to enzyme catalysts.) Increasing the amount of catalyst never increases the rate constant. Increasing the temperature will always increase the rate constant, and the rate of the reaction. If the reaction is catalyzed by an enzyme, the enzyme may denature, slowing the reaction; however, the reaction without the enzyme is considered a different reaction.

34. **D is correct.** Catalysts do not directly affect the equilibrium of a reaction. Catalysts do increase the rate of the reverse reaction as well as the forward reaction.

35. **A is correct.** When the concentration of B is doubled, the rate doesn't change. When the concentration of A is doubled, the rate doubles. The reaction is first order overall, and first order with respect to A. By choosing a trial and plugging the values into the rate law, we find that the rate constant has a value of 0.1.

36. **A is correct.** The slow step determines the rate of a reaction.

37. **C is correct.** Exothermicity concerns the thermodynamics of the reaction, and not the rate. You can ignore it. The energy of activation is the energy required for a collision of properly oriented molecules to produce a reaction. This does not change with temperature.

38. **C is correct.** A first order reaction has a constant half life. In the first 15 minutes, 16 out of 33 white dots (compound X) turned black, so 15 minutes represents approximately one half life. In the next 15 minutes, the second half life, half of the remaining 17 white dots should turn black. This represents choice C where there are 9 white dots left. Once you identify that 15 minutes is the half life, you should be able to eliminate answer A because there is no change and answer choice B and D because there are very few dots left. Even if you didn't know that a first order reaction has a constant half life, you should know that the reaction will be proportional to the concentration of white dots. In choice B and D, the rate of the reaction hasn't changed in the second 15 minutes even though the concentration of white dots has been reduced after the first 15 minutes, so this can't be right.

Copyright © 2005 Examkrackers, Inc.

39. **B is correct.** For a first order reaction the reaction rate is directly proportional to the concentration of reactant, according to the equation, rate = $k[A]$. So if the concentration of *cis*-2-butene is doubled, the reaction rate will also double. The rate constant is not affected by changes in the concentrations of reactants.

40. **B is correct.** The concentration of reactants decreases exponentially in a first order reaction. Another way of saying that is that the graph of ln(reactants) will be linear.

---

41. **D is correct.** Equilibrium will probably shift with temperature. The direction is dictated by thermodynamics. We need more information.

42. **C is correct.** The activation energy is dictated by the reaction itself and doesn't change during the reaction. We will see later that the Gibbs free energy is at a minimum when a reaction is at equilibrium.

43. **A is correct.** By Le Chatelier's principle the equilibrium would shift to the right causing an increase in the forward reaction.

44. **C is correct.** The equilibrium constant is products over reactants with the coefficients as exponents. However, reactants and products in pure liquid and solid phases generally have an exponent of zero, so they are not included in the equilibrium expression.

45. **C is correct.** Initially there are no products, so the reverse reaction begins at zero. As the reactants are used up, the forward reaction slows down. Equilibrium is the point where the rates equalize.

46. **D is correct.** A must be false because some of both solids must be present in order for equilibrium to exist. B and C are false because, as part of a solid molecule, calcium atoms have no way of leaving their respective beakers (other than a negligible amount of vapor pressure from their respective solids). D is true because when CaO in Beaker II combines with CO_2 gas in the container, $CaCO_3$ is formed in Beaker II. An equilibrium is achieved in both Beakers.

47. **A is correct.** Pure solids are not included in the equilibrium expression.

48. **A is correct.** "K_p is equal to the partial pressure of CO_2" is the equilibrium expression for this reaction. If K_p were less than the partial pressure of CO_2, the reaction would want to go to the left, but there would be no CaO to react to form $CaCO_3$. Regarding choice D, although solid CaO is required to achieve equilibrium, solid CaO could be formed with the decomposition of $CaCO_3$.

Lecture 3

49. **D is correct.** The second law of thermodynamics states that a heat engine cannot have 100% efficiency in converting heat to work in a cyclical process. An air conditioner is a heat engine running backwards. Thus an air conditioner must expel more heat than it takes in when it runs perpetually. A specially made air conditioner could initially cool the room, but to cool the room permanently, it must expel the heat to a heat reservoir.

50. **A is correct.** I. The temperature difference is directly proportional to the distance between two points of the same material.

$$\frac{Q}{t} = kA\frac{T_h - T_c}{L}$$

II. The rate of heat flow is constant throughout the blocks, or else heat would build up at the point of slowest flow. III. Since heat flow rate is constant, changing the order of the blocks won't change the rate of heat flow.

51. **C is correct.** There is no type of heat transfer called transduction. Conduction through the air would take a very long time and be very inefficient. Convection would require some type of air current or breeze. Radiation is as fast as light, and is the correct explanation.

52. **D is correct.** Unless the box and the incline are at different temperatures, there can be no heat. Energy transfer due to friction is work.

53. **D is correct.** Work is not a state function, thus we must know the path in order to calculate it.

Copyright © 2005 Examkrackers, Inc.

54. **B is correct.** The rate at which heat is conducted is directly proportional to the difference in temperatures between the hot and cold reservoirs. In December, the difference is $25 - 5 = 20$ degrees. That's the largest difference on the table.

55. **D is correct.** Since the container is at rest and has constant volume, no work is done.

56. **A is correct.** The efficiency of a thermodynamic process describes what percent of the input energy is converted into work. No thermodynamic process can be 100 percent efficient.

---

57. **B is correct.** To find the enthalpy of the reaction we use the following formula:

$$\Delta H°_{\text{reaction}} = \Delta H_f°{}_{\text{products}} - \Delta H_f°{}_{\text{reactants}}$$

The table gives these enthalpies. Don't forget that enthalpy is an extensive process, so quantity matters. We must multiply the enthalpies by the number of moles formed for each molecule. The enthalpy of formation of O_2 is zero, like that of any other molecule in its elemental form at 298 K.

58. **D is correct.** The definition of enthalpy is: $H \equiv U + PV$

59. **A is correct.** A catalyst affects the kinetics of a reaction and not the thermodynamics.

60. **B is correct.** Altering the ratio of the rates of a reaction will change the equilibrium. Removing thermal energy from an exothermic reaction will <u>probably</u> push it forward according to Le Chatelier's principle, since heat is a product. Answer C and D concern catalysts and will not change the ratio of the forward and reverse reaction.

61. **B is correct.** This is Hess's law. We reverse the equation for graphite, so that graphite is a product. In doing so, we must also reverse the sign of the enthalpy. Now we add the two equations and their enthalpies. Don't forget that we must multiply by two for the two moles. Enthalpy is an extensive property.

62. **C is correct.** Condensation must occur to form liquid water. Condensation is an exothermic process, so the formation of liquid water should be more exothermic than the formation of water vapor. The standard enthalpy of formation of water vapor will not be an endothermic process, so D is wrong.

63. **D is correct.** The reaction coordinate diagram below shows the energy of activation for an exothermic reaction is greater than for an endothermic reaction.

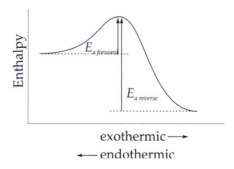

64. **A is correct.** Increasing the temperature increases the energy available to both the forward and the reverse reactions, enabling both to more easily overcome the activation energy. Just so you know, because the reverse reaction is endothermic, its rate will increase more. That's what causes the increase in the concentration of reactants predicted by LeChatelier's law.

---

65. **D is correct.** According to the equation $\Delta G = \Delta H - T\Delta S$, to guarantee that a reaction is spontaneous, enthalpy of the system must decrease and entropy of the system must increase.

66. **A is correct.** The entropy of the universe will increase in a spontaneous reaction. The entropy of a system may or may not increase.

67. **D is correct.** Energy is always required to break a bond.

68. **D is correct.** The process of building a bridge is an ordering process.

Copyright © 2005 Examkrackers, Inc.

Exam Explanations

69. **A is correct.** Since the number of moles of gas is decreasing with the forward reaction, positional entropy is decreasing. This almost always means that overall system entropy is decreasing. Since the MCAT doesn't distinguish between positional entropy and any other kind of entropy, you can always view a reaction with decreasing number of gas particles as decreasing in entropy and vice versa.

70. **D is correct.** Bonds are formed when water condenses, so energy is released and ΔH is negative. The water molecules become less random, so ΔS is negative. Condensation occurs spontaneously at 25°C (room temperature), so ΔG is negative. Notice that you can answer this question without being given any numbers.

71. **A is correct.** $\Delta G = \Delta H - T\Delta S$. For a spontaneous reaction, ΔG must be negative. As T is increased, the negative part of the equation increases in magnitude. If T is increased enough, eventually ΔG will switch from positive to negative. Changing the pressure will have no effect on a nongaseous reaction that takes place in a solution.

72. **D is correct.** At the boiling point, benzene is in equilibrium between the liquid and gas phases. At equilibrium, ΔG for a reaction is equal to zero. S is positive for the reaction shown because gases are more random than liquids.

Lecture 4

73. **C is correct.** One liter of water weighs 1 kg; one liter of this solution weighs 1.006 kilograms. If we assume that the volume of water changes very little when NaCl is added, then about 0.006 kg, or 6 g, of NaCl are in each liter of solution. The molecular weight of NaCl is 58.6. 6 grams is about 0.1 moles. (By the way, even if the salt increased the volume of 1 liter of solution by 10 cubic centimeters, the molarity would still be slightly greater than 0.099 M. So this is a good approximation. Remember, for dilute solutions, the volume of the solute is negligible.)

74. **D is correct.** Remember that like dissolves like. Water is polar, and will dissolve polar and ionic substances. A, B, C are ions, ionic compounds, or capable of hydrogen bonding. Carbon tetrachloride is a nonpolar molecule.

75. **A is correct.** For all practical purposes, choices A and B are the same. However, since the question asks you to compare them, a one molar solution is 1 mole of NaCl in slightly less than a liter of water. This is because the NaCl requires some volume. A one molal solution is one mole in one full liter of water. (This question assumes that a liter of water has a mass of 1 kg. This is true at 1 atm. and approximately 3°C. Water at 1 atm. is at its most dense state at a temperature of slightly over 3°C.) There are 55.5 moles of water in a liter (grams/molecular weight = moles). 1/100 = 0.01 and 1/50 = 0.02. Thus a solution with a mole fraction of 0.01 is closer to a 0.5 molar solution than a 1 molar solution. The last answer choice is less than one mole of NaCl in one liter of water.

76. **D is correct.** You should know that 1 atm is equal to 760 torr. Since the partial pressure of nitrogen is 600, the mole fraction of nitrogen is 0.79. This means that the percentages given are by particle and not by mass. D would be true if the percentages were based on mass. If you chose B, you need to go back to Lecture 3 and review standard molar volume.

77. **C is correct.** No solution is formed, so either B or C must be correct. B is not true.

78. **D is correct.** First calculate the number of moles of $MgCl_2$

$$\text{moles} = \text{grams}/MW = 19 \text{ g}/95 \text{ g/mol} = 0.2 \text{ mol}$$

0.2 moles of $MgCl_2$ will dissociate to produce 0.4 moles of Cl^- ions.

$$[Cl^-] = \text{moles}/\text{liters} = 0.4 \text{ mol}/0.5 \text{ L} = 0.8 \ M$$

79. **B is correct.** First find the number of moles of HCl.

$$\text{moles} = (\text{mol/L})(L) = (3 \text{ mol/L})(0.8 \ L) = 2.4 \text{ moles}$$

Now find the number of liters needed to make the solution 1 molar

$$L = \text{mol}/\text{mol/L} = 2.4 \text{ mol}/1 \ M = 2.4 \text{ L}$$

Now be careful. You already have 0.8 liters of solution, so in order to get 2.4 L, you have to add 1.6 L of water.

Copyright © 2005 Examkrackers, Inc.

80. **B is correct.** A strong electrolyte is a substance that dissociates completely in water to form ions, which can then conduct electricity. Carbon dioxide does not dissociate to form ions so it is not an electrolyte.

81. **D is correct.** The change in entropy is positive in solution formation and Gibbs free energy is negative in a spontaneous reaction. From $\Delta G = \Delta H_{sol} - T\Delta S$ we see that the heat of solution may be either positive or negative in this case. The heat of hydration is the separation of water molecules (which requires energy) and the formation of bonds between the ions and water molecules (which releases energy). Thus, the value of the heat of hydration could be either positive or negative. The actual heat of hydration is –783 kJ/mol making the heat of solution +3 kJ/mol.

82. **A is correct.** At constant pressure, change in enthalpy is equal to heat.

83. **C is correct.** The vapor pressure of solution might be lower than just one of the pure substances but not the other. You can see this from the graph below.

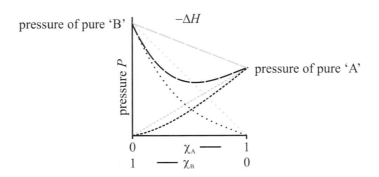

84. **B is correct.** You should notice that B and C are opposites, so one of them must be the answer. Molecules break free of the surface of a liquid and add to the vapor pressure when they have sufficient kinetic energy to break the intermolecular bonds.

85. **C is correct.** The solution had to deviate from Raoult's law and therefore could not be ideal. Since it deviated negatively from Raoult's law, the heat of solution is exothermic.

86. **B is correct.** In an ideal solution, the vapor pressure will be somewhere in between the vapor pressures of the solute and the solvent, depending on their relative mole fractions.

87. **D is correct.** Try testing the answer choices to see which one is right.

$$(0.2)(800 \text{ mmHg}) + (0.8)(300 \text{ mmHg}) = 400 \text{ mmHg}.$$

88. **C is correct.** If heat is released, the solvation process must be exothermic. The breaking of bonds is an endothermic process and the forming of bonds is an exothermic process, so in order for the process to be exothermic overall, the bonds formed must be stronger than the bonds that were broken.

89. **D is correct.** Think in terms of mole fraction. The concentration of solvent is at a minimum when the concentration of solute is at a maximum.

90. **C is correct.** This is the common ion effect (very important for the MCAT).

91. **D is correct.** We can compare the solubilities in one liter of water. For the compounds that dissociate into two parts, the smallest K_{sp} will be the least soluble and first to precipitate. This is $BaSO_4$. We don't have to compare $BaSO_4$ with Ag_2SO_4 because Ag_2SO_4 dissociates into three particles. This means that if their K_{sp}s were equal, then Ag_2SO_4 would be more soluble than $BaSO_4$. However, the K_{sp} for $BaSO_4$ is much lower, so we know for sure that it is less soluble.

92. **C is correct.** Gases become more soluble under greater pressure and lower temperatures. The pressure must be the partial pressure of the soluble gas. Adding an inert gas would not change the partial pressure of oxygen in this example. Shaking the can is adding energy, and is similar to heating the can. Think about shaking a can of soda.

Copyright © 2005 Examkrackers, Inc.

93. **C is correct.** The solubility of $BaCO_3$ in 3 liters of water is found from the equilibrium expression:

$$K_{sp} = [Ba^{2+}][CO_3^{2-}]$$
$$1.6 \times 10^{-9} = [x][x]$$
$$x = 4 \times 10^{-5}$$

This is the saturated concentration in mol/L. We multiply this by 3 liters to get the total number of moles.

94. **A is correct.** The solubility product is created by multiplying the concentrations of the products of the solvation while turning the coefficients into exponents.

95. **A is correct.** The K_{sp} expression is as follows.

$$K_{sp} = [Pb^{2+}][Cl^-]^2$$

For every $PbCl_2$ in solution, there is 1 Pb^{2+} and 2 Cl^-. So $[Pb^{2+}] = x$ and $[Cl^-] = 2x$.

$$K_{sp} = (x)(2x)^2 = (x)(4x^2) = 4x^3$$

96. **B is correct.** NaF is very soluble, so when it is added to the solution, it will introduce more Na^+ and F^- ions. The introduction of extra F^- ions will shift the CaF_2 equilibrium toward solid CaF_2, which removes Ca^{2+} ions from the solution.

Lecture 5

97. **D is correct.** First figure out the heat evolved by the reaction using $q = mc\Delta T$ =>

$$q = 250 \text{ grams } x \text{ } 4.18 \text{ J/g } °C \text{ } x \text{ } 1 \text{ } °C \approx 1050 \text{ joules}$$

Next divide by moles of NaCl (20 grams is about 1/3 of a mole). This gives you 3150 joules, which is equal to 3 kJ. Since the temperature went down, the reaction is endothermic with positive enthalpy. Notice all the rounding. This problem should have been done with very little math.

98. **A is correct.** Remember, $\Delta E = w + q$. There is no work done because there is no change in volume in a bomb calorimeter. Thus, the total change in energy is heat. Heat is not enthalpy. Heat equals enthalpy at constant pressure. The pressure is not constant in a bomb calorimeter.

99. **B is correct.** I is false because objects cannot contain heat, and because the same amount of the same substance can have the same amount of energy and be at different temperatures. Nevertheless, this is a treading the MCAT edge of required knowledge. Don't feel too bad if you chose C. II is false. Different phases will have different specific heats. III is true.

100. **D is correct.** A, B, and C are false. Temperature is proportional to kinetic energy not just velocity, so more mass per molecule does not make a difference. Boiling point does not make sense; substance A might be water and substance B ice. Answer C mistakenly relies upon speed and not kinetic energy for temperature. D is the correct choice by process of elimination. The more ways that a substance has to absorb energy, the more heat it can absorb with the least change in temperature.

101. **D is correct.** No energy transfer takes place, so there is no heat or work.

102. **C is correct.** Aluminum has the largest value for specific heat, which means that it can absorb the most energy while showing the smallest temperature change.

103. **A is correct.** Since the specific heat for Au is one-third as large as the specific heat for Cu, one-third as much heat will be required to get the same temperature change.

104. **B is correct.** Use the equation $q = mc\Delta T$. The change in temperature is $31 - 26 = 5$. Don't forget to convert 1.8 kJ into 1800 J.

$$m = q/c\Delta T = (1800)/(0.90)(5) = 400 \text{ } g.$$

Copyright © 2005 Examkrackers, Inc.

105.   **D is correct.** We can solve this problem by summing the q's on the heat curve. The heat is positive because heat is added to the system.

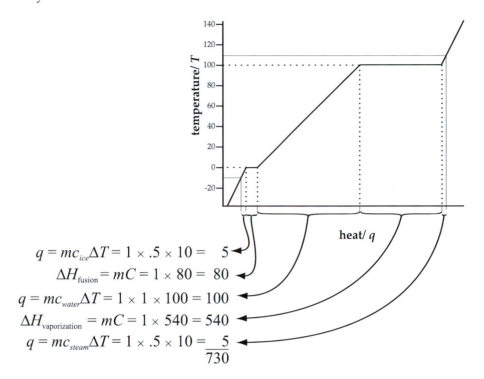

$$q = mc_{ice}\Delta T = 1 \times .5 \times 10 = 5$$
$$\Delta H_{fusion} = mC = 1 \times 80 = 80$$
$$q = mc_{water}\Delta T = 1 \times 1 \times 100 = 100$$
$$\Delta H_{vaporization} = mC = 1 \times 540 = 540$$
$$q = mc_{steam}\Delta T = 1 \times .5 \times 10 = \underline{5}$$
$$730$$

106.   **B is correct.** The added energy goes into breaking bonds, and as is demonstrated by the heat curve above, the temperature remains constant until all the ice is melted. Entropy increases moving to the right on the heat curve.

107.   **C is correct.** This is just a phase diagram with pressure on a log scale. There are many ways to manipulate the phase diagram. Don't be intimidated. Try to compare it to what you know.

108.   **C is correct.** Above the critical point, liquid and vapor water have the same density. The critical temperature will be the highest temperature on the graph where the two lines meet.

109.   **A is correct.** The area in the dashed line is the point where water is changing phase. Like along line RS, in the dashed line area water and steam exist in equilibrium.

110.   **B is correct.** The heat of fusion is the amount of heat that must be added to convert one mole of a substance completely from solid to liquid. Benzene has a molecular mass of 78, so the sample contains 1 mole. The flat line on the heating curve represents the heat being added while the phase changes from solid to liquid, so the heat of fusion can be found by measuring the length of the flat line. So 14.4 kJ – 3.5 kJ = 10.9 kJ.

111.   **D is correct.** At the boiling point, any added energy is used to break intermolecular bonds and not to increase kinetic energy, so while the water is boiling, there is no temperature increase.

112.   **A is correct.** Heating the solid will raise its temperature which will eventually melt it. Compressing the solid will raise the pressure on the solid which will most likely keep it a solid. A few substances like water will melt under pressure, but for most solids, pressure changes a liquid to a solid. It is the random kinetic energy of the molecules of a solid and not the uniform translational motion kinetic energy of the solid that increases its temperature and would make it melt.

113.   **A is correct.** Boiling point elevation is a colligative property. The more particles the higher the boiling point. NaCl dissociates so that the normality is twice the molarity. Thus, the least number of particles will be in 0.5 M glucose solution.

114.   **C is correct.** The osmotic pressure will not create a difference in the buoyant force. The equation for buoyant force ($F_b = \rho V g$) does not include osmotic pressure. Seawater has greater density because salts are heavier than water, and the salt added does not create an appreciable difference in volume.

Copyright © 2005 Examkrackers, Inc.

Exam Explanations

115. **B is correct.** You must recognize from the formula that glycerol does not dissociate; it is not ionic. Then use $\Delta T = K_f m$, which gives you a molality of 10. Molality is moles of solute divided by kg of solvent. Assume that 1 liter of water has a mass of 1 kg. Thus 100 moles of glycerol are required. Glycerol has a molecular weight of 62 g/mol. 6200 g = 6.2 kg.

116. **B is correct.** The reaction is exothermic because the temperature increased. An exothermic reaction makes stronger bonds. Stronger bonds lower vapor pressure. A lower vapor pressure means more energy is needed to raise the vapor pressure to equal atmospheric pressure. Thus, a lower vapor pressure means a higher boiling point.

117. **C is correct.** The question has a lot of extra information to mislead you. A high value for h indicates a high osmotic pressure in the solution. From the formula for osmotic pressure, $\Pi = iMRT$, we know that a high osmotic pressure corresponds to a high molarity. A high molarity means many particles per gram of protein placed into the solution. Thus a high osmotic pressure means a low molecular weight.

118. **D is correct.** The freezing point depression formula is $\Delta T = kmi$. We know that k is 1.86. The molar mass of $CaCl_2$ is 111, so there are 3 moles of salt in 1 kg of water and m is 3. $CaCl_2$ dissociates into 3 particles, so i is 3.

$$\Delta T = (1.86)(3)(3) = 16.7°C$$

119. **A is correct.** The freezing point expression is $\Delta T = kmi$. The solute is non-polar, so i is 1 and we can leave it out. Now let's remember the definition of molality.

$$m = \text{(moles of solute)}/\text{(kg of solvent)}$$
$$\text{but (moles of solute)} = \text{(grams of solute)}/\text{(molar mass of solute)}$$
$$\text{Substituting, we get } \Delta T = (k)\text{(grams of solute)}/\text{(molar mass of solute)(kg of solvent)}$$
$$\text{If you solve for the molar mass, you get choice A.}$$

120. **D is correct.** Boiling point is a colligative property, which means that it depends only on the number of particles in solution, not on their specific properties. Both NaF and KCl dissociate completely into 2 particles each, so they will have the same effect on the boiling point of water.

Lecture 6

121. **B is correct.** The conjugate acid is the molecule after it accepts a proton.

122. **C is correct.** By definition, a Lewis base donates a pair of electrons.

123. **C is correct.** NH_4^+ is an acid. The strongest base is the conjugate of the weakest acid.

124. **A is correct.** An amino acid can act as an acid or a base depending upon the pH. Although the conjugate base of sulfuric acid is amphoteric, sulfuric acid cannot accept a proton and is not amphoteric.

125. **A is correct.** The electron withdrawing group will further polarize the O-H bond, and polarization increases acidity in aqueous solution.

126. **B is correct.** The pH of solution B is 7. The pH of solution A is between 4 and 5. The difference in pH must be between 7 – 5 = 2 and 7 – 4 = 3. Choice B is the only one in that range.

127. **B is correct.** In a coordinate covalent bond, one atom donates an electron pair to share with another atom. In this case, ammonia has the unbonded pair to donate to boron, so ammonia is the Lewis base and boron is the Lewis acid.

128. **A is correct.** In Reaction 1, water accepts a proton to become H_3O^+, so it is acting as a Bronsted-Lowry base. In Reaction 2, water gives up a proton to become OH⁻, so it acts as a Bronsted-Lowry acid.

---

129. **D is correct.** K_b is the reaction of the conjugate base with water.

130. **B is correct.** HBr dissociates completely, so the concentration of H⁺ ions will be equal to the concentration of solution. The $-\log(0.1) = 1$.

Copyright © 2005 Examkrackers, Inc.

131. **C is correct**. The K_b for $NaHCO_3$ is $K_w/K_a \approx \_ \times 10^{-7}$. We can set up the equilibrium expression:

$$K_b = \frac{[OH^-][H_2CO_3]}{[HCO_3^-]}$$

$$0.25 \times 10^{-7} = \frac{[x][x]}{[1 - x]}$$ This x is insignificant.

$$2.5 \times 10^{-8} = x^2$$

$$1.5 \times 10^{-4} = x$$

Thus, the pOH = between 3 and 4. Subtracting from 14, the pH = between 10 and 11.

132. **D is correct**. Each unit of pH is a tenfold increase of acidity.

133. **D is correct**. You should recognize F⁻ as the conjugate base of a weak acid. Choices A and B are conjugates of strong acids, and thus weaker bases. Choice C is an acid.

134. **B is correct**. BrO⁻ is the conjugate base of HBrO, so you can find the base dissociation constant K_b by dividing. $1 \times 10^{-14}/2 \times 10^{-9}$. You get 0.5×10^{-5}, which is the same as 5×10^{-6}.

135. **C is correct**. If the pH is 10, the pOH must be 4. If the pOH is 4, then the hydroxide ion concentration must be 10^{-4} M.

136. **D is correct**. Acetate ion, $C_2H_3O_2^-$, is the conjugate base of a weak acid, so it will act as a base in solution. Sodium ion, Na^+, is the conjugate acid of a strong base, so it is neutral in solution.

---

137. **D is correct**. The pH starts basic so a base is being titrated. It ends very acidic so a strong acid is titrating.

138. **B is correct**. A buffer is made from equal amounts of an acid and its conjugate. The buffer works best when the pH = pK_a. $-\log(8.3 \times 10^{-7})$ = between 6 and 7. 8.3 is close to ten, making the pK_a closer to 6.

139. **A is correct**. An indicator generally changes color within plus or minus one pH point of its pK_a.

140. **B is correct**. The concentration of the conjugate base of the first acid is the greatest at the first equivalence point.

141. **C is correct**. The equivalence point of a titration of a weak acid with a strong base will always be greater than 7. It is the same as adding the conjugate base of the acid to pure water. 14 is way too basic. Pure 1 M NaOH has a pH of 14.

142. **C is correct**. A buffered solution is formed when equal amounts of a weak acid and its conjugate base are present in a solution. Acetic acid is a weak acid and the acetate ion is its conjugate.

143. **D is correct**. HCO_3^- can act as a Bronsted Lowry acid and give up a hydrogen ion to become CO_3^{2-}. It can also act as a Lewis base and donate an electron pair to a hydrogen ion to become H_2CO_3. It is amphoteric because it can act as an acid or base. It is not polyprotic because it has only one hydrogen.

144. **B is correct**. From the Henderson-Hasselbalch equation, you can see that when a weak acid and its conjugate base are present in a solution in equal amounts, the pH will be equal to the pK_a. If you take the negative logarithm of 8.0×10^{-5}, it will be between 4 and 5. That's choice B.

Lecture 7

145. **C is correct**. Each oxygen has an oxidation state of –2, and hydrogen has an oxidation state of +1. In order for the ion to have a 1– charge, the sulfur must have a +6 oxidation state. (Notice that oxidation states are given as +n, and actual charges are given as n+.)

146. **C is correct**. Aluminum begins as +3 and ends as 0, while carbon begins as 0 and ends as +4.

Copyright © 2005 Examkrackers, Inc.

Exam Explanations

147. **A is correct.** The Zn is oxidized from an oxidation state of 0 to +2. Thus, it is the reducing agent.

148. **A is correct.** Both A and D cannot be true, so the answer must be A or D. The trickiest part of this problem is to know that lead is comfortable at +2 and sulfur, being in the oxygen family, is comfortable at –2; thus these are their oxidation states when they are together. But when they are with oxygen, the –2 of the oxygen rules.

149. **D is correct.** An example of where this is false is:

$$2HCl + Zn \rightarrow ZnCl_2 + H_2$$

Here each atom of the reducing agent, zinc, loses two electrons, and the hydrogen atom of the oxidizing agent, HCl, gains one electron. Of course, there must be two hydrogens for each zinc.

150. **D is correct.** The two oxygens in NO_2^- have a total oxidation number of –4, so nitrogen must have an oxidation number of +3 to get a total of –1 on the polyatomic ion. . The three oxygens in NO_3^- have a total oxidation number of –6, so nitrogen must have an oxidation number of +5 to get a total of –1 on the polyatomic ion. Since the oxidation state is increasing from +3 to +5, electrons are being lost and oxidation is taking place.

151. **D is correct.** None of the oxidation states are changed during the course of this acid-base neutralization reaction, so no redox takes place.

152. **A is correct.** Don't forget, the oxidation states for Cl and Br in Cl_2 and Br_2 are zero by definition because the two elements are in their uncombined states. Chlorine gains electrons, so it is reduced. Since it is reduced, it is the oxidizing agent. Bromine loses electrons, so it is oxidized.

---

153. **D is correct.** Positive ions move across the salt bridge to the cathode. You can remember this because the salt bridge is used to balance the charges. Since negative electrons move to the cathode, positive ions must balance the charge by moving to the cathode.

154. **C is correct.** The forward and reverse reaction rates are only equal at equilibrium, and their rate constants are rarely equal.

155. **B is correct.** This question requires knowledge of the equation: $\Delta G° = -RT \ln(K)$. This equation is a statement about the relationship between $\Delta G°$ and K at a specific temperature. If $\Delta G° = 0$, then $K = 1$. The standard state for an aqueous solution is $1\,M$ concentrations.

156. **A is correct.** The strongest reducing agent is the one most easily oxidized; thus we must reverse the equations and the signs of the potentials.

157. **D is correct.** Although a both a Galvanic cell and an electrolytic cell can have a positive potential, only an electrolytic cell can have a negative potential.

158. **C is correct.** The potential given are reduction potentials. Since copper is reduced, we can use its potential (0.15 V) as written. Tin is oxidized, so we have to change the sign before we calculate. The total potential is 0.15 V + 0.14 V = 0.29 V. Notice that we ignore the coefficients when we do cell potential calculations.

159. **A is correct.** You can use the Nernst equation here, or you can just think about LeChatelier's law. As the concentration of products increases, the reaction will become less spontaneous. The less spontaneous the reaction, the lower the reaction potential.

160. **B is correct.** A galvanic cell generates power via a spontaneous reaction, so $\Delta G°$ must be less than zero. From the expression $\Delta G° = -RT\ln(K)$, you can figure out that if $\Delta G°$ is negative, then K must be greater than 1.

Copyright © 2005 Examkrackers, Inc.

161. **C is correct**. Reactions in galvanic cells are always spontaneous. To find the reaction for this cell we must flip the more negative half reaction. Now we have a spontaneous cell.

$$Al^{3+} + 3e^- \rightarrow Al \qquad -1.66$$
$$\underline{Mg \rightarrow Mg^{2+} + 2e^- \qquad 2.37}$$
$$0.71$$

We also have to multiply the aluminum reaction by 2 and the magnesium reaction by 3. Notice, however, that we do not multiply their potentials.

$$2Al^{3+} + 3Mg \rightarrow 3Mg^{2+} + 2Al \qquad E° = 0.71 \text{ V}$$

Since the potential for this cell does not equal this, the conditions must not be standard.

162. **C is correct**. Reduction always takes place at the cathode in any cell. This means that the cathode gains electrons.

163. **D is correct**. A concentration cell is a special type of galvanic cell. It is always spontaneous. The concentrations in the cell even out at equilibrium.

164. **D is correct**. In this cell the cathode has the greater concentration because electrons flow toward it to reduce the number of cations. Also in a concentration cell $E° = 0$, since the reduction half reaction is simply the reverse of the oxidation half reaction. $n = 1$ because only one electron is transferred in each reaction. x/y must be a fraction so that the log will be negative and E will be positive. Thus we have:

$$E = -(0.06/1)\log(0.1/y) = 0.12$$

$$y = 10 \text{ so that } x/y = 10^{-2}.$$

165. **B is correct**. Use units to solve the problem. We want to go from current to grams. Current is C/s. F is coulombs per mol of electrons. For every mol of electrons there is one mol of silver. The molecular weight of silver is 107.8 g/mol

$$C/s \ x \ s = C \quad => \quad C \ x \ mol/C = mol \quad => \quad mol \ x \ grams/mol = grams$$

so:

$$i \ x \ t \ x \ (1/F) \ x \ 107.8 = grams$$

166. **A is correct**. Remember, $I = Q/t$. The charge Q is $(96,500)(0.01) = 965$ C. The time t in seconds is $(5)(60) = 300$. So $Q/t = 965/300 = 3$. The answer is rounded to 3 because there is only 1 significant digit in some of the numbers used in the calculation.

167. **B is correct**. If a voltage is applied to a solution containing Na^+ and H_2O, the H_2O will take the electrons first because it has a larger reduction potential. As long as there is H_2O present, the aqueous sodium will not react.

168. **C is correct**. Ag^{2+} gains an electron to become Ag^+, so it is reduced (LEO says GER). Reduction takes place at the cathode (ANOX/REDCAT).

Exam Explanations

Copyright © 2005 Examkrackers, Inc.

Copyright © 2005 Examkrackers, Inc.

INDEX

Copyright © 2005 Examkrackers, Inc.

Copyright © 2005 Examkrackers, Inc.

Copyright © 2005 Examkrackers, Inc.

Copyright © 2005 Examkrackers, Inc.

Copyright © 2005 Examkrackers, Inc.

Copyright © 2005 Examkrackers, Inc.

Copyright © 2005 Examkrackers, Inc.

Copyright © 2005 Examkrackers, Inc.

11 Full Length
MCAT Verbal Exams
in the
NEW MCAT FORMAT

674 MCAT verbal questions in total!

**16 solid hours
of MCAT verbal testing!**

**2,696 explanations
for correct
and incorrect
answer choices!**

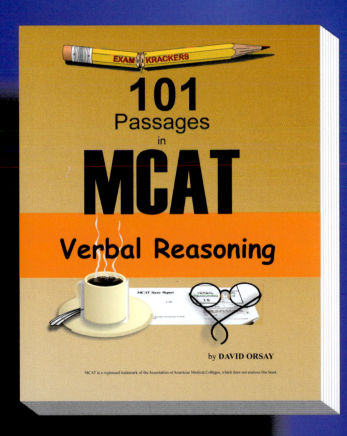

**101 MCAT
verbal reasoning
passages!**

**Twelve tear-our answer sheets
for simulation accuracy!**

An Unedited Student Review of This Book

The following review of this book was written by Teri R—. from New York. Teri scored a 43 out of 45 possible points on the MCAT. She is currently attending UCSF medical school, one of the most selective medical schools in the country.

"The Examkrackers MCAT books are the best MCAT prep materials I've seen-and I looked at many before deciding. The worst part about studying for the MCAT is figuring out what you need to cover and getting the material organized. These books do all that for you so that you can spend your time learning. The books are well and carefully written, with great diagrams and really useful mnemonic tricks, so you don't waste time trying to figure out what the book is saying. They are concise enough that you can get through all of the subjects without cramming unnecessary details, and they really give you a strategy for the exam. The study questions in each section cover all the important concepts, and let you check your learning after each section. Alternating between reading and answering questions in MCAT format really helps make the material stick, and means there are no surprises on the day of the exam-the exam format seems really familiar and this helps enormously with the anxiety. Basically, these books make it clear what you need to do to be completely prepared for the MCAT and deliver it to you in a straightforward and easy-to-follow form. The mass of material you could study is overwhelming, so I decided to trust these books—I used nothing but the Examkrackers books in all subjects and got a 13-15 on Verbal, a 14 on Physical Sciences, and a 14 on Biological Sciences. Thanks to Jonathan Orsay and Examkrackers, I was admitted to all of my top-choice schools (Columbia, Cornell, Stanford, and UCSF). I will always be grateful. I could not recommend the Examkrackers books more strongly. Please contact me if you have any questions."

Sincerely,
Teri R—

About the Author

Jonathan Orsay is uniquely qualified to write an MCAT preparation book. He graduated on the Dean's list with a B.A. in History from Columbia University. While considering medical school, he sat for the real MCAT three times from 1989 to 1996. He scored in the 90 percentiles on all sections before becoming an MCAT instructor. He has lectured in MCAT test preparation for thousands of hours and across the country for every MCAT administration since August 1994. He has taught premeds from such prestigious Universities as Harvard and Columbia. He was the editor of one of the best selling MCAT prep books in 1996 and again in 1997. Orsay is currently the Director of MCAT for Examkrackers. He has written and published the following books and audio products in MCAT preparation: "Examkrackers MCAT Physics"; "Examkrackers MCAT Chemistry"; "Examkrackers MCAT Organic Chemistry"; "Examkrackers MCAT Biology"; "Examkrackers MCAT Verbal Reasoning & Math"; "Examkrackers 1001 questions in MCAT Physics", "Examkrackers MCAT Audio Osmosis with Jordan and Jon".